BITES
OF
TERROR

For London

Copyright © 2020 by Cuddles and Rage

Library of Congress Cataloging in Publication Number: 2019914892

ISBN: 978-1-68369-164-8

Printed in China

Typeset in Fright Night and Supernett

Designed by Andie Reid
Production management by John J. McGurk

Quirk Books
215 Church Street
Philadelphia, PA 19106
quirkbooks.com

10 9 8 7 6 5 4 3 2 1

BITES OF TERROR

10 FRIGHTFULLY DELICIOUS TALES

BY CUDDLES AND RAGE

QUIRK BOOKS
PHILADELPHIA

FOREWORD

"How do you guys do it?"

That was the first question I asked Liz and Jimmy Reed about their work. I wasn't talking about the astonishing world building they've done as Cuddles and Rage, a brilliant storytelling duo that examines the human condition through stories about anthropomorphic cupcakes, veggies, and snacks who live rich, full, hilarious, and often relatable lives. I wasn't asking about their photography, which has a clean, retro vibe that captures the eye and the imagination. The biggest mystery of Liz and Jimmy's work isn't the way they create eerily human personalities for their characters, nor is it the jaw-dropping amount of detail in their scenes. It's their collaborative process, their individual talents combining seamlessly to create a world that feels fully realized.

After meeting them at a film festival and then following them on Instagram, watching their short films on YouTube, and purchasing their artwork, which adorn several spots in my house, I'm delighted that they're bringing their Richard Scarry—esque "foodiverse" to *Bites of Terror*, a horror anthology that serves as the perfect banquet for their particular brand of adorable and delicious mayhem.

An arcane but affable host who tells cautionary tales with gruesome plot twists is a tradition practically as old as eating itself, and with *Bites of Terror* these creators earn a spot in a storytelling continuum: Aesop, the Brothers Grimm, Rod Serling, and Cuddles and Rage. What's more, this particular endeavor falls into an uncanny space all its own: horror stories filled with the kind of existential dread that adults will relate to in an adorable, kid-friendly package.

"How do you guys do it?" I'm not sure they ever gave me a real answer, perhaps because it's a hopeless question. Their creative process is uniquely their own; one might as well ask a master baker how they've executed the perfect dessert. Liz and Jimmy operate intuitively as one unit, and it's as rare as it is amazing to behold. And maybe that's all we need to know. We needn't concern ourselves with how the anthropomorphic donuts (and cakes and fruits and veggies) get made; they exist and we're lucky to have them. Knowing too much about the process might diminish the magic—and the magic in these pages is something to be treasured, respected, and preserved.

PHIL NOBILE JR.
Editor in Chief, *Fangoria* magazine

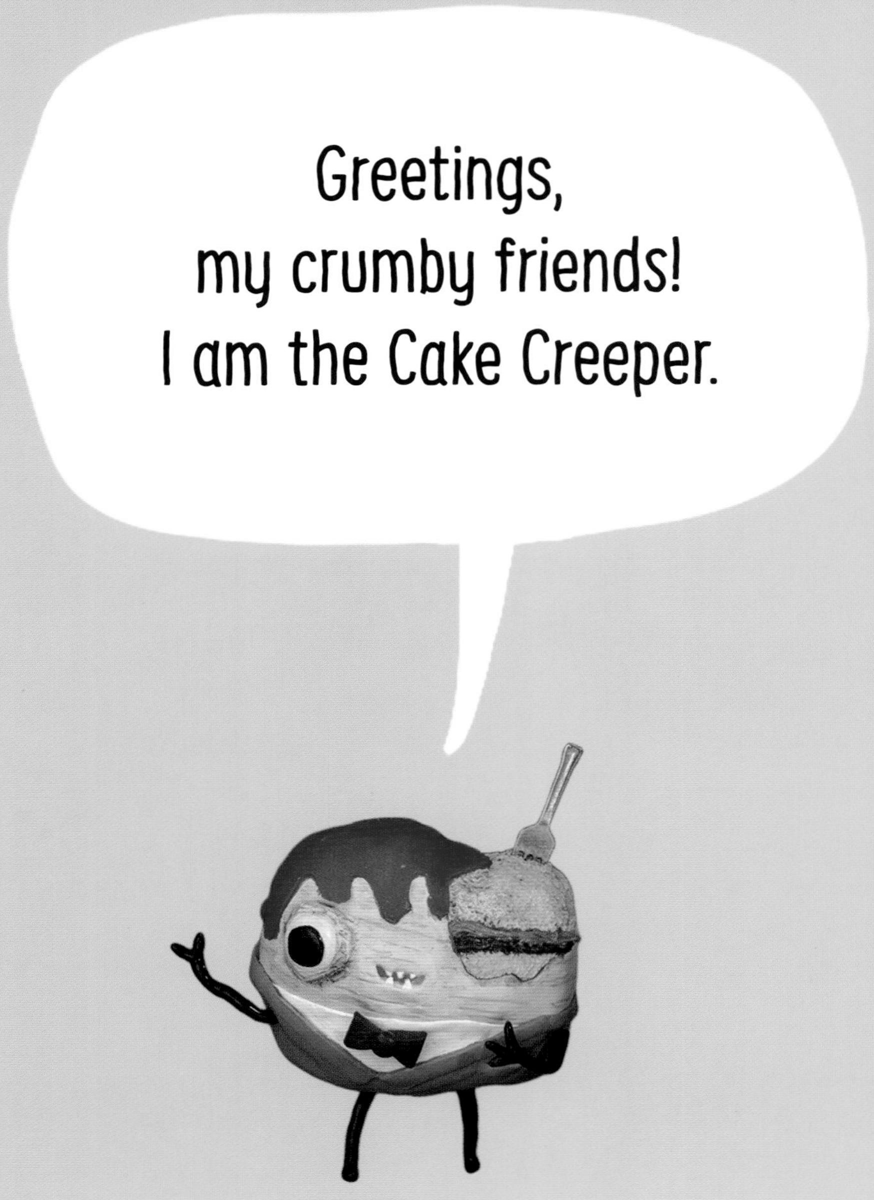
Greetings, my crumby friends! I am the Cake Creeper.

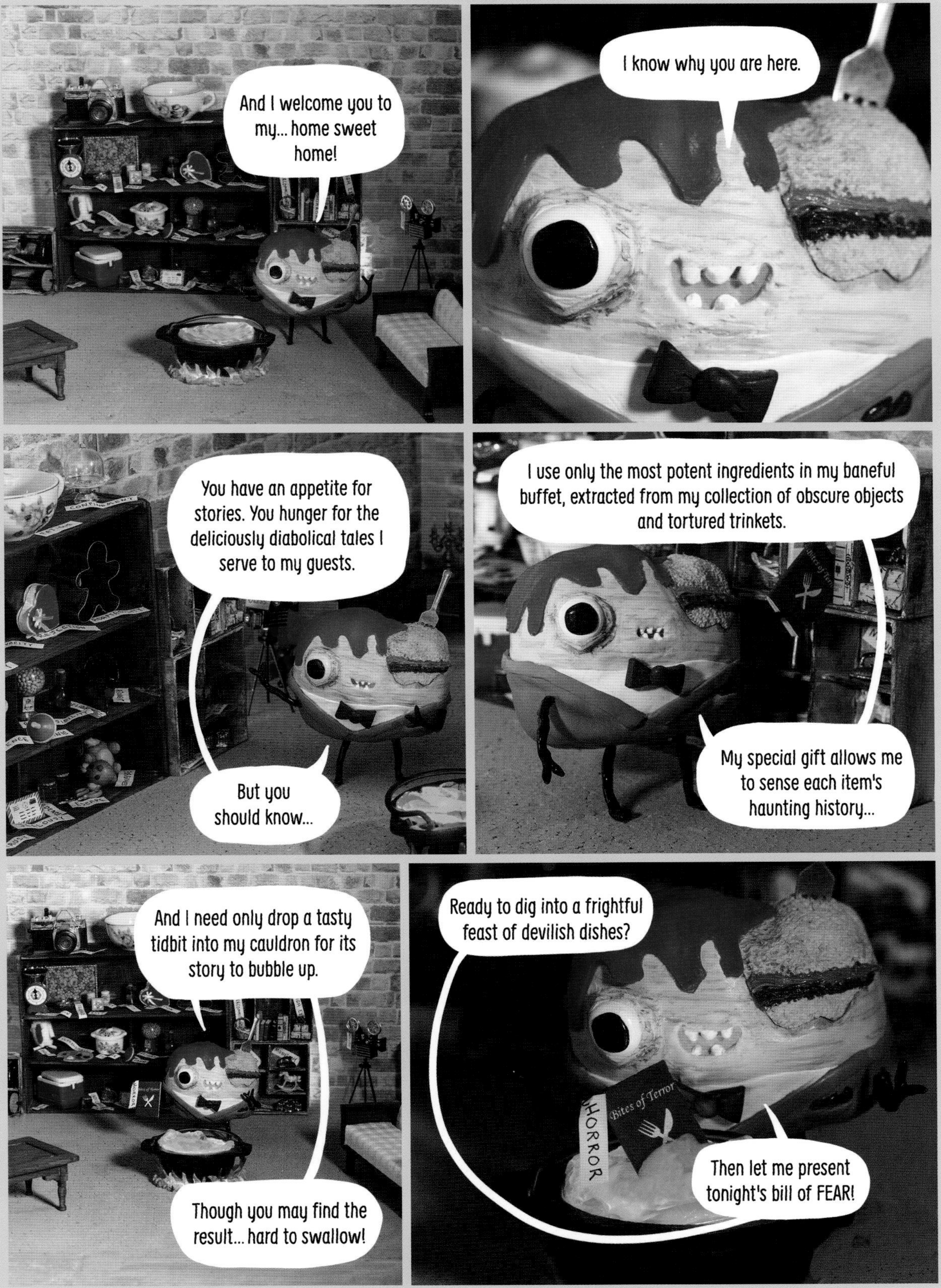
And I welcome you to my... home sweet home!
I know why you are here.
You have an appetite for stories. You hunger for the deliciously diabolical tales I serve to my guests.
But you should know...
I use only the most potent ingredients in my baneful buffet, extracted from my collection of obscure objects and tortured trinkets.
My special gift allows me to sense each item's haunting history...
And I need only drop a tasty tidbit into my cauldron for its story to bubble up.
Though you may find the result... hard to swallow!
Ready to dig into a frightful feast of devilish dishes?
HORROR
Bites of Terror
Then let me present tonight's bill of FEAR!

OUR PRIX FIXE MENU

STARTERS

ONE MORE SWIM   16
Desperation and delusion
in a creamy dressing of doom

REAP WHAT YOU SOW   26
Foolishness blended
with anxiety and misery

DEVILED EGG   40
Carefully balanced dark
and light instincts unified
by anxiety and animosity

MAINS

PIZZA PARTY MASSACRE   52
A violent fusion of murder
and vengeance in a crust
of freshly baked terror

POTLUCK   64
A generous serving of
treachery, lightly seasoned
with deception and fear

DON'T CRY   74
A tangy emulsion of suspicion,
distrust, disgust, and derision

DESSERTS

MAKE A WISH   90
Regret and ennui sprinkled
with complacency

DEATH BY CHOCOLATE   100
Deep mystery spiked with
dark secrets and a sharp layer
of fatality

UNFORTUNATE COOKIE   112
Hubris served on a bed of
locally sourced damnation

PRESERVED   128
Flavorful essence of obsession
floating in a rich broth of irony

ACKNOWLEDGMENTS   144

STARTERS

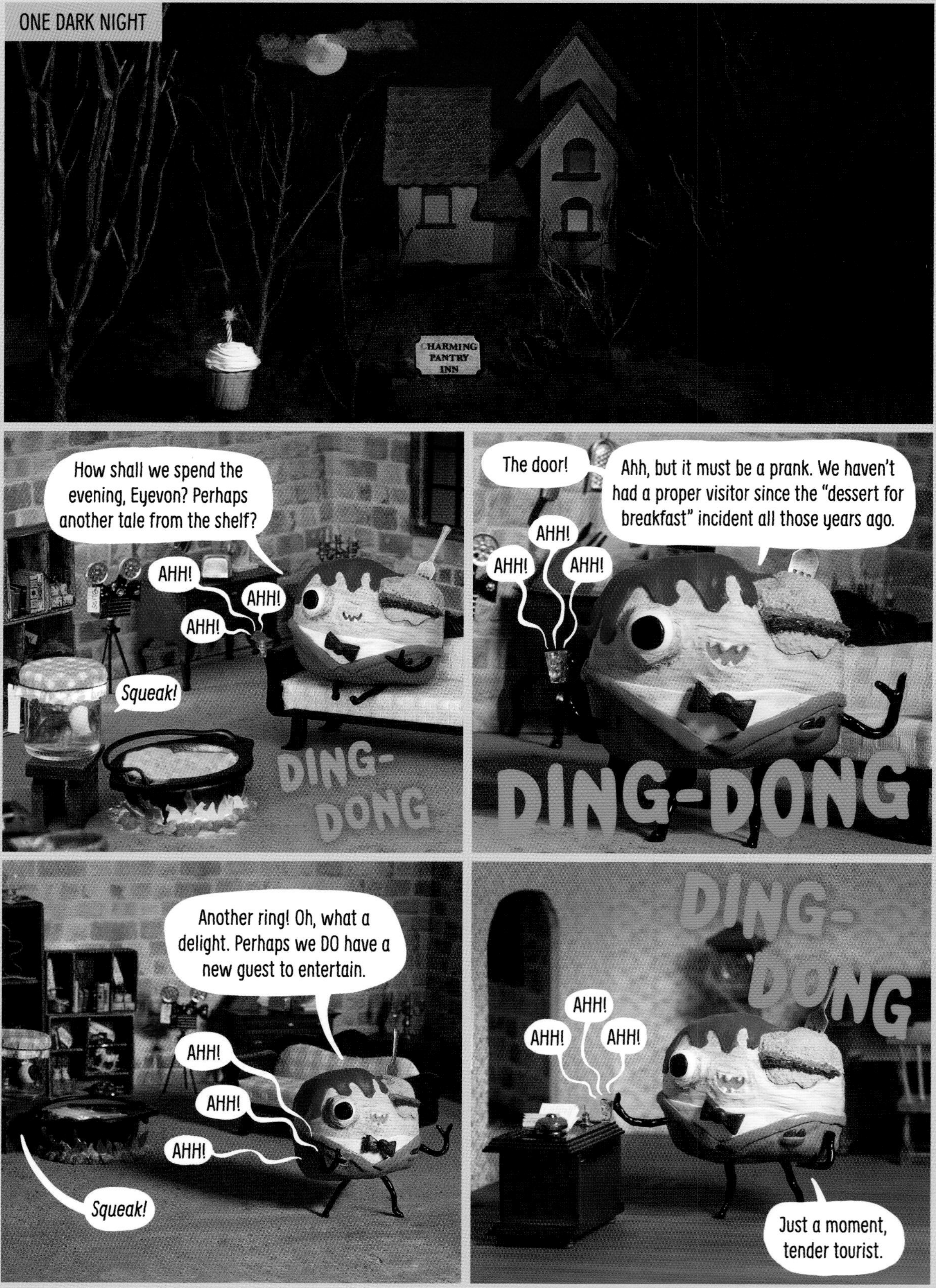
ONE DARK NIGHT
CHARMING PANTRY INN
How shall we spend the evening, Eyevon? Perhaps another tale from the shelf?
AHH!
AHH!
AHH!
Squeak!
DING-DONG
The door!
Ahh, but it must be a prank. We haven't had a proper visitor since the "dessert for breakfast" incident all those years ago.
AHH!
AHH!
AHH!
DING-DONG
Another ring! Oh, what a delight. Perhaps we DO have a new guest to entertain.
AHH!
AHH!
AHH!
Squeak!
DING-DONG
AHH!
AHH!
AHH!
Just a moment, tender tourist.

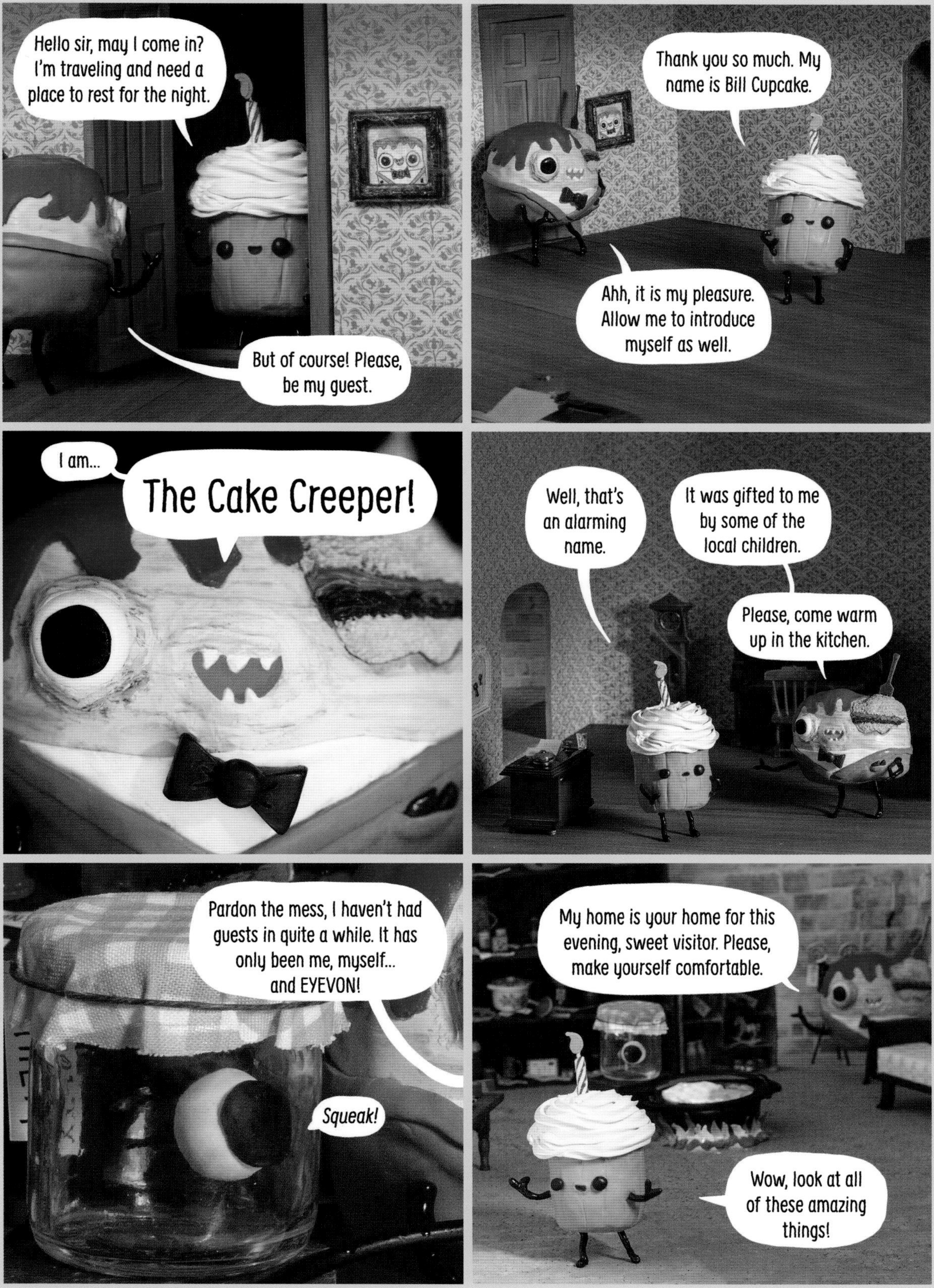
Hello sir, may I come in? I'm traveling and need a place to rest for the night.
But of course! Please, be my guest.
Thank you so much. My name is Bill Cupcake.
Ahh, it is my pleasure. Allow me to introduce myself as well.
I am...
The Cake Creeper!
Well, that's an alarming name.
It was gifted to me by some of the local children.
Please, come warm up in the kitchen.
Pardon the mess, I haven't had guests in quite a while. It has only been me, myself... and EYEVON!
Squeak!
My home is your home for this evening, sweet visitor. Please, make yourself comfortable.
Wow, look at all of these amazing things!

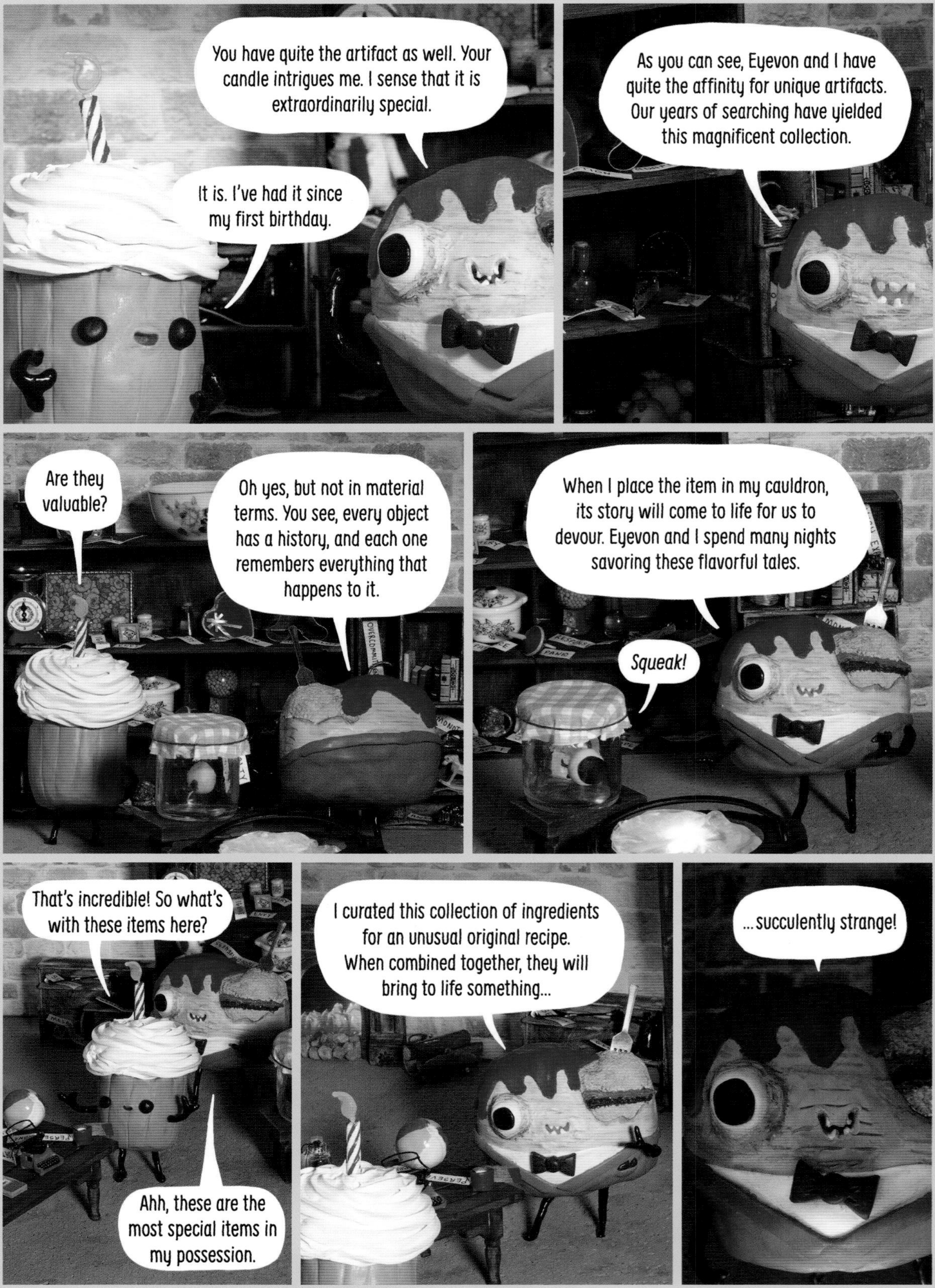
You have quite the artifact as well. Your candle intrigues me. I sense that it is extraordinarily special.
It is. I've had it since my first birthday.
As you can see, Eyevon and I have quite the affinity for unique artifacts. Our years of searching have yielded this magnificent collection.
Are they valuable?
Oh yes, but not in material terms. You see, every object has a history, and each one remembers everything that happens to it.
When I place the item in my cauldron, its story will come to life for us to devour. Eyevon and I spend many nights savoring these flavorful tales.
Squeak!
That's incredible! So what's with these items here?
Ahh, these are the most special items in my possession.
I curated this collection of ingredients for an unusual original recipe. When combined together, they will bring to life something...
...succulently strange!

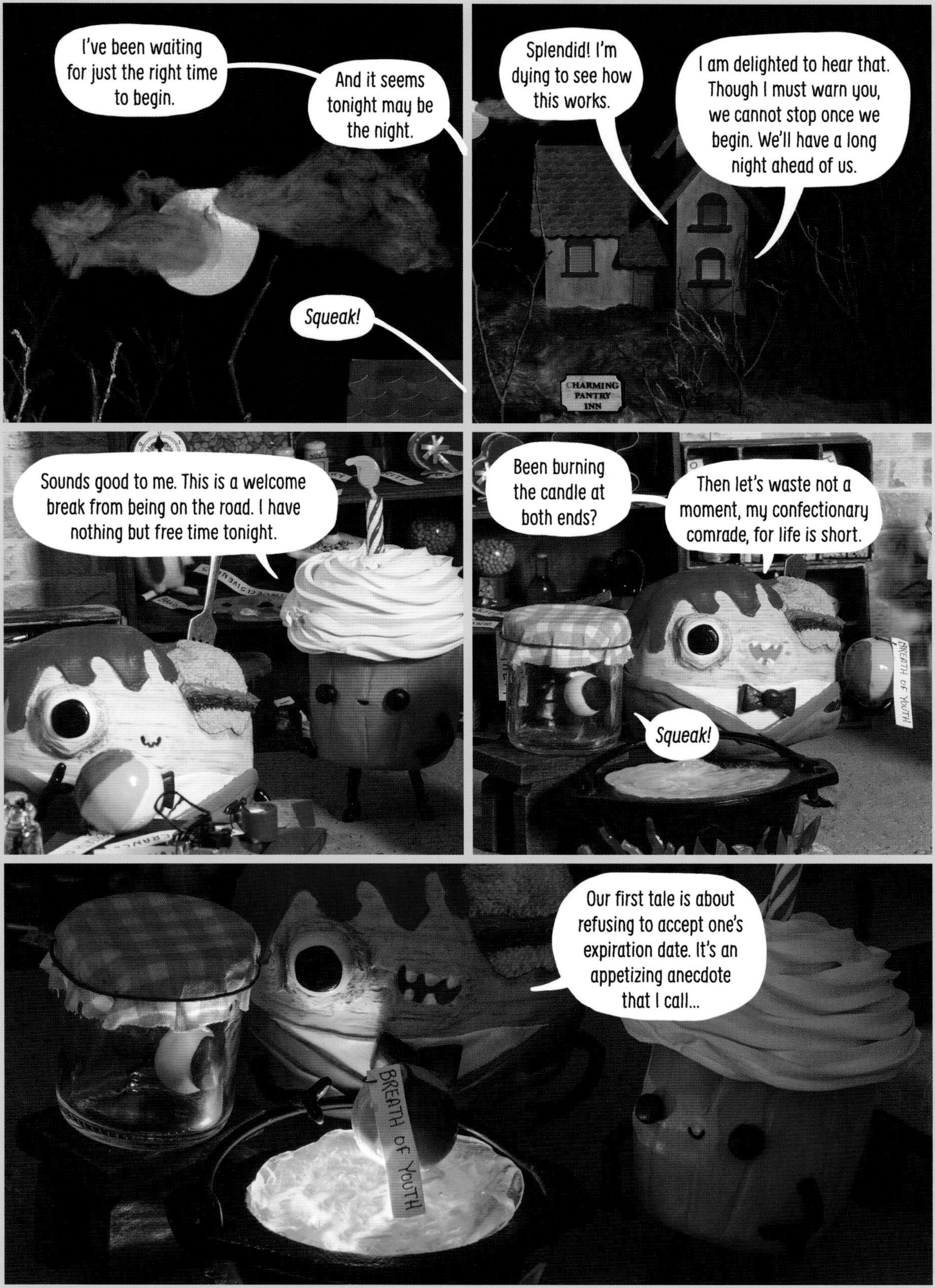
I've been waiting for just the right time to begin.
And it seems tonight may be the night.
Squeak!
Splendid! I'm dying to see how this works.
I am delighted to hear that. Though I must warn you, we cannot stop once we begin. We'll have a long night ahead of us.
CHARMING PANTRY INN
Sounds good to me. This is a welcome break from being on the road. I have nothing but free time tonight.
Been burning the candle at both ends?
Then let's waste not a moment, my confectionary comrade, for life is short.
Squeak!
BREATH of YOUTH
Our first tale is about refusing to accept one's expiration date. It's an appetizing anecdote that I call...
BREATH of YOUTH

ONE MORE SWIM

I think we got it all, Paul.

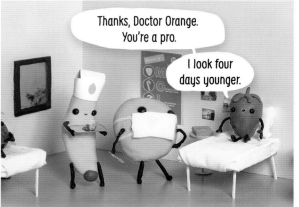

Thanks, Doctor Orange. You're a pro.

I look four days younger.

I do what I can. Get some rest tonight. The lab results should be back tomorrow.

That's good news, Paul.

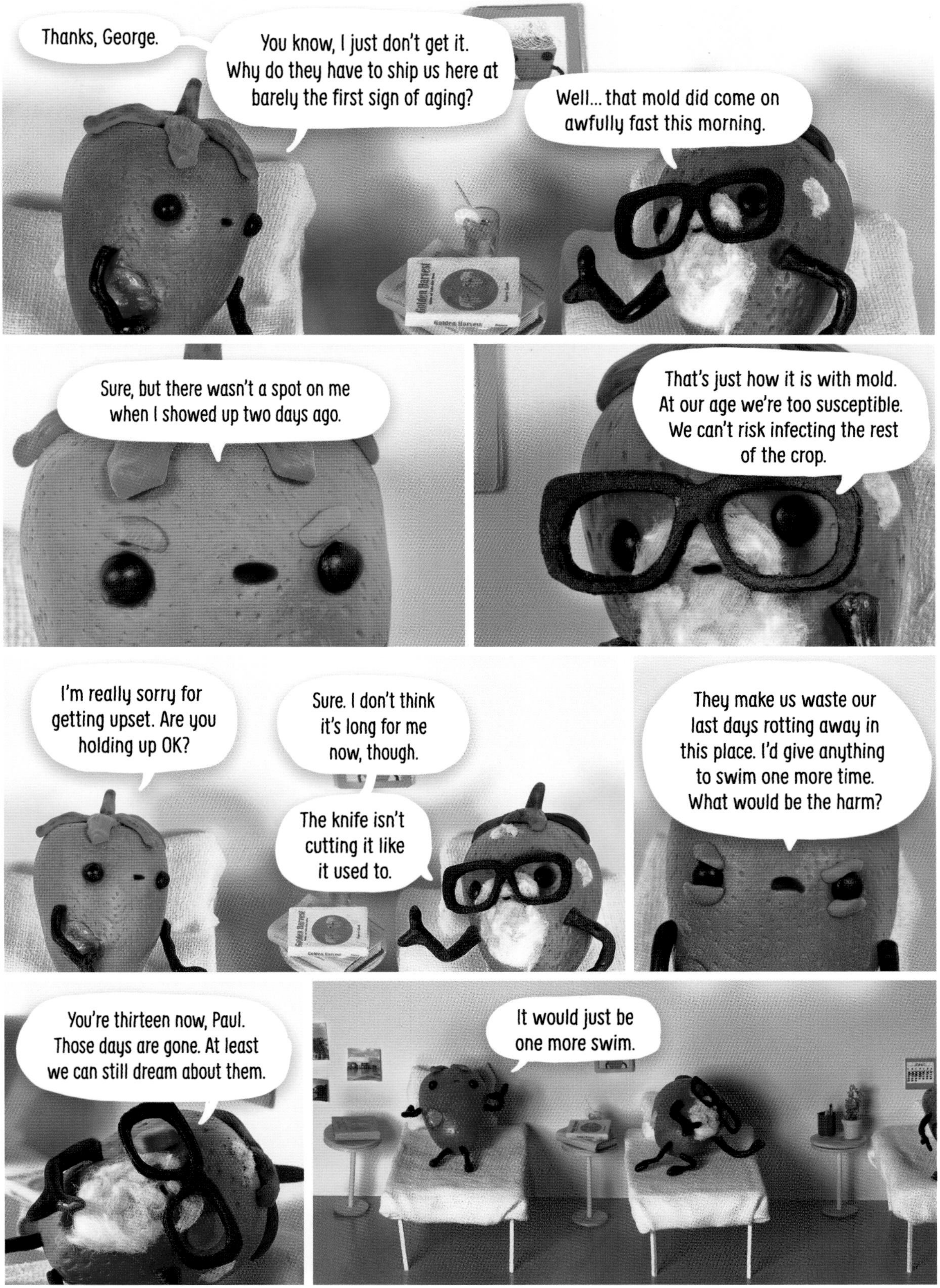
Thanks, George.
You know, I just don't get it. Why do they have to ship us here at barely the first sign of aging?
Well... that mold did come on awfully fast this morning.
Sure, but there wasn't a spot on me when I showed up two days ago.
That's just how it is with mold. At our age we're too susceptible. We can't risk infecting the rest of the crop.
I'm really sorry for getting upset. Are you holding up OK?
Sure. I don't think it's long for me now, though.
The knife isn't cutting it like it used to.
They make us waste our last days rotting away in this place. I'd give anything to swim one more time. What would be the harm?
You're thirteen now, Paul. Those days are gone. At least we can still dream about them.
It would just be one more swim.

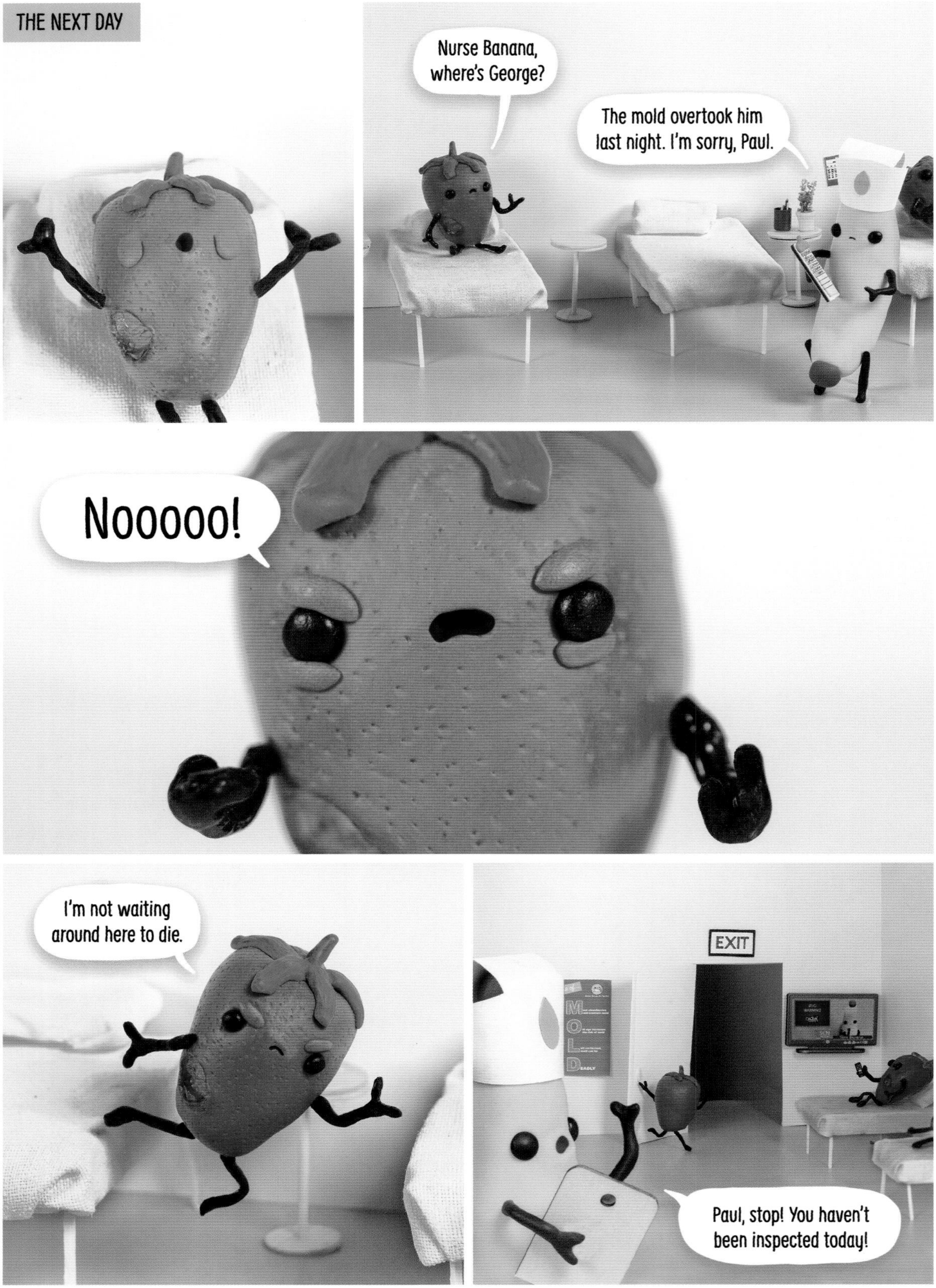
THE NEXT DAY
Nurse Banana, where's George?
The mold overtook him last night. I'm sorry, Paul.
Nooooo!
I'm not waiting around here to die.
EXIT
Paul, stop! You haven't been inspected today!

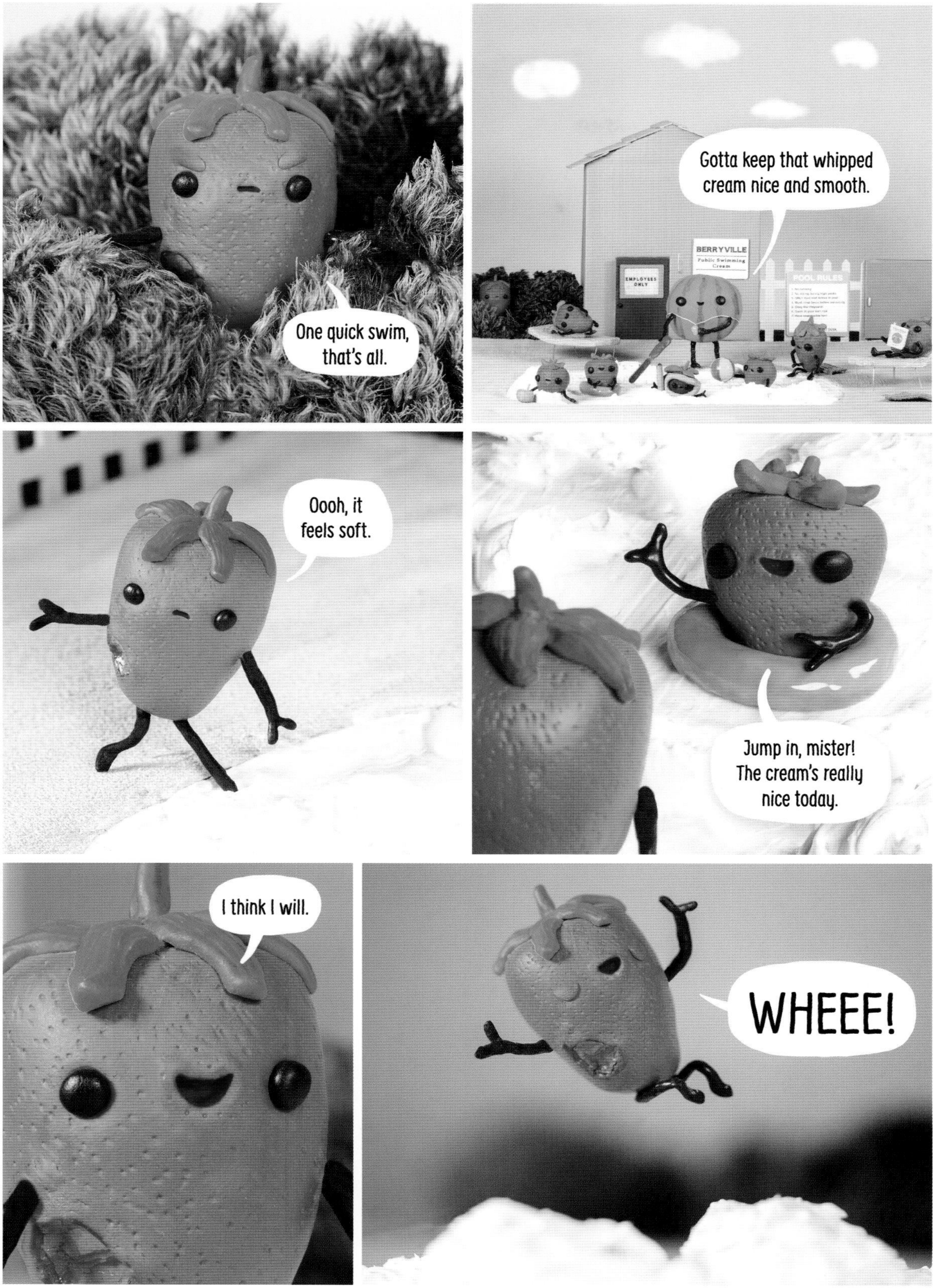

One quick swim,
that's all.
Gotta keep that whipped
cream nice and smooth.
BERRYVILLE
Public Swimming
Cream
EMPLOYEES
ONLY
POOL RULES
Oooh, it
feels soft.
Jump in, mister!
The cream's really
nice today.
I think I will.
WHEEE!

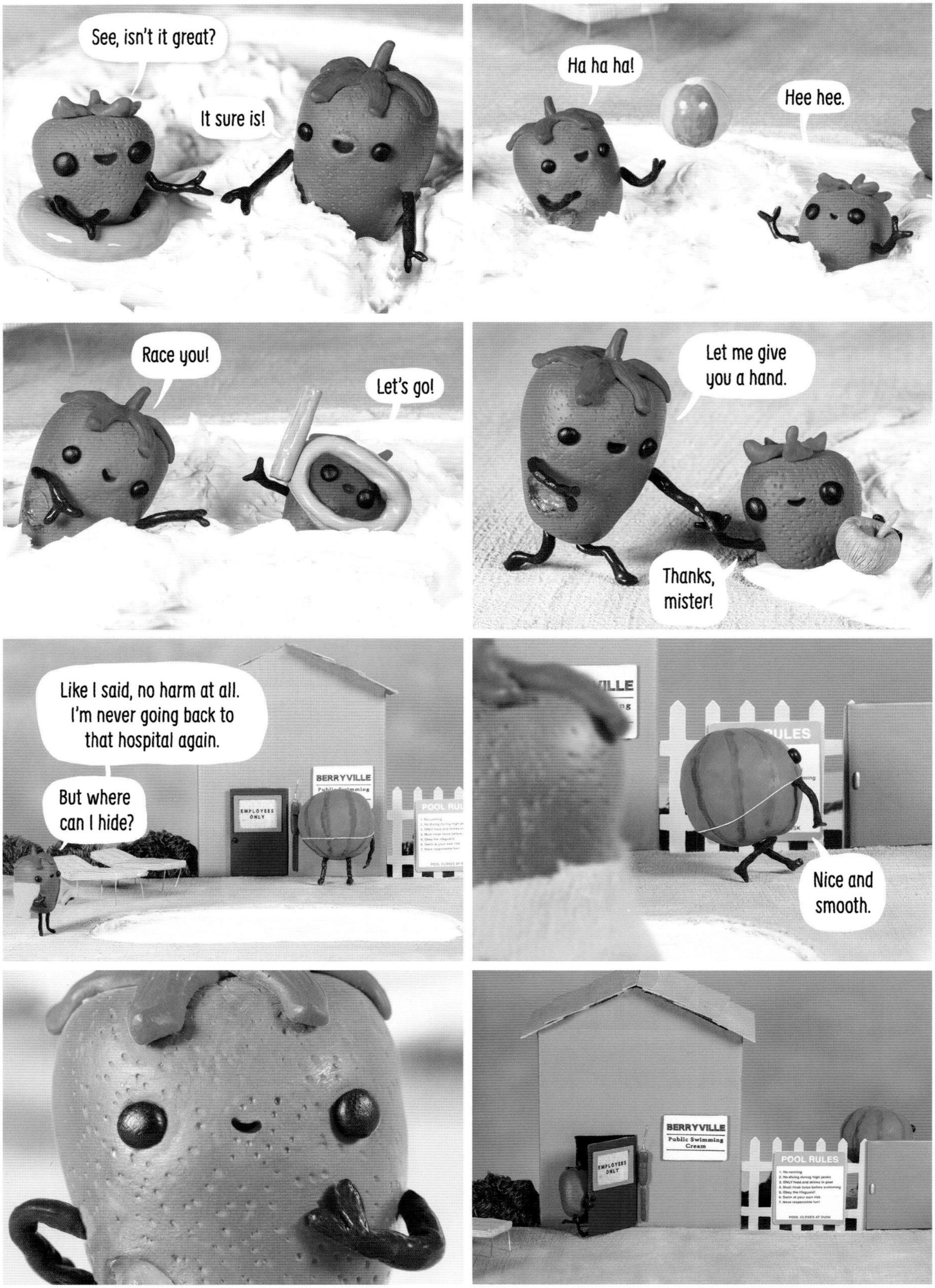
See, isn't it great?
It sure is!
Ha ha ha!
Hee hee.
Race you!
Let's go!
Let me give you a hand.
Thanks, mister!
Like I said, no harm at all. I'm never going back to that hospital again.
But where can I hide?
BERRYVILLE
EMPLOYEES ONLY
POOL RULES
Nice and smooth.
BERRYVILLE
Public Swimming
Cream
EMPLOYEES ONLY
POOL RULES
POOL CLOSES AT DUSK

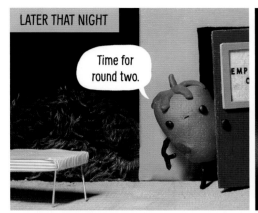

LATER THAT NIGHT
Time for round two.
Hey, what are you still doing here this late?
EMPLOYEES ONLY
BERRYVILLE
Public Swimming Cream
POOL RULES
Ugh, my side hurts. I think it's a cramp.
Let me see.
Mold! But... you're too young! Where did it come from?
I don't know, but I think I need a doctor.
5. Obey the lifeguard!
Come on, I'll take you.

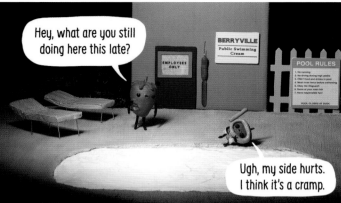

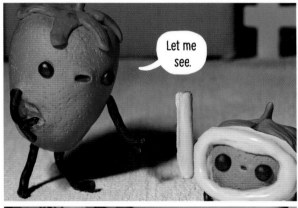

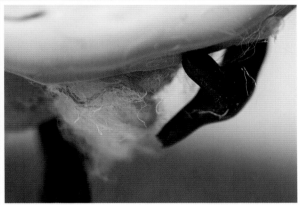

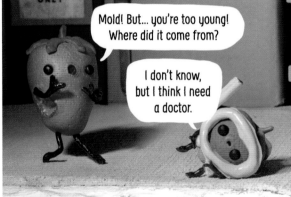

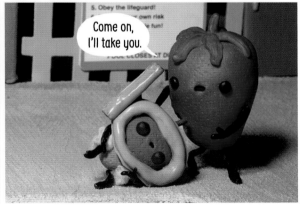

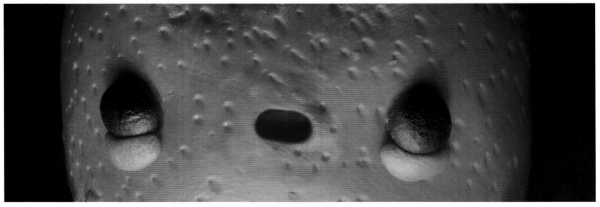

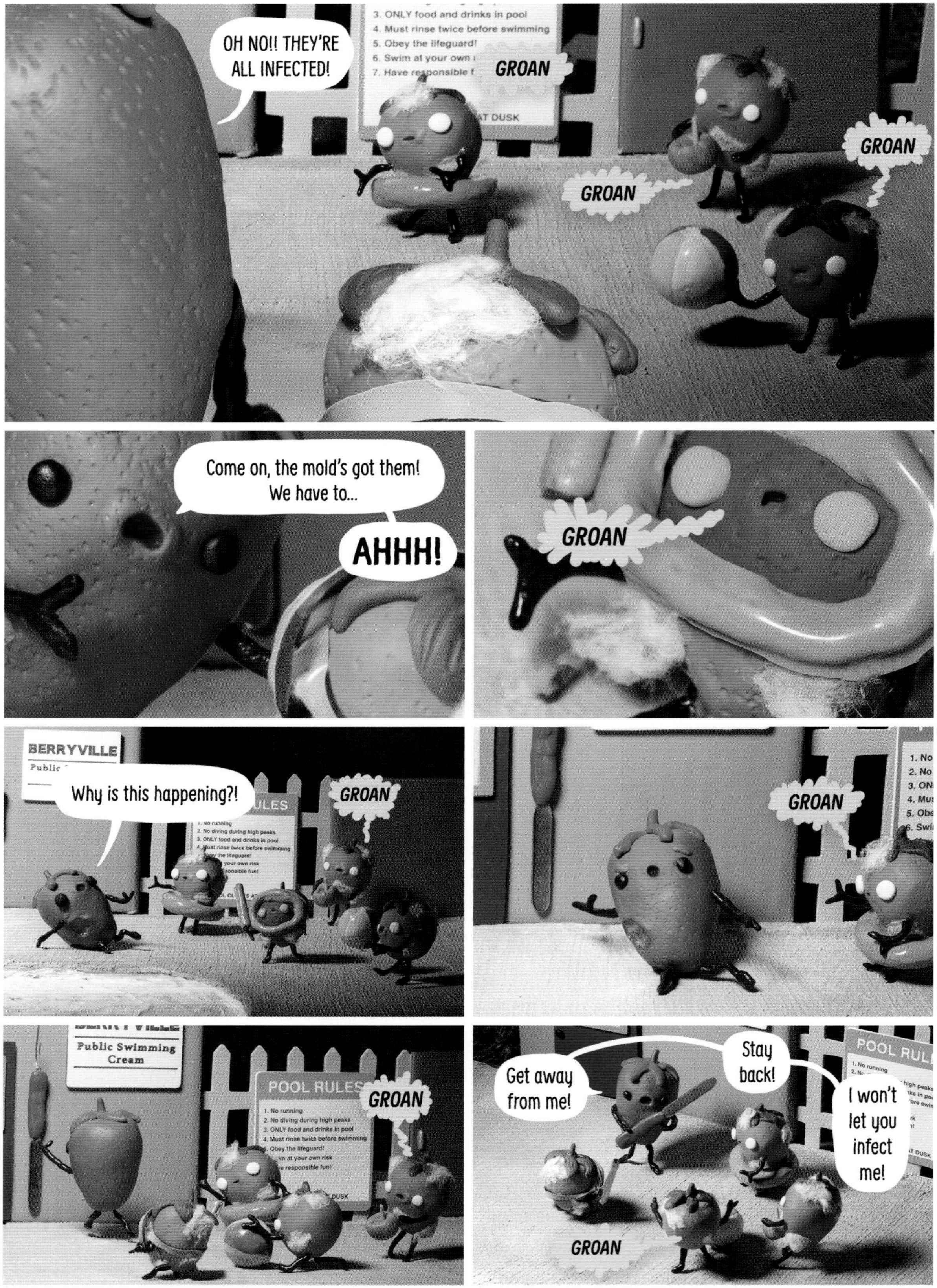
OH NO!! THEY'RE ALL INFECTED!
GROAN
GROAN
GROAN
Come on, the mold's got them! We have to...
AHHH!
GROAN
BERRYVILLE
Why is this happening?!
GROAN
GROAN
Public Swimming Cream
POOL RULES
1. No running
2. No diving during high peaks
3. ONLY food and drinks in pool
4. Must rinse twice before swimming
GROAN
Get away from me!
Stay back!
I won't let you infect me!
GROAN

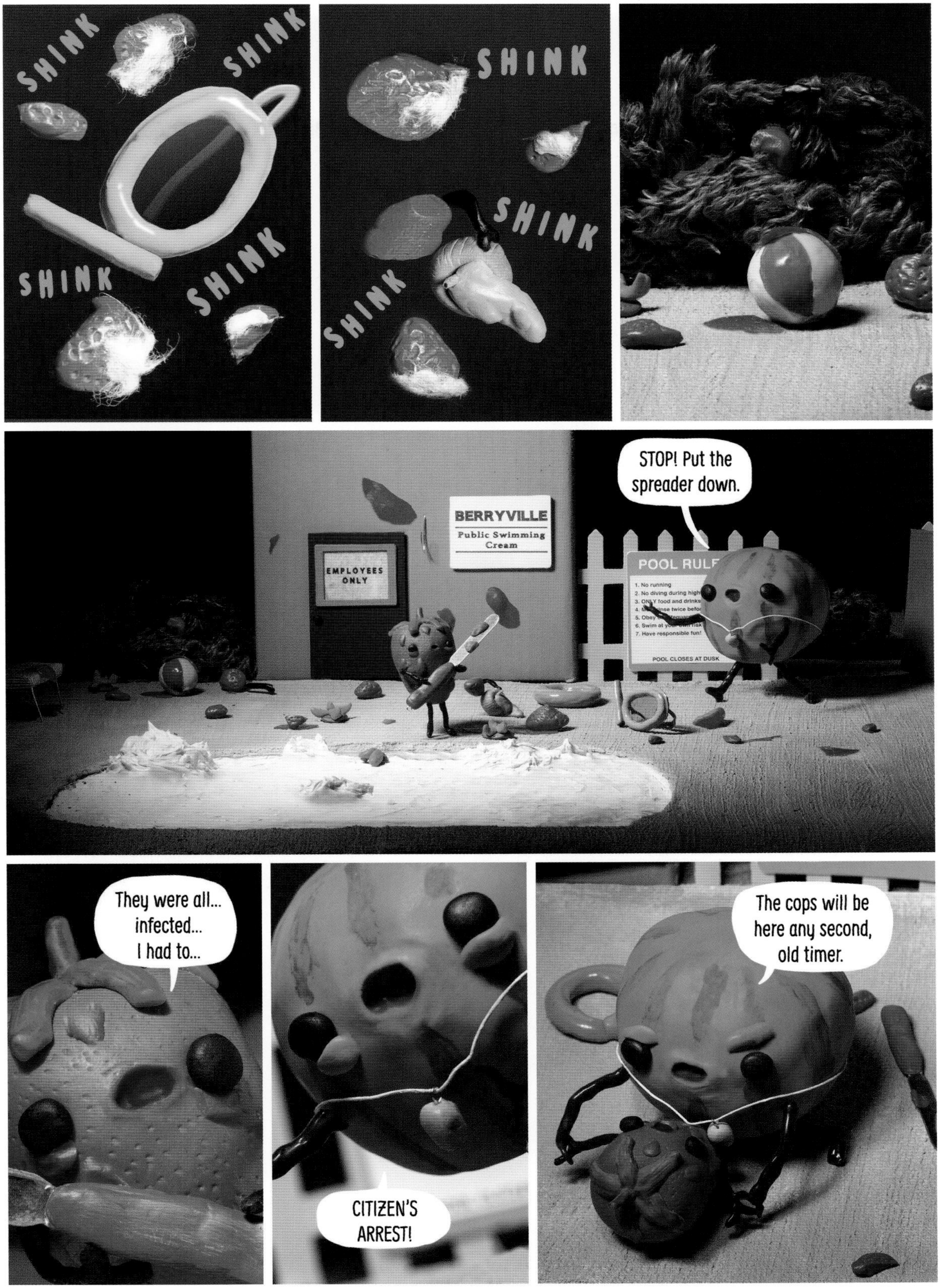
SHINK
SHINK
SHINK
SHINK
SHINK
SHINK
SHINK
EMPLOYEES ONLY
BERRYVILLE
Public Swimming Cream
POOL RULES
POOL CLOSES AT DUSK
STOP! Put the spreader down.
They were all... infected... I had to...
CITIZEN'S ARREST!
The cops will be here any second, old timer.

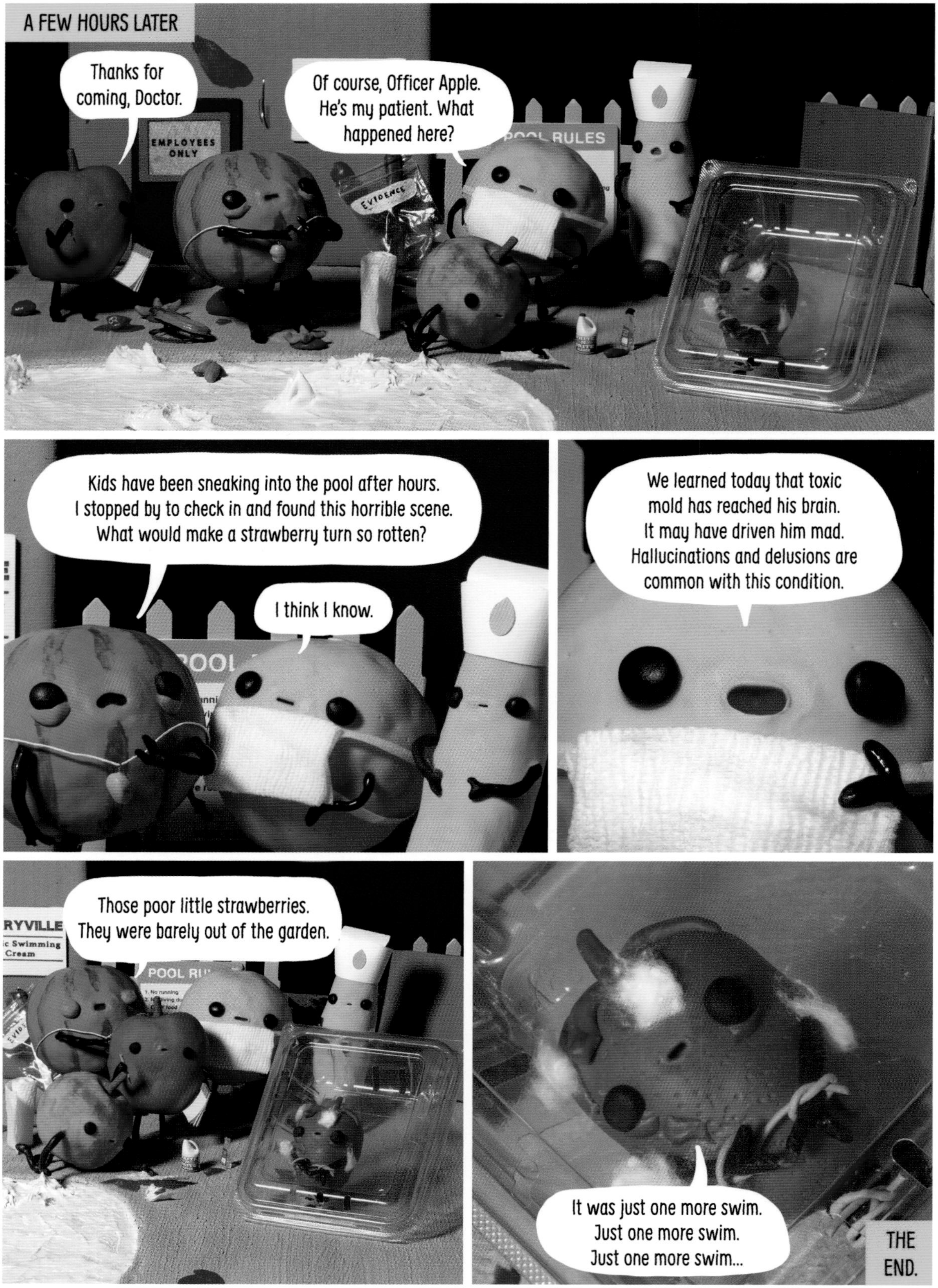
A FEW HOURS LATER
Thanks for coming, Doctor.
Of course, Officer Apple. He's my patient. What happened here?
EMPLOYEES ONLY
EVIDENCE
POOL RULES
Kids have been sneaking into the pool after hours. I stopped by to check in and found this horrible scene. What would make a strawberry turn so rotten?
I think I know.
We learned today that toxic mold has reached his brain. It may have driven him mad. Hallucinations and delusions are common with this condition.
Those poor little strawberries. They were barely out of the garden.
It was just one more swim. Just one more swim. Just one more swim...
THE END.

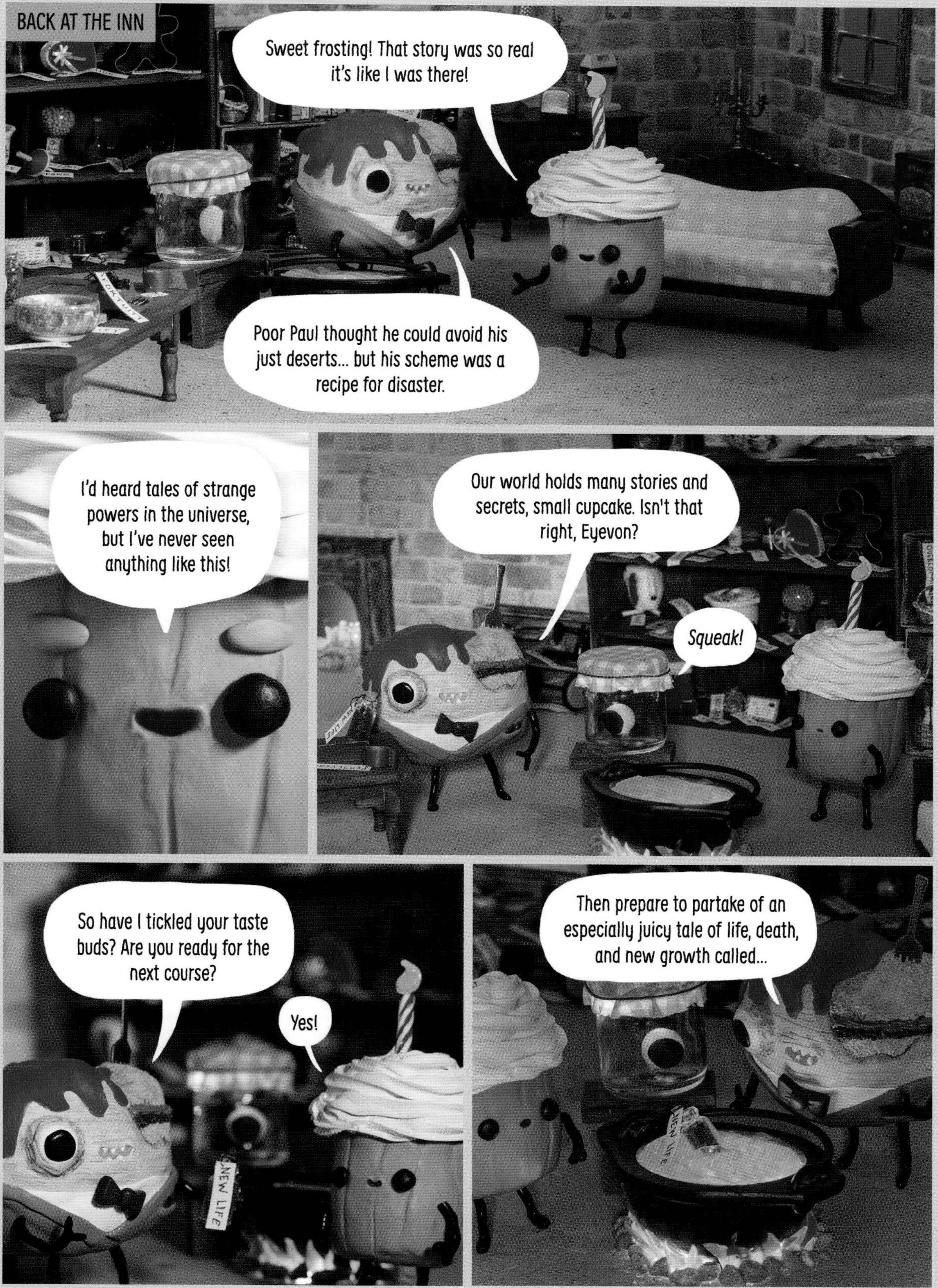
BACK AT THE INN
Sweet frosting! That story was so real it's like I was there!
Poor Paul thought he could avoid his just deserts... but his scheme was a recipe for disaster.
I'd heard tales of strange powers in the universe, but I've never seen anything like this!
Our world holds many stories and secrets, small cupcake. Isn't that right, Eyevon?
Squeak!
So have I tickled your taste buds? Are you ready for the next course?
Yes!
Then prepare to partake of an especially juicy tale of life, death, and new growth called...

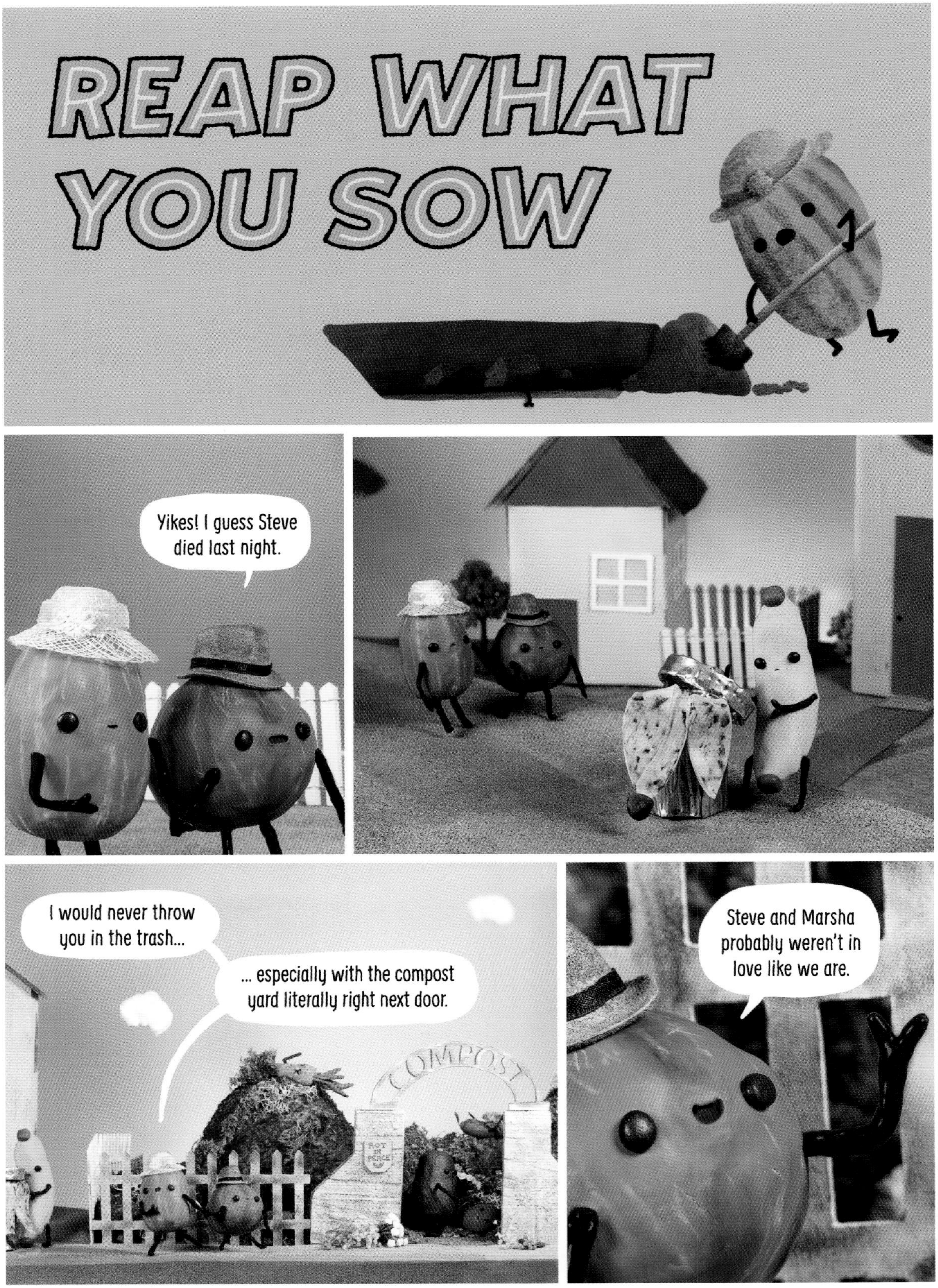
REAP WHAT YOU SOW
Yikes! I guess Steve died last night.
I would never throw you in the trash...
... especially with the compost yard literally right next door.
COMPOST
ROT IN PEACE
Steve and Marsha probably weren't in love like we are.

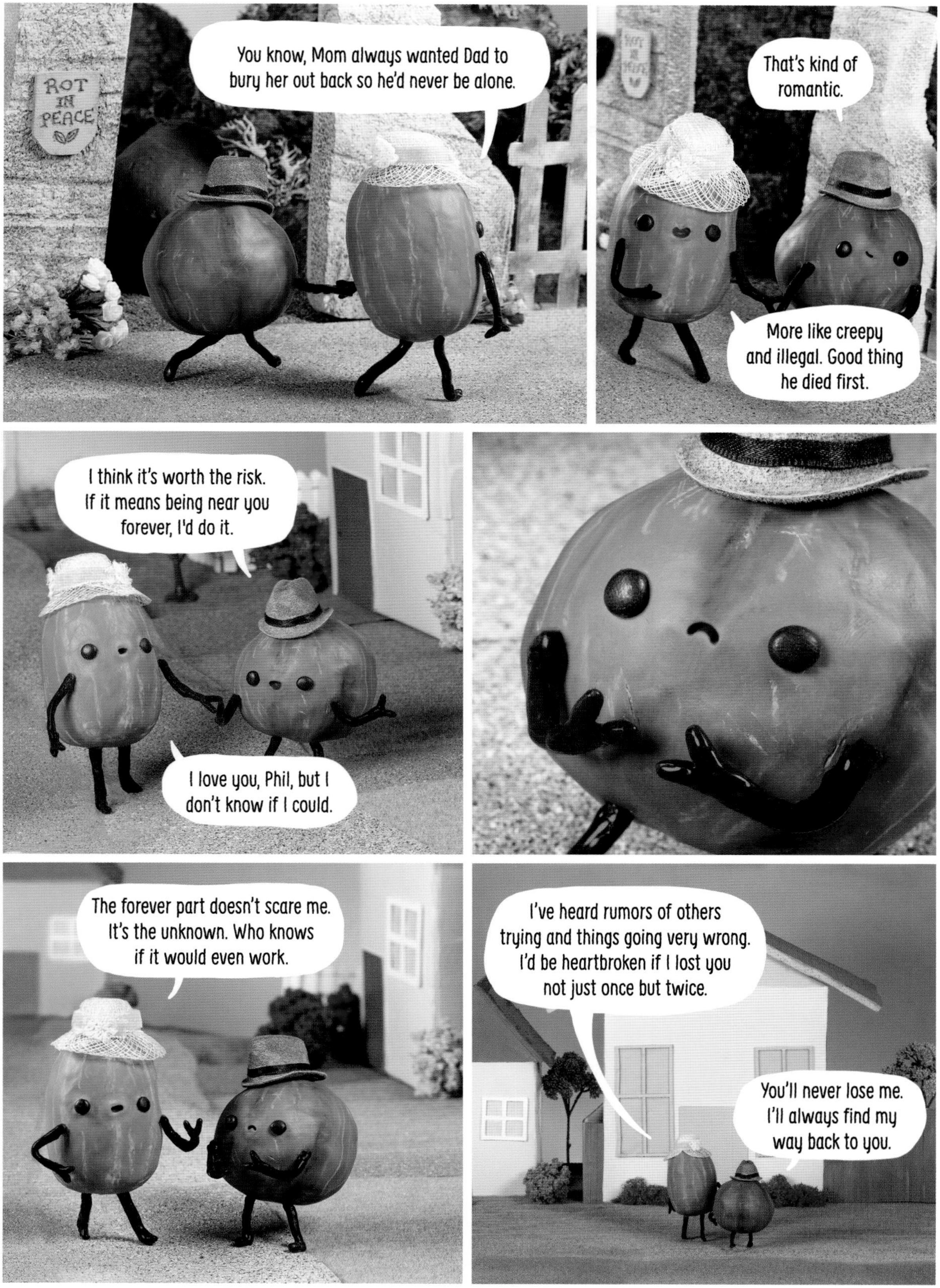
ROT IN PEACE
You know, Mom always wanted Dad to bury her out back so he'd never be alone.
That's kind of romantic.
More like creepy and illegal. Good thing he died first.
I think it's worth the risk. If it means being near you forever, I'd do it.
I love you, Phil, but I don't know if I could.
The forever part doesn't scare me. It's the unknown. Who knows if it would even work.
I've heard rumors of others trying and things going very wrong. I'd be heartbroken if I lost you not just once but twice.
You'll never lose me. I'll always find my way back to you.

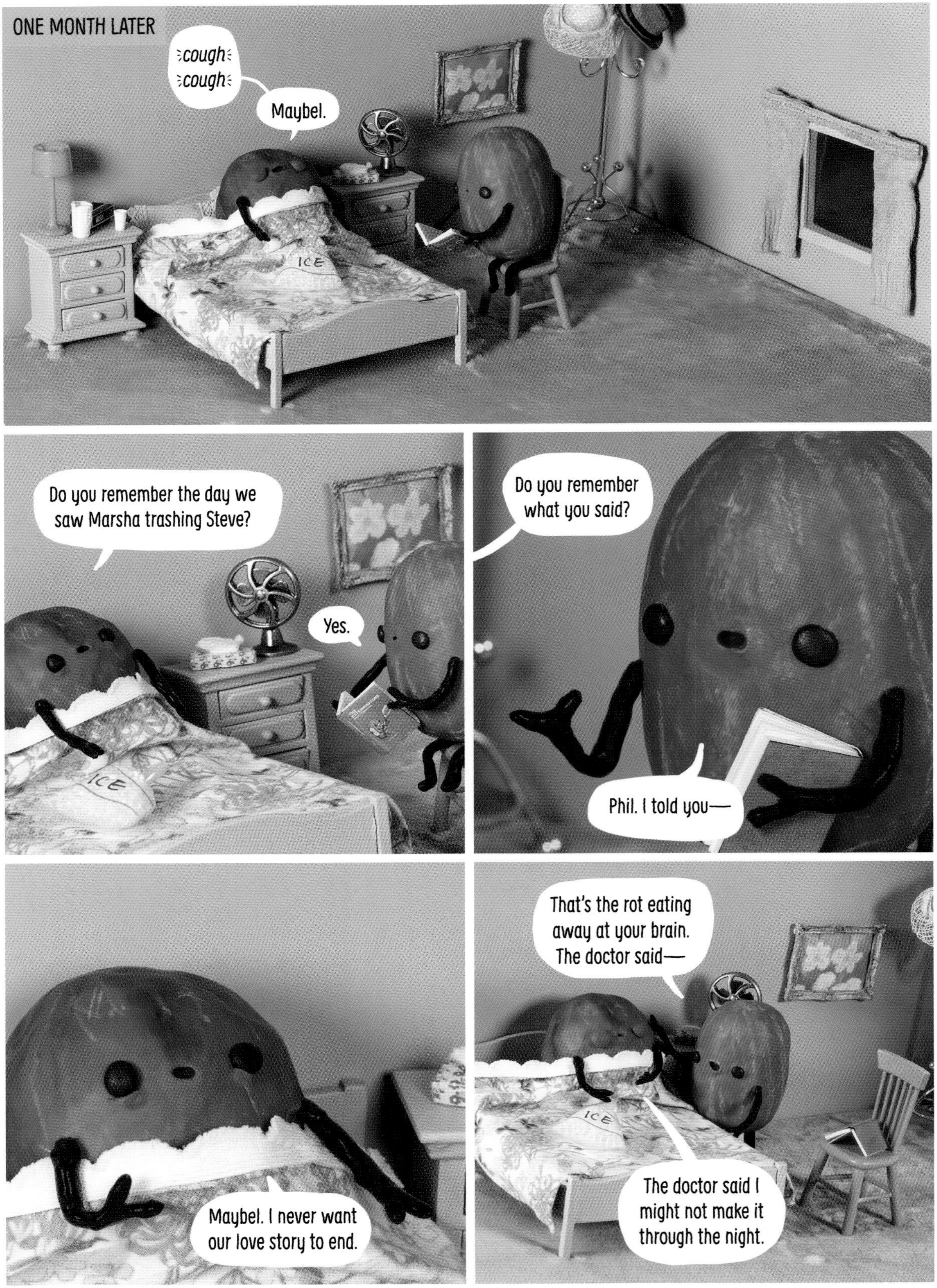
ONE MONTH LATER
cough cough
Maybel.
Do you remember the day we saw Marsha trashing Steve?
Yes.
Do you remember what you said?
Phil. I told you—
Maybel. I never want our love story to end.
That's the rot eating away at your brain. The doctor said—
The doctor said I might not make it through the night.

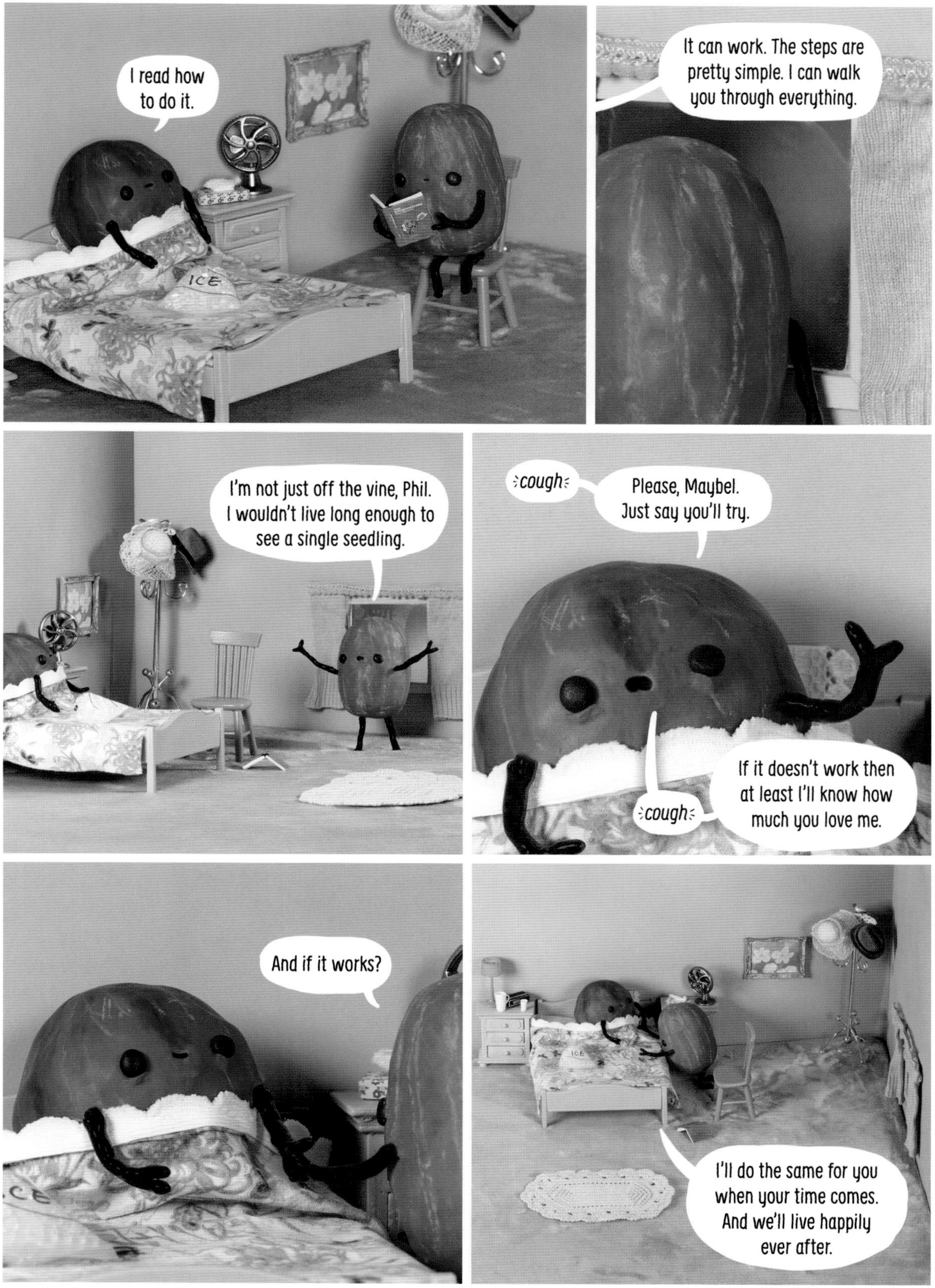

I read how to do it.
It can work. The steps are pretty simple. I can walk you through everything.
I'm not just off the vine, Phil. I wouldn't live long enough to see a single seedling.
cough
Please, Maybel. Just say you'll try.
cough
If it doesn't work then at least I'll know how much you love me.
And if it works?
I'll do the same for you when your time comes. And we'll live happily ever after.

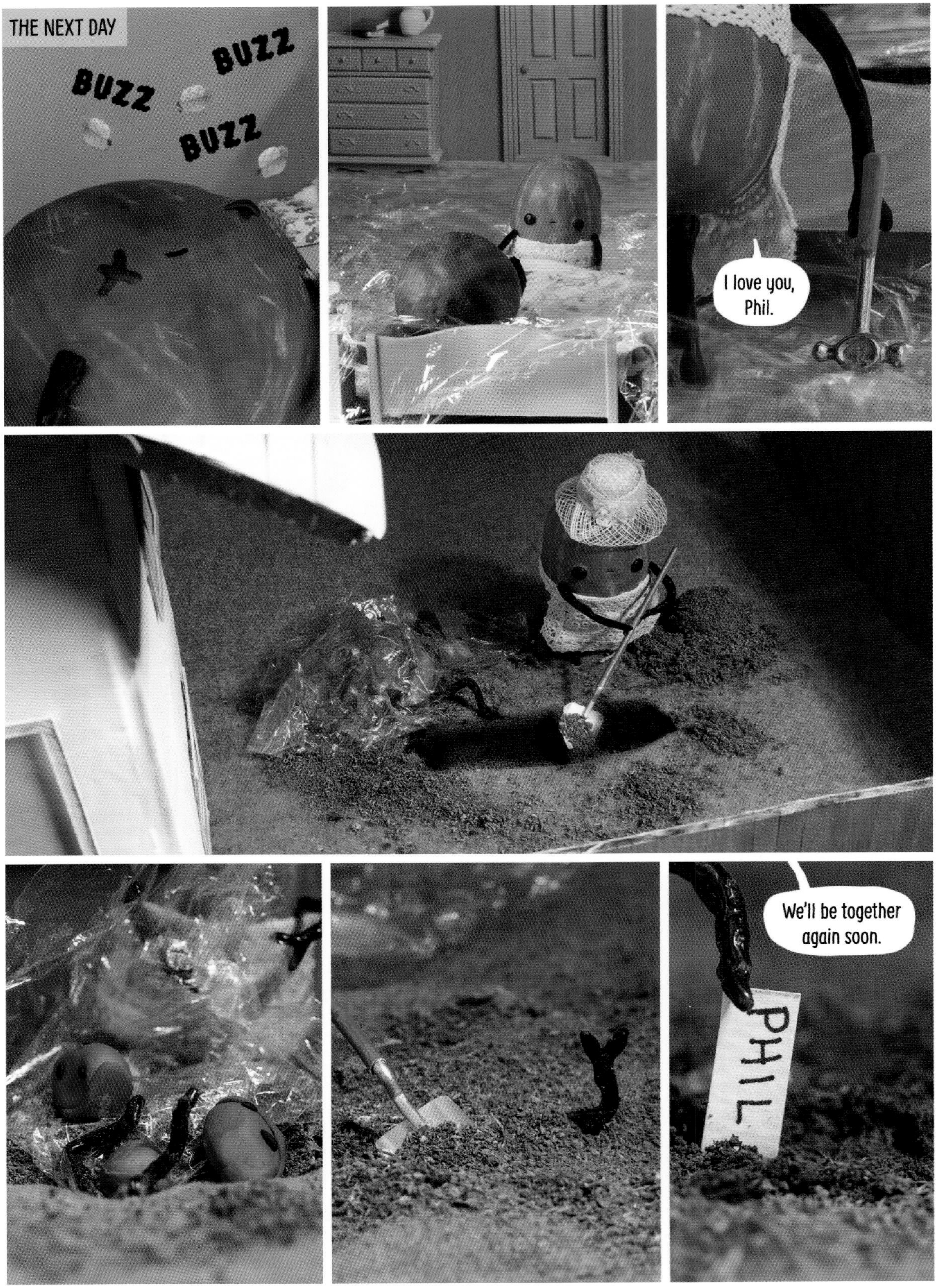
THE NEXT DAY
BUZZ
BUZZ
BUZZ
I love you, Phil.
We'll be together again soon.
PHIL

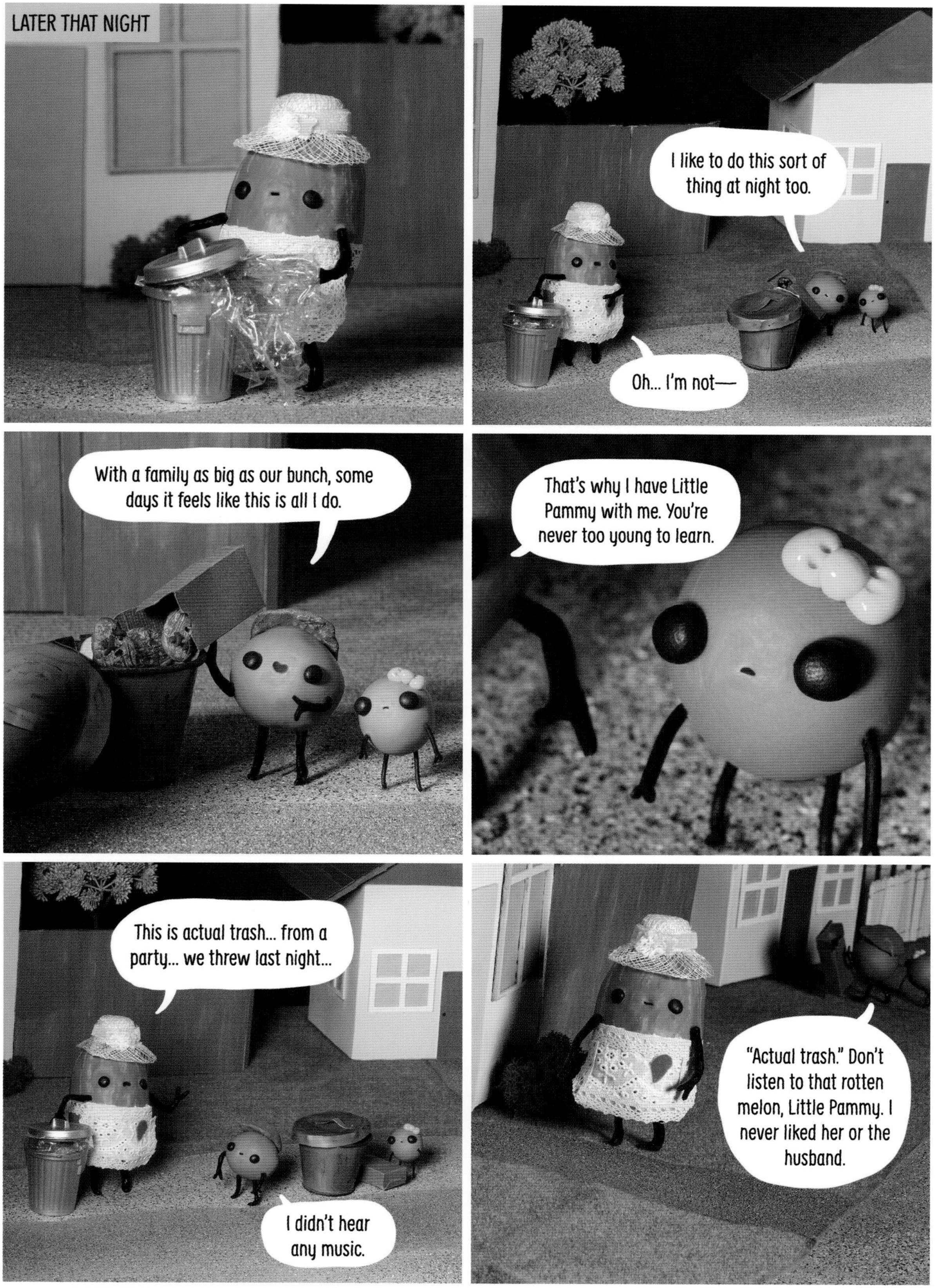
LATER THAT NIGHT
I like to do this sort of thing at night too.
Oh... I'm not—
With a family as big as our bunch, some days it feels like this is all I do.
That's why I have Little Pammy with me. You're never too young to learn.
This is actual trash... from a party... we threw last night...
I didn't hear any music.
"Actual trash." Don't listen to that rotten melon, Little Pammy. I never liked her or the husband.

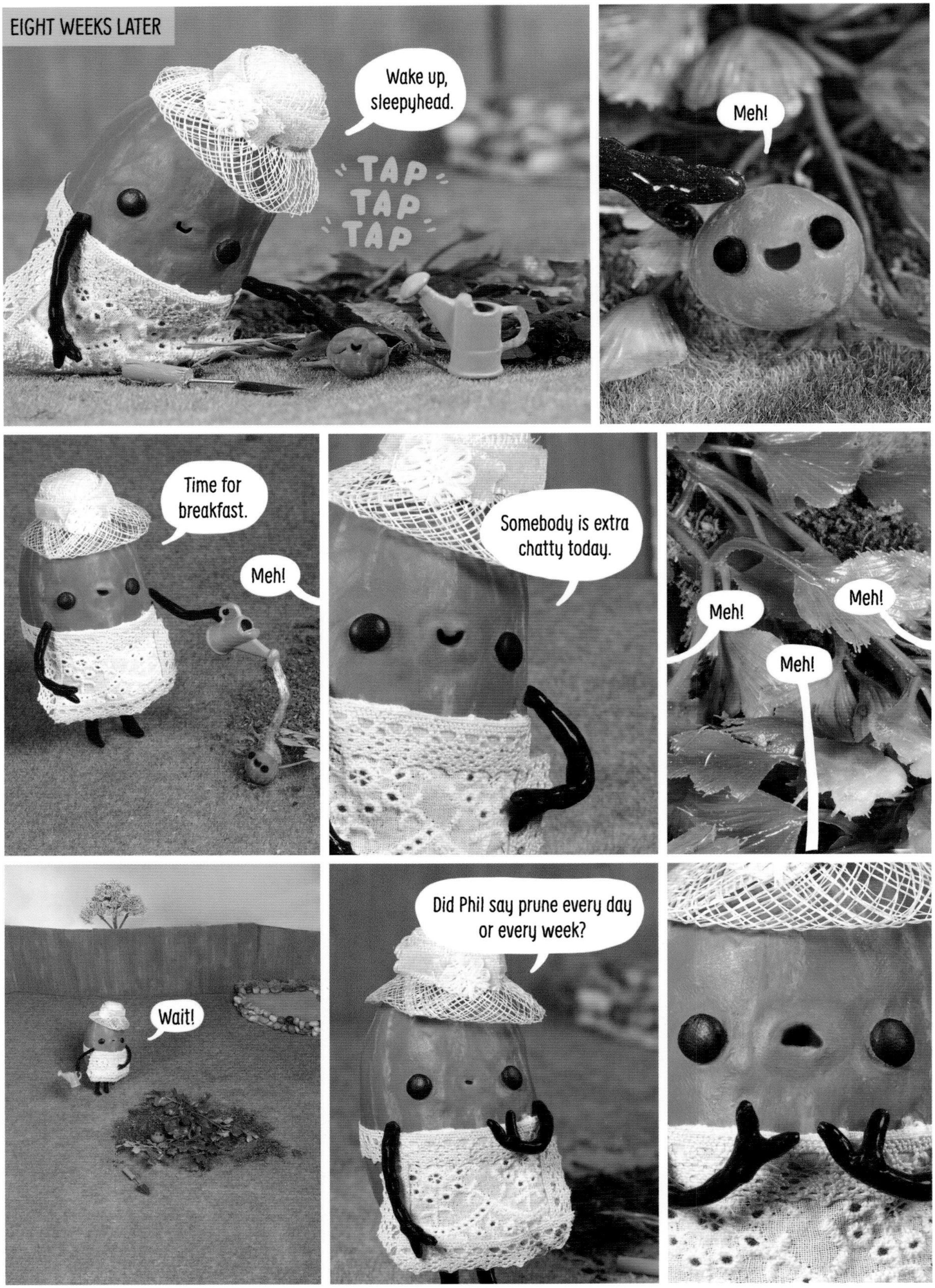
EIGHT WEEKS LATER
Wake up, sleepyhead.
TAP TAP TAP
Meh!
Time for breakfast.
Meh!
Somebody is extra chatty today.
Meh!
Meh!
Meh!
Wait!
Did Phil say prune every day or every week?

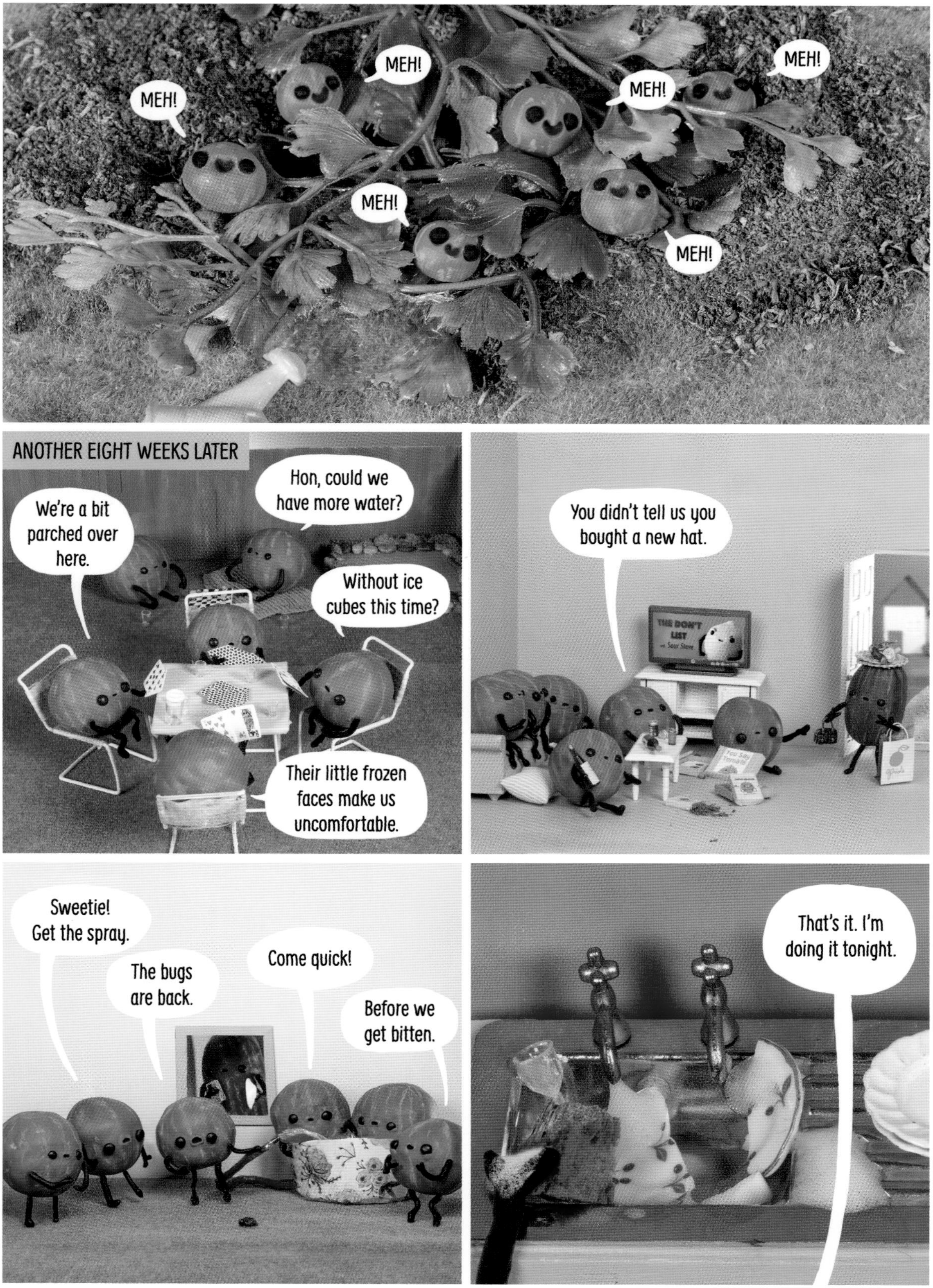
MEH!
MEH!
MEH!
MEH!
MEH!
MEH!
MEH!
ANOTHER EIGHT WEEKS LATER
We're a bit parched over here.
Hon, could we have more water?
Without ice cubes this time?
Their little frozen faces make us uncomfortable.
You didn't tell us you bought a new hat.
Sweetie! Get the spray.
The bugs are back.
Come quick!
Before we get bitten.
That's it. I'm doing it tonight.

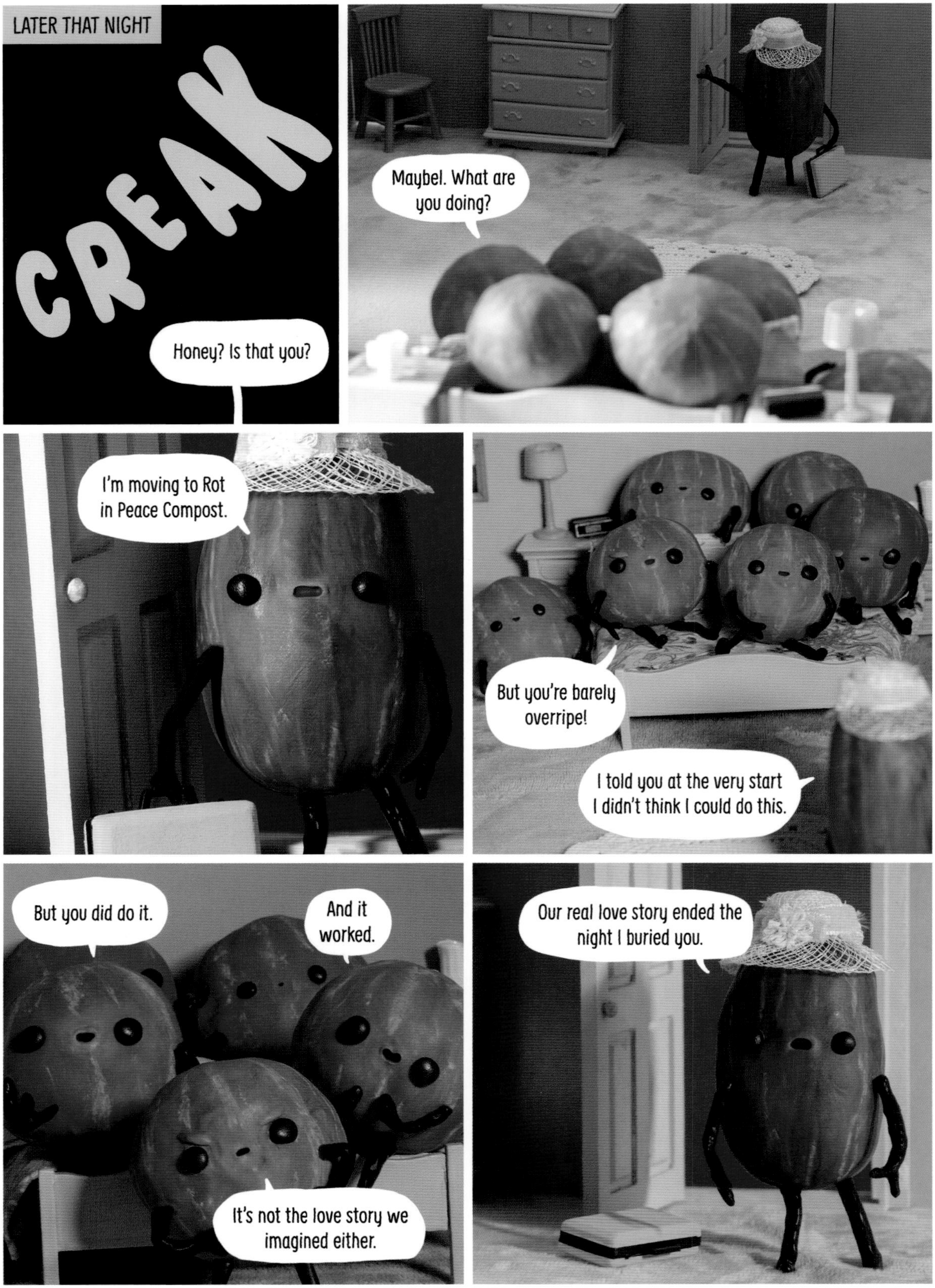
LATER THAT NIGHT
CREAK
Honey? Is that you?
Maybel. What are you doing?
I'm moving to Rot in Peace Compost.
But you're barely overripe!
I told you at the very start I didn't think I could do this.
But you did do it.
And it worked.
It's not the love story we imagined either.
Our real love story ended the night I buried you.

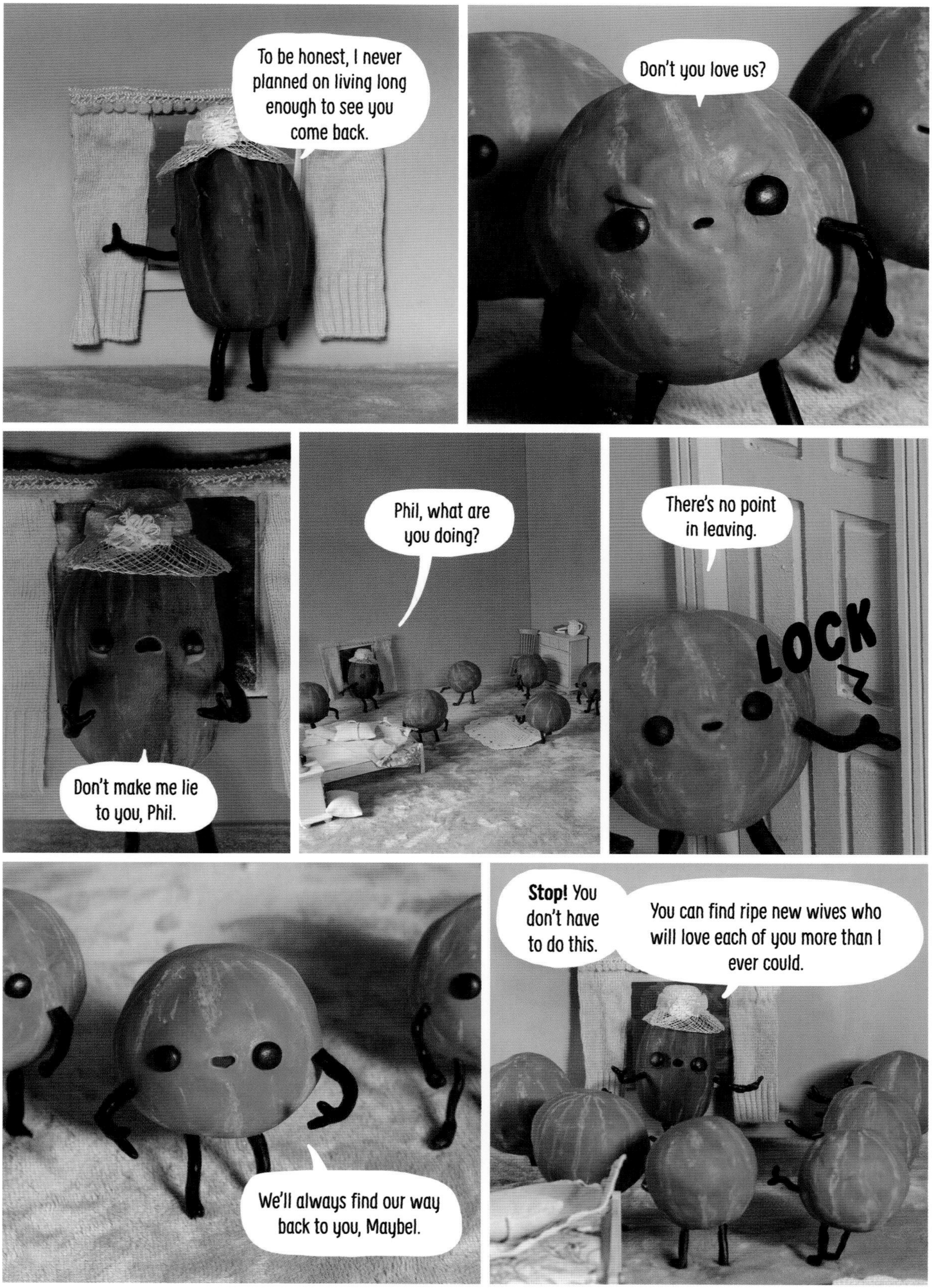
To be honest, I never planned on living long enough to see you come back.
Don't you love us?
Don't make me lie to you, Phil.
Phil, what are you doing?
There's no point in leaving.
LOCK
We'll always find our way back to you, Maybel.
Stop! You don't have to do this.
You can find ripe new wives who will love each of you more than I ever could.

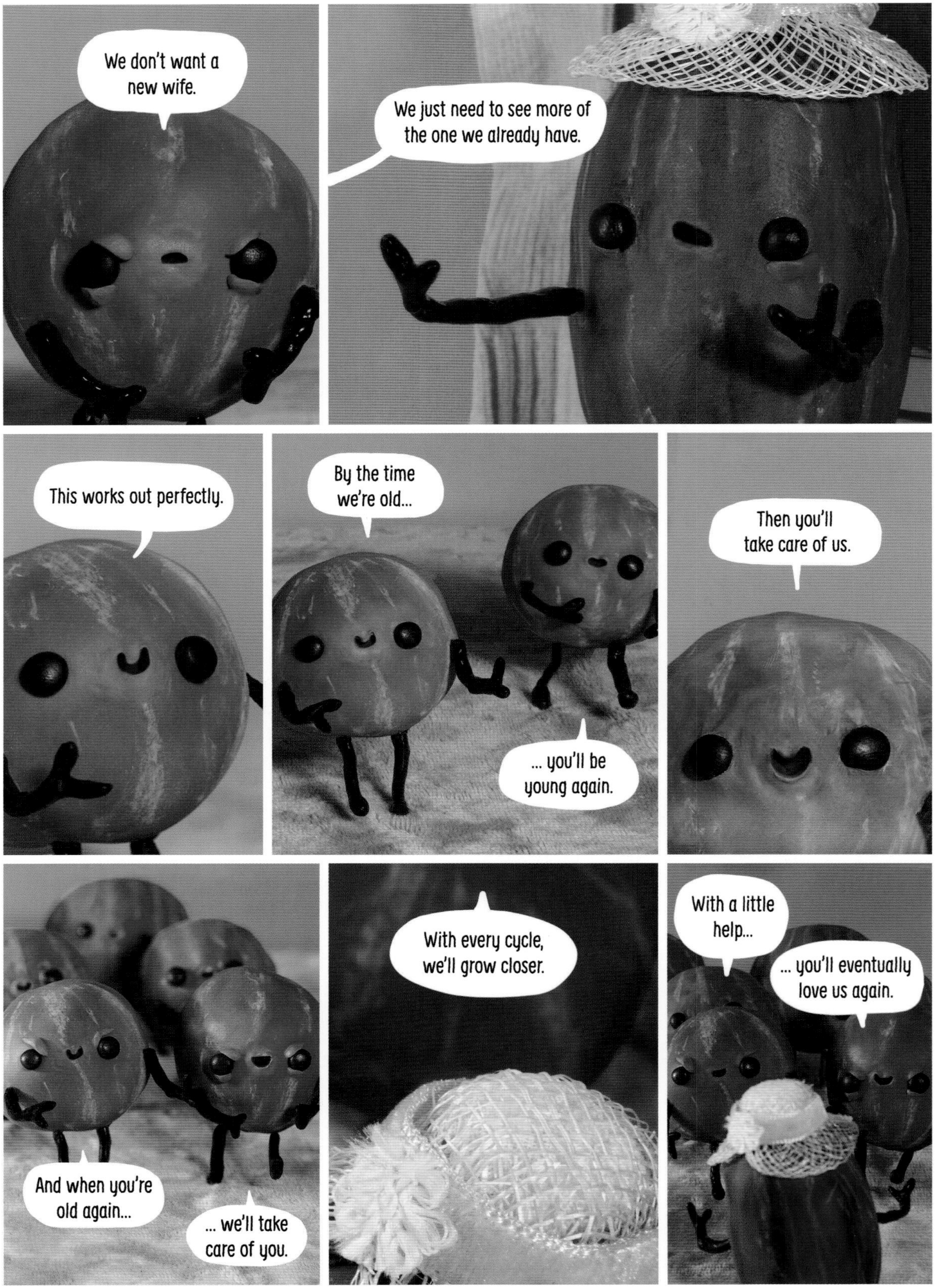
We don't want a new wife.
We just need to see more of the one we already have.
This works out perfectly.
By the time we're old...
... you'll be young again.
Then you'll take care of us.
And when you're old again...
... we'll take care of you.
With every cycle, we'll grow closer.
With a little help...
... you'll eventually love us again.

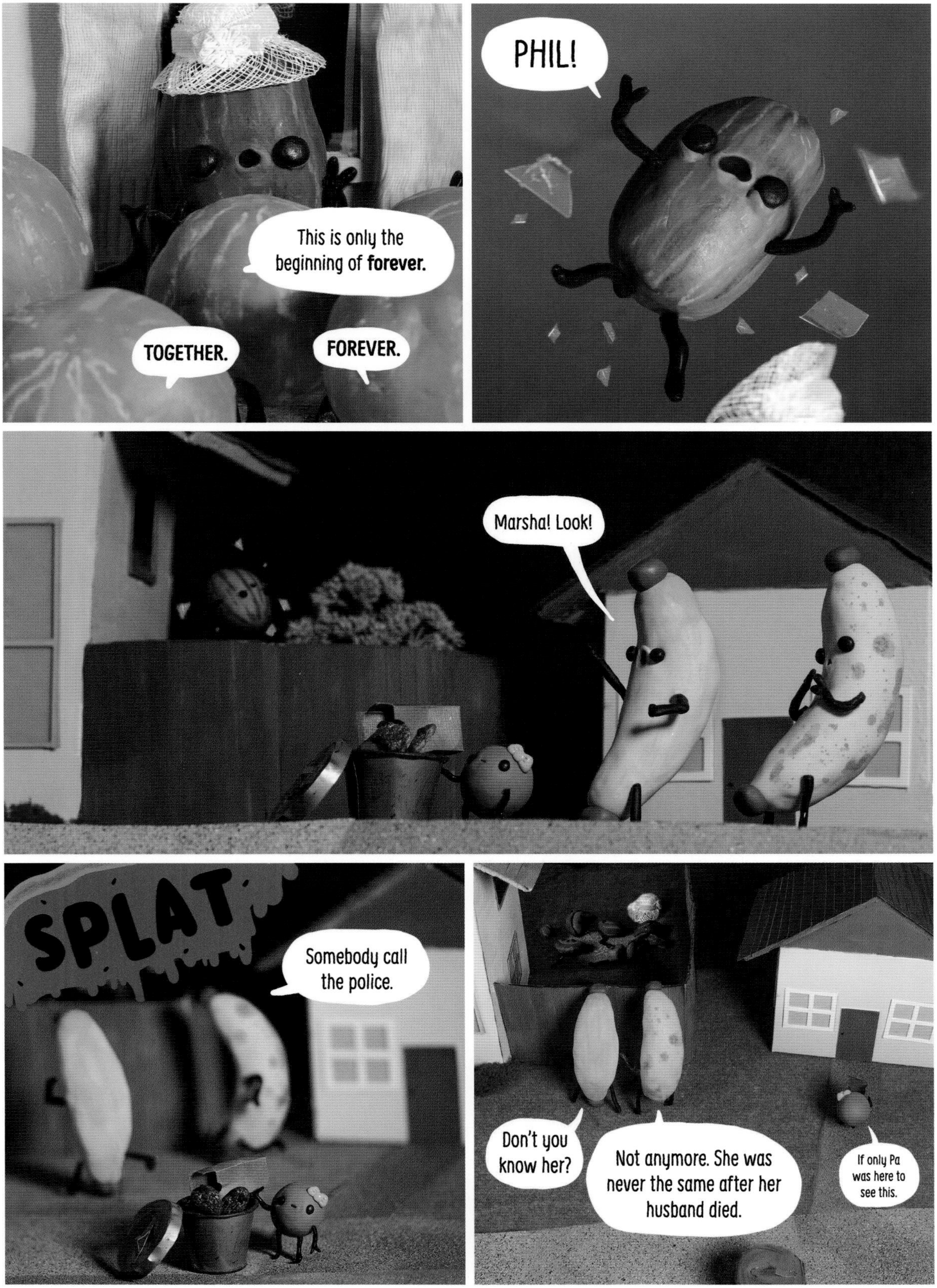
This is only the beginning of forever.
TOGETHER.
FOREVER.
PHIL!
Marsha! Look!
SPLAT
Somebody call the police.
Don't you know her?
Not anymore. She was never the same after her husband died.
If only Pa was here to see this.

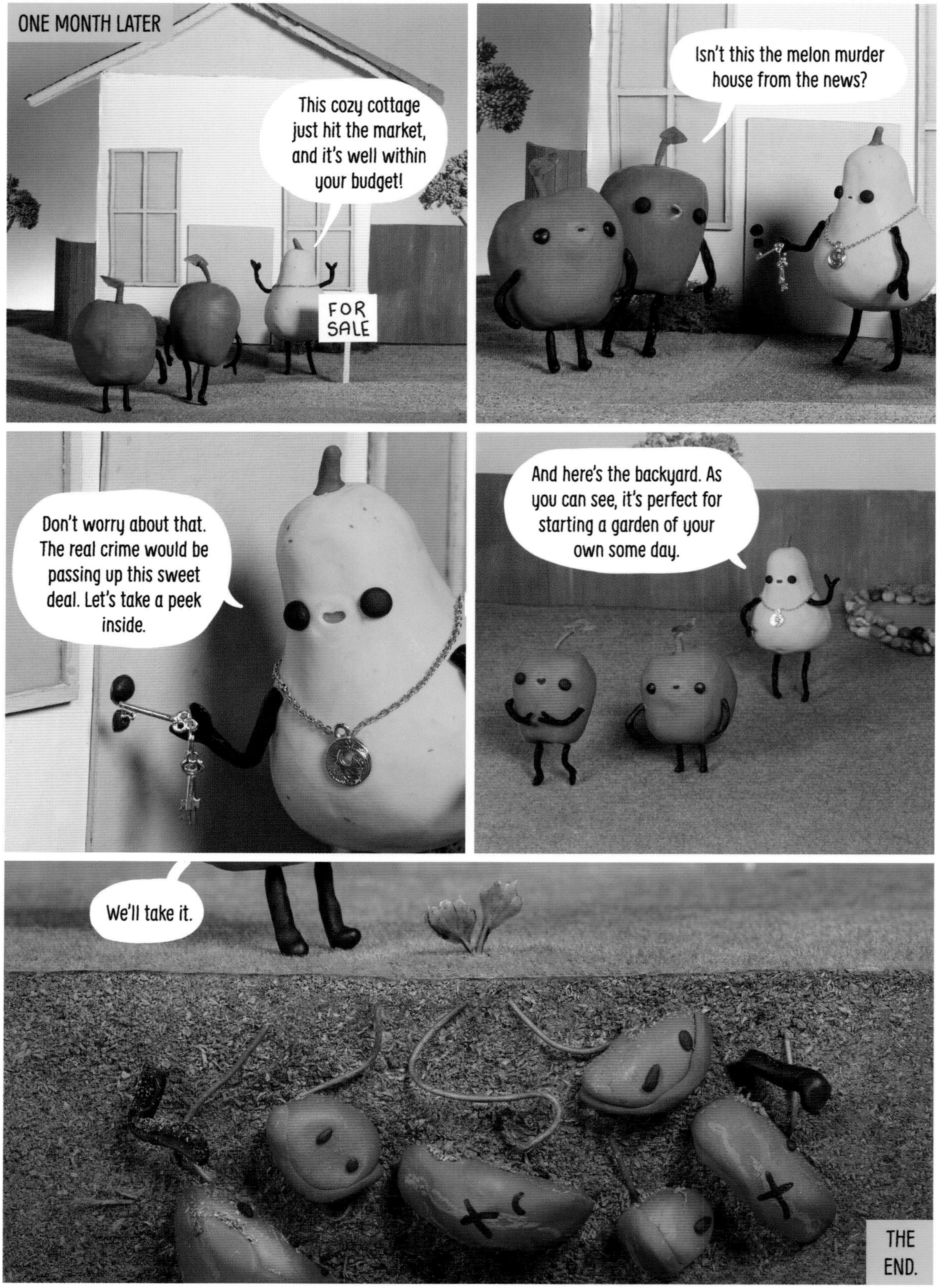
ONE MONTH LATER
This cozy cottage just hit the market, and it's well within your budget!
FOR SALE
Isn't this the melon murder house from the news?
Don't worry about that. The real crime would be passing up this sweet deal. Let's take a peek inside.
And here's the backyard. As you can see, it's perfect for starting a garden of your own some day.
We'll take it.
THE END.

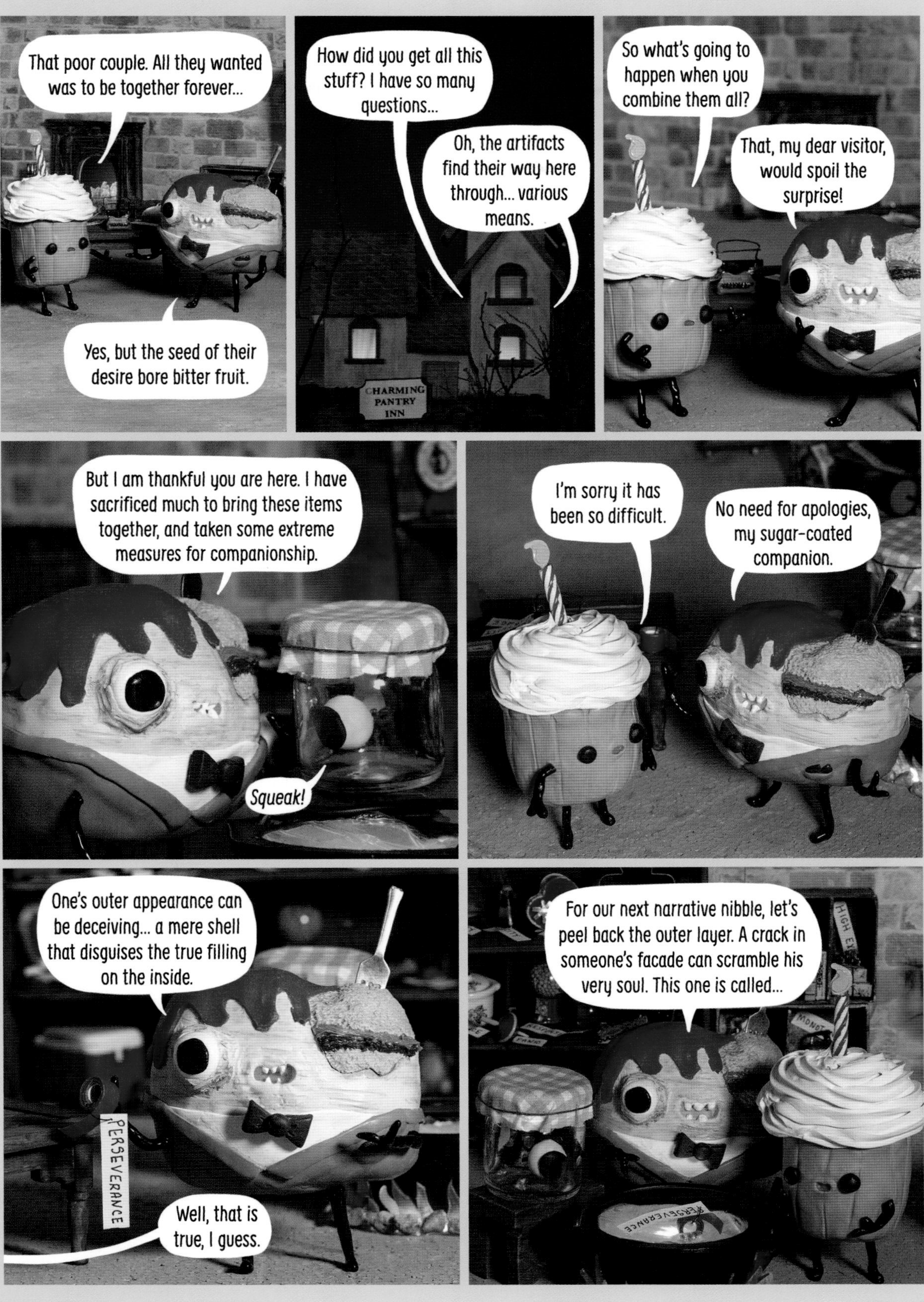
That poor couple. All they wanted was to be together forever...
Yes, but the seed of their desire bore bitter fruit.
How did you get all this stuff? I have so many questions...
Oh, the artifacts find their way here through... various means.
CHARMING PANTRY INN
So what's going to happen when you combine them all?
That, my dear visitor, would spoil the surprise!
But I am thankful you are here. I have sacrificed much to bring these items together, and taken some extreme measures for companionship.
Squeak!
I'm sorry it has been so difficult.
No need for apologies, my sugar-coated companion.
One's outer appearance can be deceiving... a mere shell that disguises the true filling on the inside.
PERSEVERANCE
Well, that is true, I guess.
For our next narrative nibble, let's peel back the outer layer. A crack in someone's facade can scramble his very soul. This one is called...

DEVILED EGG

OK Brad, take it easy on me. I'm just here to pick up some new defense skills.

Come on, Rupert. Live a little.

MASTER DOUGH
SPARRING GYMNASIU

CODE OF THE GYM

RESPECT ONE ANOTHER
YOUR SPRINKLES AND FROSTING
MUST BE CLEANED UP BY YOU

NO RAW MEATS

BRING PERSONAL WEAPONS
AT YOUR OWN RISK

KEEP SHENANIGANS TO A MINIMUM

HAVE FUN!

Thank You for Training
with
Master Dough!

SWISH

Haha! A total miss.

Now let's see you dodge this.

Please, don't!

SWOOSH

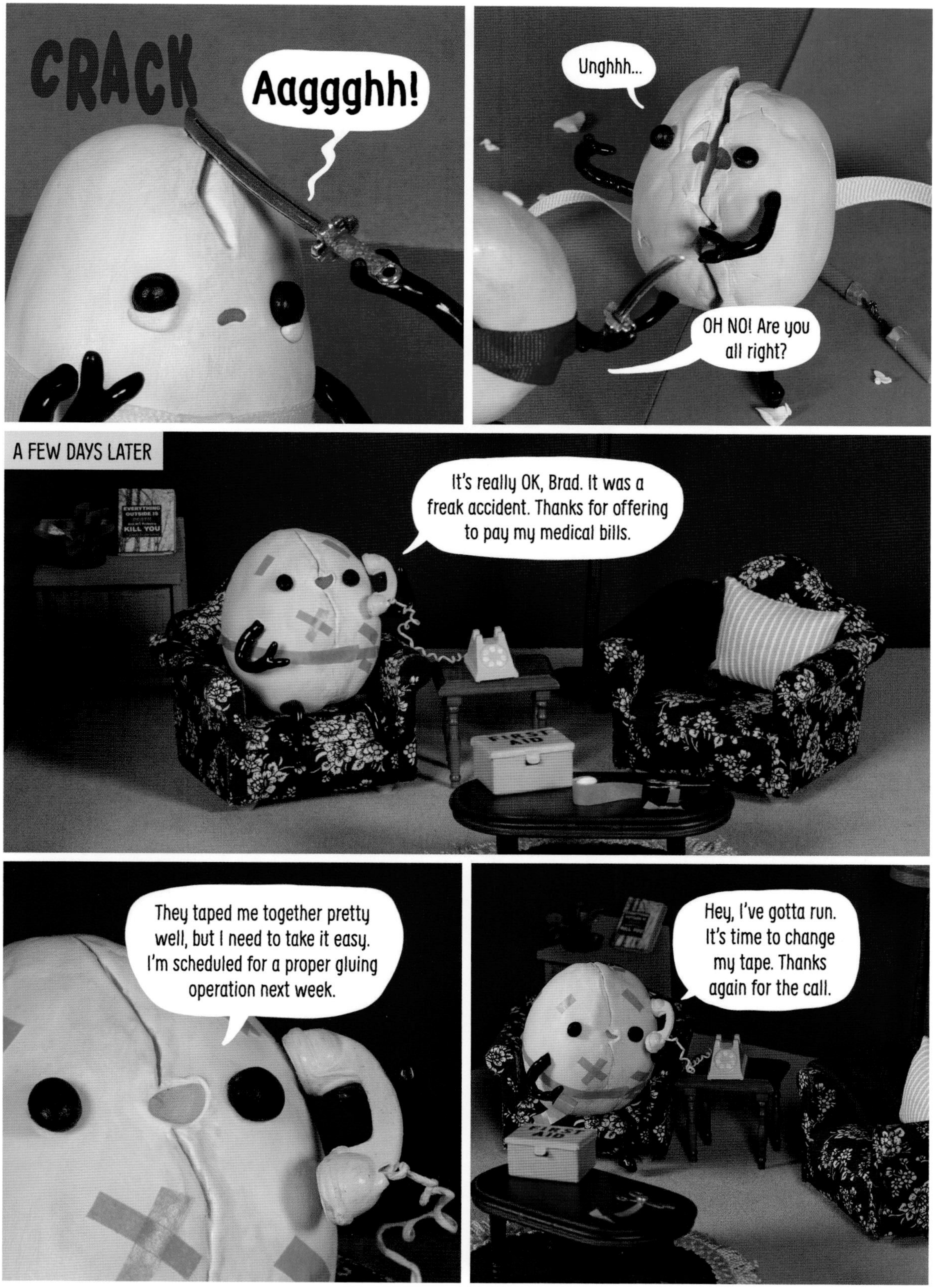
CRACK
Aaggghh!
Unghhh...
OH NO! Are you all right?
A FEW DAYS LATER
EVERYTHING OUTSIDE IS
KILL YOU
It's really OK, Brad. It was a freak accident. Thanks for offering to pay my medical bills.
FIRST AID
They taped me together pretty well, but I need to take it easy. I'm scheduled for a proper gluing operation next week.
Hey, I've gotta run. It's time to change my tape. Thanks again for the call.
FIRST AID

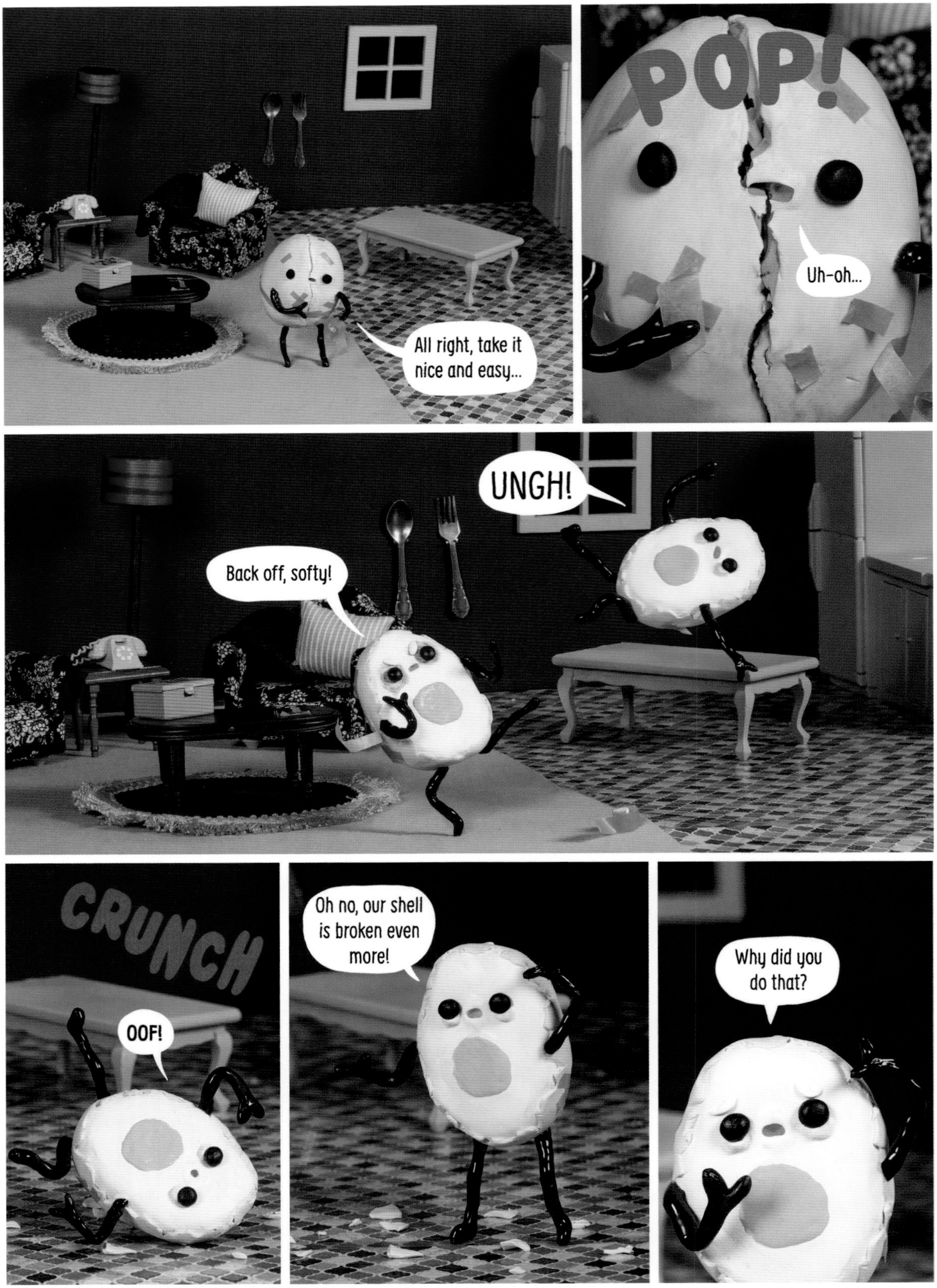
All right, take it nice and easy...
POP!
Uh-oh...
UNGH!
Back off, softy!
CRUNCH
OOF!
Oh no, our shell is broken even more!
Why did you do that?

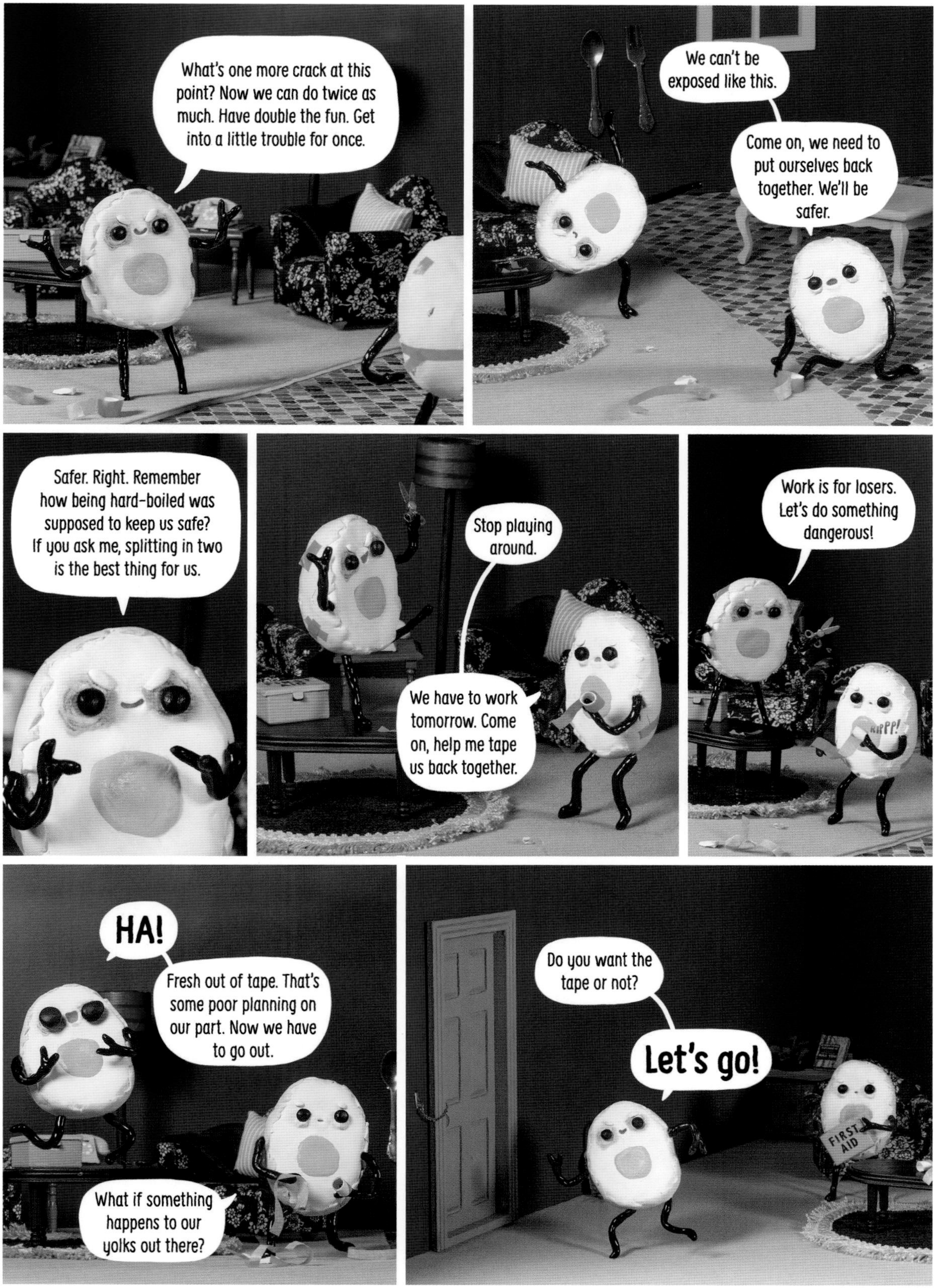

What's one more crack at this point? Now we can do twice as much. Have double the fun. Get into a little trouble for once.
We can't be exposed like this.
Come on, we need to put ourselves back together. We'll be safer.
Safer. Right. Remember how being hard-boiled was supposed to keep us safe? If you ask me, splitting in two is the best thing for us.
Stop playing around.
We have to work tomorrow. Come on, help me tape us back together.
Work is for losers. Let's do something dangerous!
RIPPP!
HA!
Fresh out of tape. That's some poor planning on our part. Now we have to go out.
What if something happens to our yolks out there?
Do you want the tape or not?
Let's go!
FIRST AID

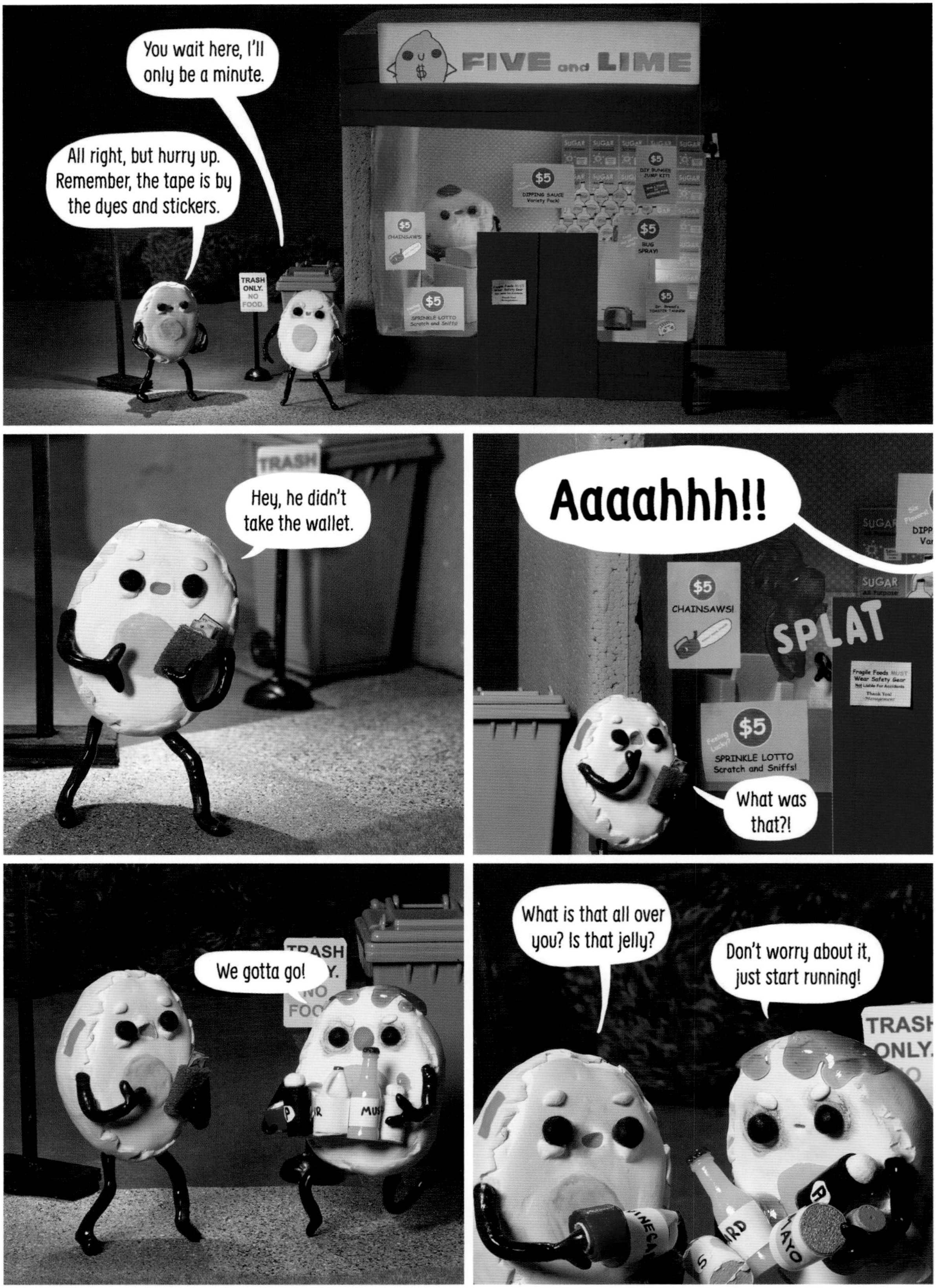

FIVE and LIME
You wait here, I'll only be a minute.
All right, but hurry up. Remember, the tape is by the dyes and stickers.
TRASH ONLY. NO FOOD.
$5 CHAINSAWS!
$5 DIPPING SAUCE Variety Pack!
$5 BUG SPRAY!
$5 SPRINKLE LOTTO Scratch and Sniffs!
Hey, he didn't take the wallet.
Aaaahhh!!
SPLAT
Fragile Foods MUST Wear Safety Gear
What was that?!
We gotta go!
What is that all over you? Is that jelly?
Don't worry about it, just start running!

OK, now tell me what happened.

You're really not going to like it.

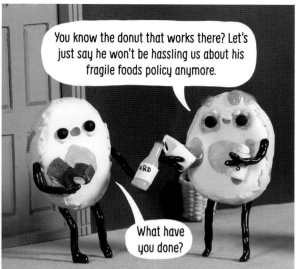

You know the donut that works there? Let's just say he won't be hassling us about his fragile foods policy anymore.

What have you done?

I did what I had to.

You did what you **wanted** to. You better not have hurt him.

Come on, aren't you tired of being a sensitive little goody two-shoes? We're out of our shell now.

It's not too late. We can fix this. Please, let's go back to being one whole, normal egg.

What are you making?! Stop doing that right now!

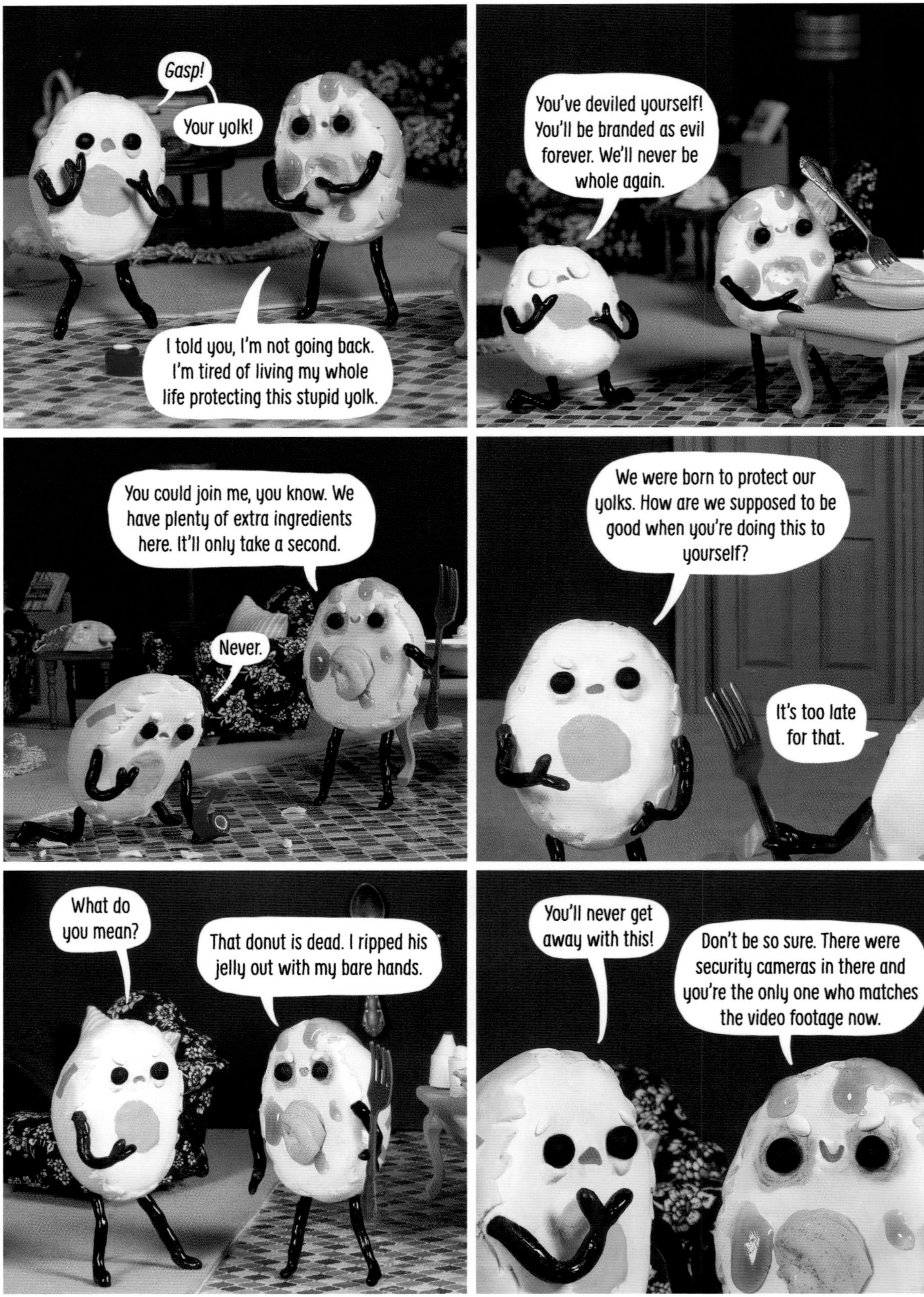

Gasp!
Your yolk!
I told you, I'm not going back. I'm tired of living my whole life protecting this stupid yolk.
You've deviled yourself! You'll be branded as evil forever. We'll never be whole again.
You could join me, you know. We have plenty of extra ingredients here. It'll only take a second.
Never.
We were born to protect our yolks. How are we supposed to be good when you're doing this to yourself?
It's too late for that.
What do you mean?
That donut is dead. I ripped his jelly out with my bare hands.
You'll never get away with this!
Don't be so sure. There were security cameras in there and you're the only one who matches the video footage now.

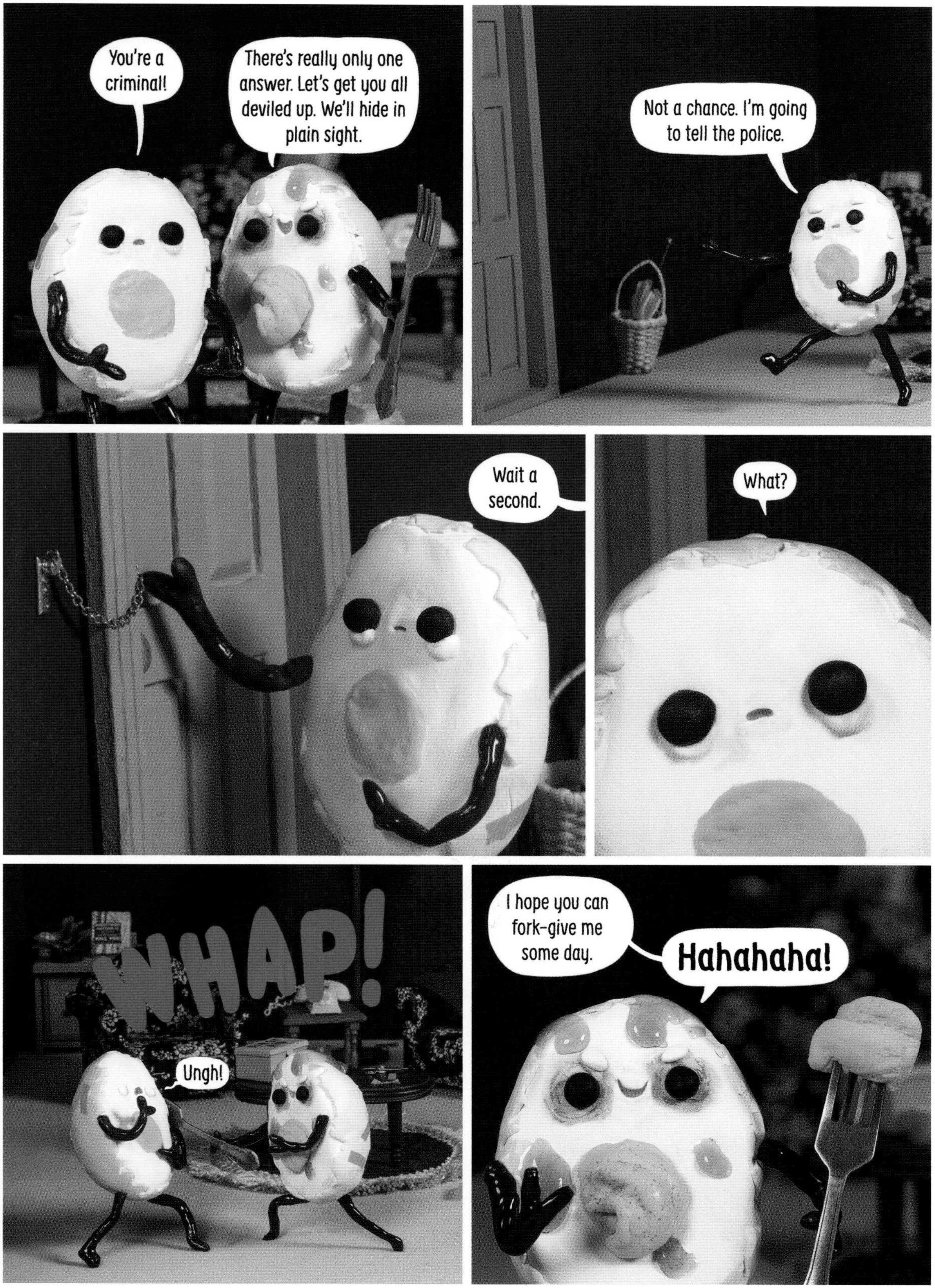

You're a criminal!
There's really only one answer. Let's get you all deviled up. We'll hide in plain sight.
Not a chance. I'm going to tell the police.
Wait a second.
What?
WHAP!
Ungh!
I hope you can fork-give me some day.
Hahahaha!

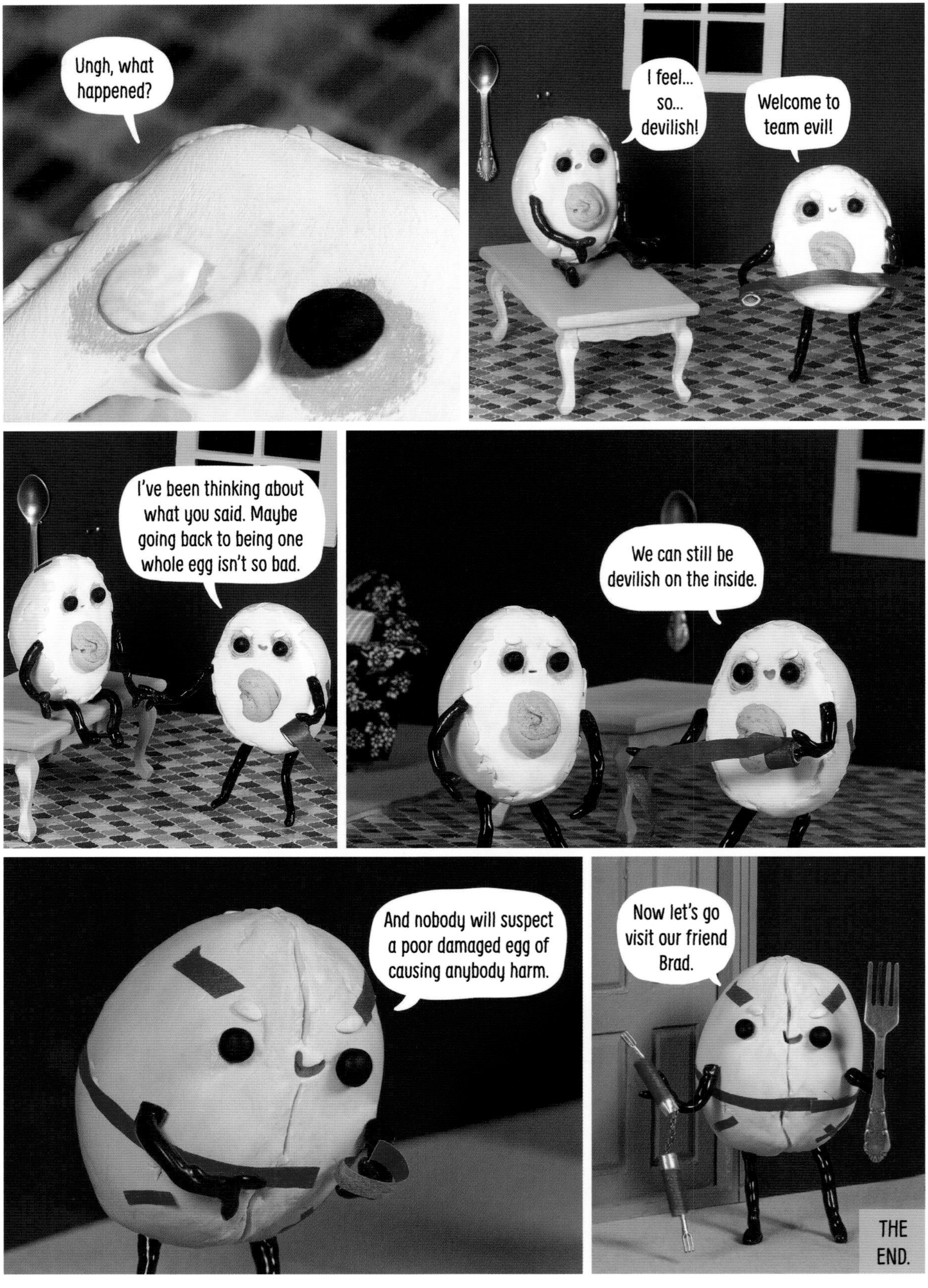

Ungh, what happened?
I feel... so... devilish!
Welcome to team evil!
I've been thinking about what you said. Maybe going back to being one whole egg isn't so bad.
We can still be devilish on the inside.
And nobody will suspect a poor damaged egg of causing anybody harm.
Now let's go visit our friend Brad.
THE END.

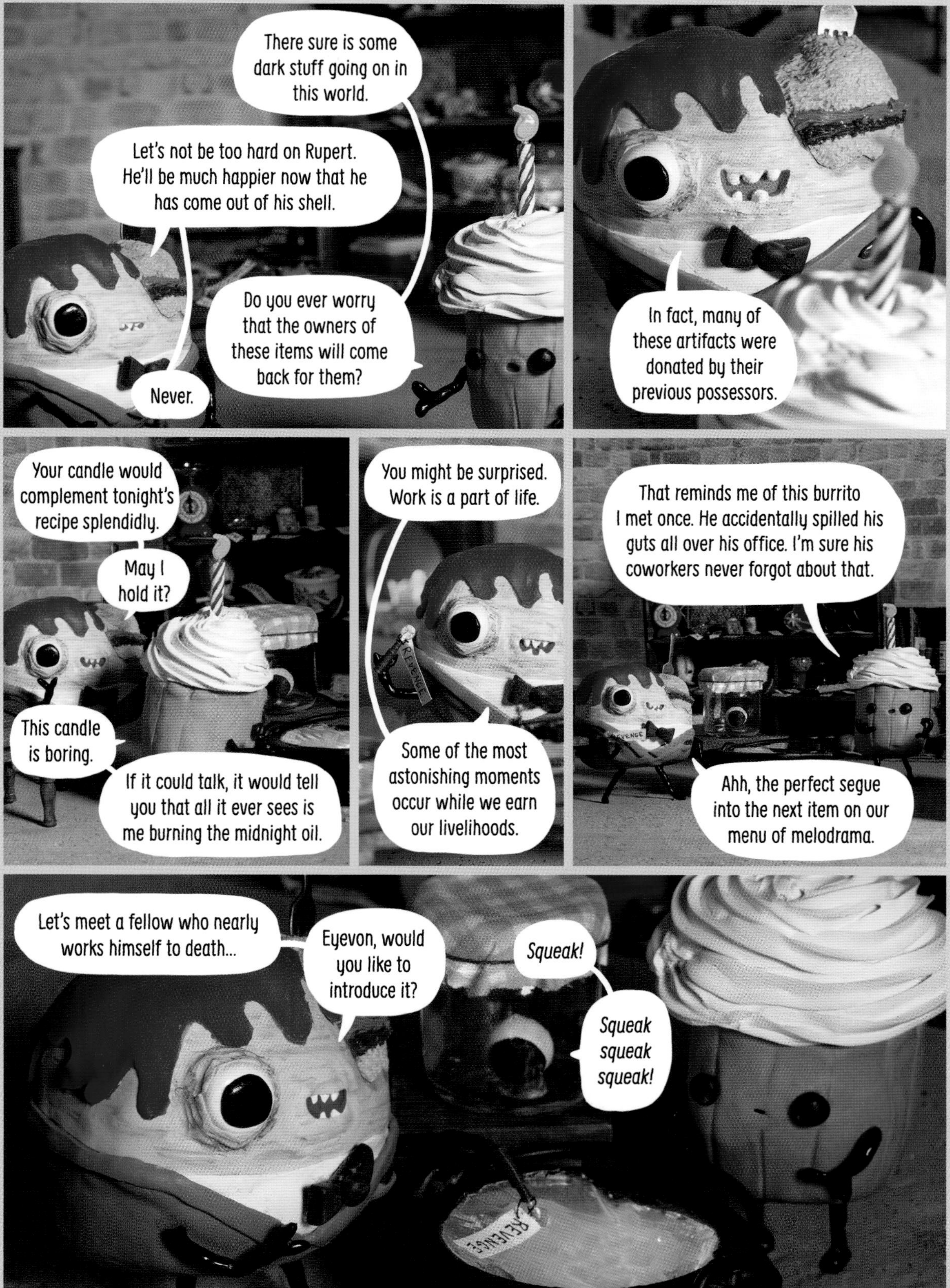
There sure is some dark stuff going on in this world.
Let's not be too hard on Rupert. He'll be much happier now that he has come out of his shell.
Do you ever worry that the owners of these items will come back for them?
Never.
In fact, many of these artifacts were donated by their previous possessors.
Your candle would complement tonight's recipe splendidly.
May I hold it?
This candle is boring.
If it could talk, it would tell you that all it ever sees is me burning the midnight oil.
You might be surprised. Work is a part of life.
REVENGE
Some of the most astonishing moments occur while we earn our livelihoods.
That reminds me of this burrito I met once. He accidentally spilled his guts all over his office. I'm sure his coworkers never forgot about that.
Ahh, the perfect segue into the next item on our menu of melodrama.
Let's meet a fellow who nearly works himself to death...
Eyevon, would you like to introduce it?
Squeak!
Squeak squeak squeak!
REVENGE

MAINS

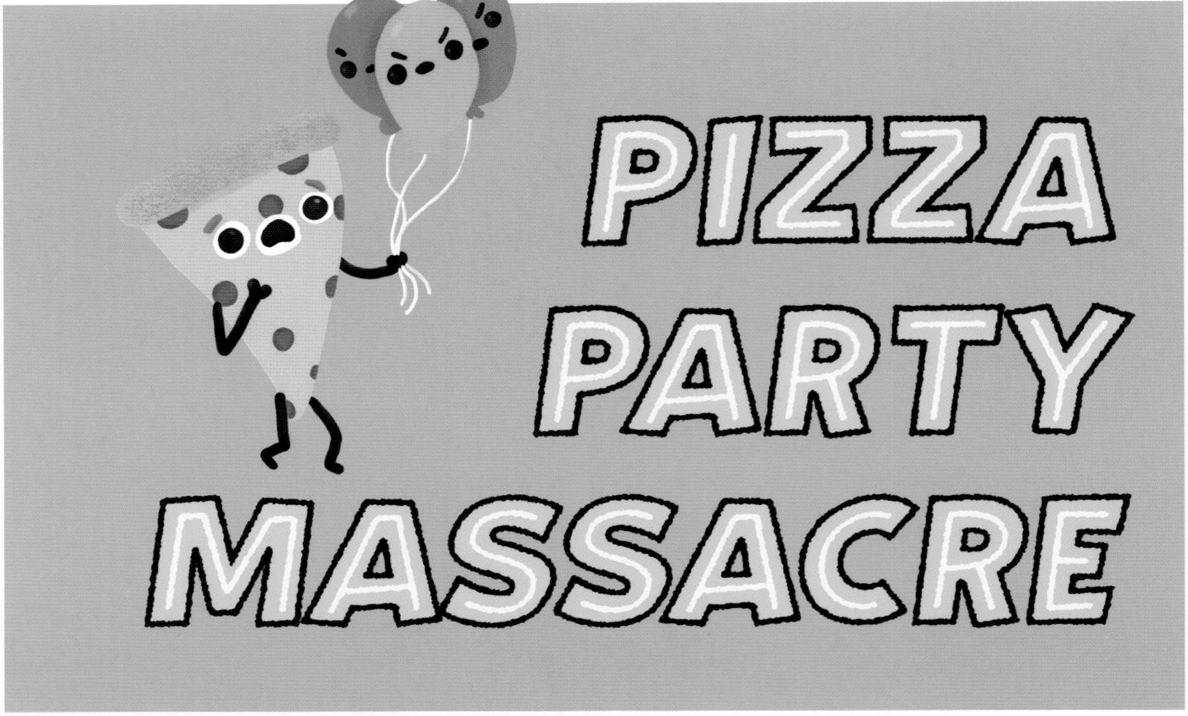
PIZZA PARTY MASSACRE

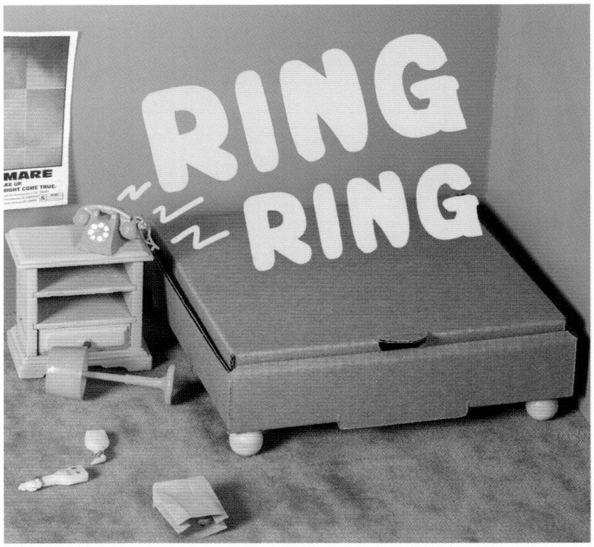
RING
RING

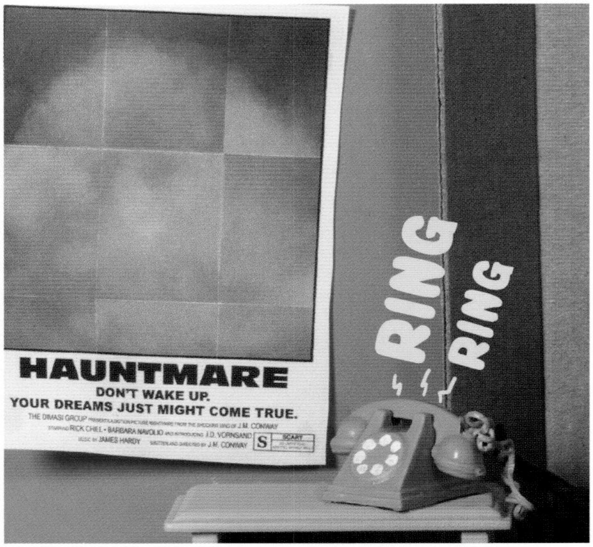
HAUNTMARE
DON'T WAKE UP.
YOUR DREAMS JUST MIGHT COME TRUE.
RING
RING

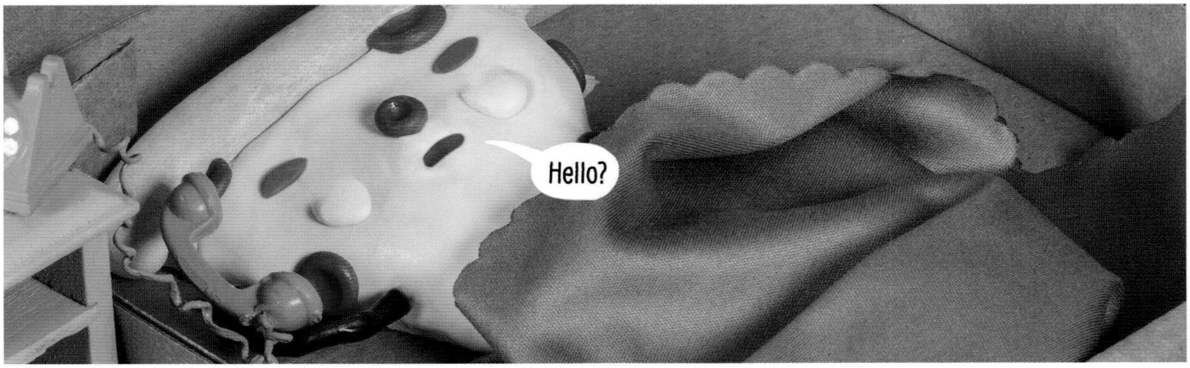
Hello?

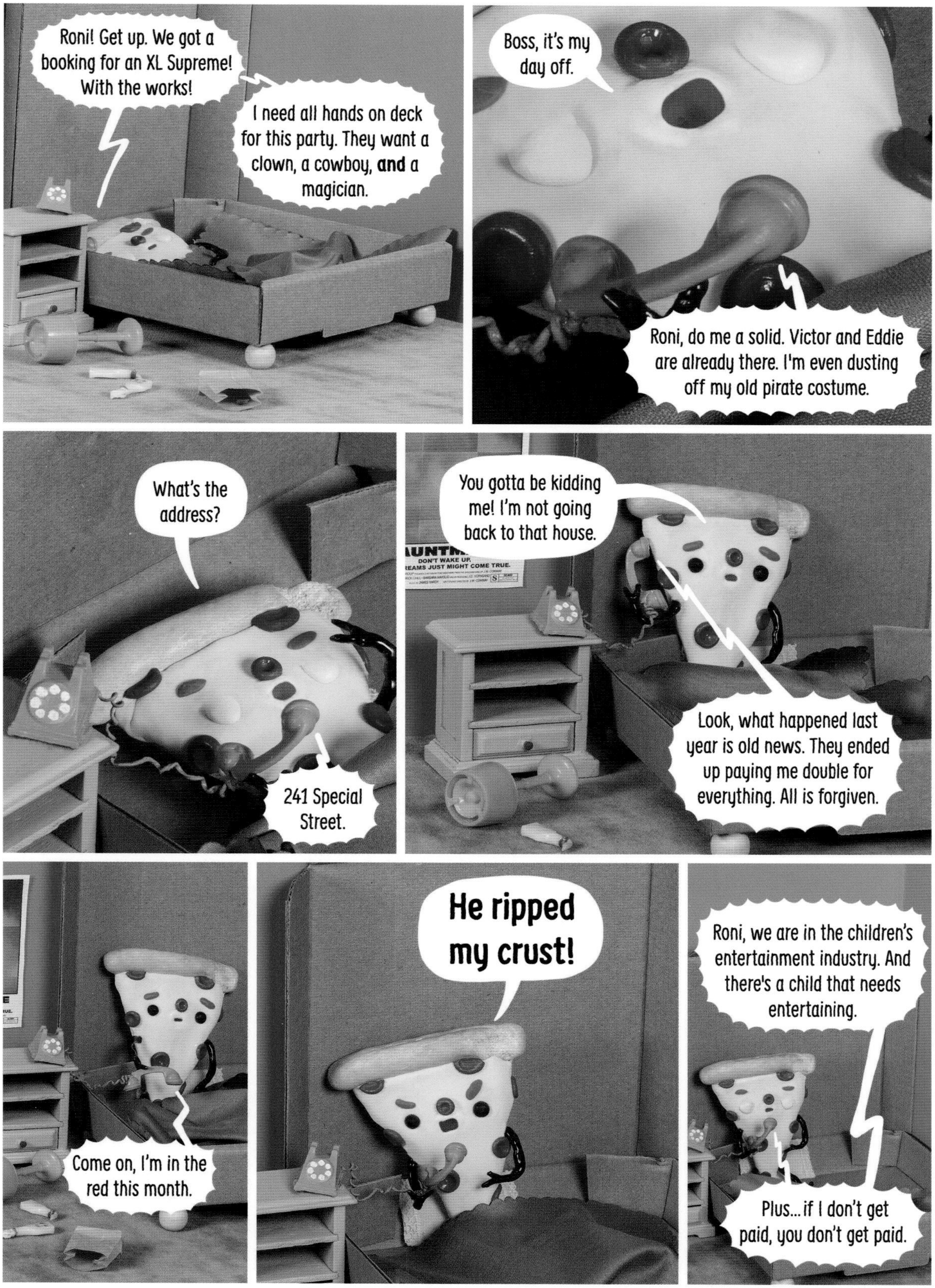
Roni! Get up. We got a booking for an XL Supreme! With the works!
I need all hands on deck for this party. They want a clown, a cowboy, **and** a magician.
Boss, it's my day off.
Roni, do me a solid. Victor and Eddie are already there. I'm even dusting off my old pirate costume.
What's the address?
241 Special Street.
You gotta be kidding me! I'm not going back to that house.
Look, what happened last year is old news. They ended up paying me double for everything. All is forgiven.
Come on, I'm in the red this month.
He ripped my crust!
Roni, we are in the children's entertainment industry. And there's a child that needs entertaining.
Plus...if I don't get paid, you don't get paid.

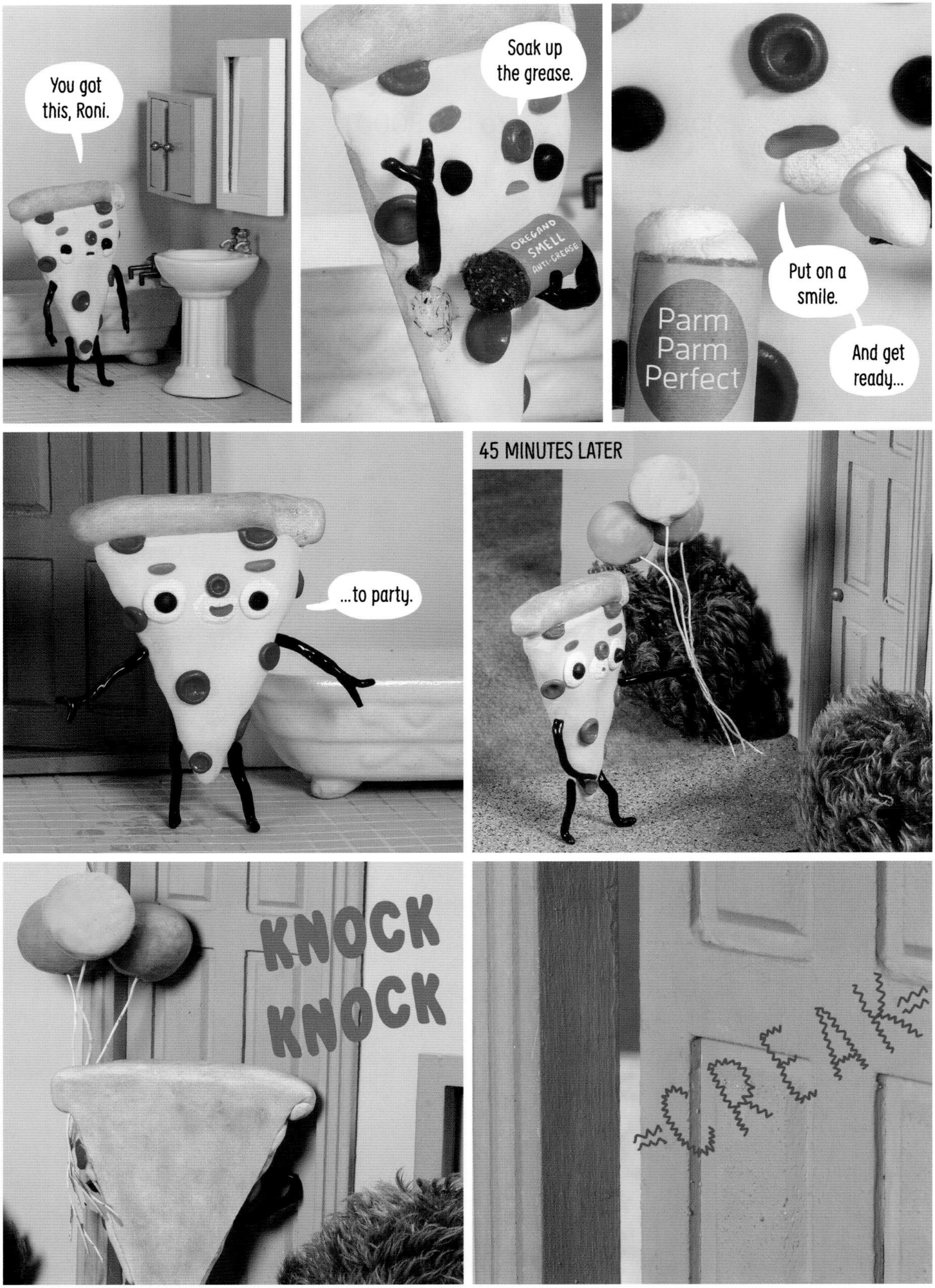
You got this, Roni.
Soak up the grease.
OREGANO SMELL ANTI-GREASE
Parm Parm Perfect
Put on a smile.
And get ready...
...to party.
45 MINUTES LATER
KNOCK KNOCK

Hello?
It's Party Party Pizza. Where fun comes to you in thirty minutes or less.
I'm here for the XL Supreme.
RONI!
Victor?
SMACK!
CHEESE AND PEPPERS!

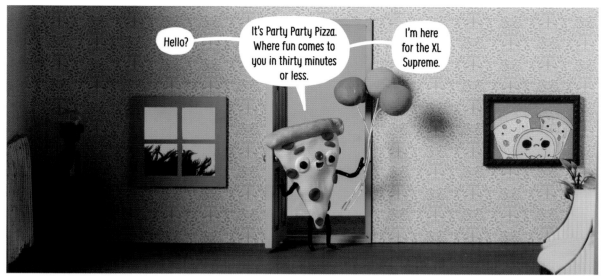

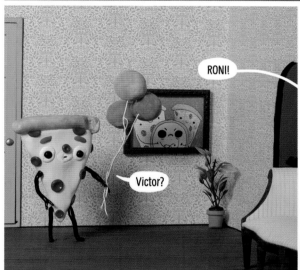

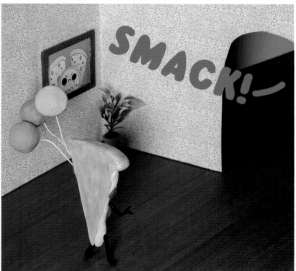

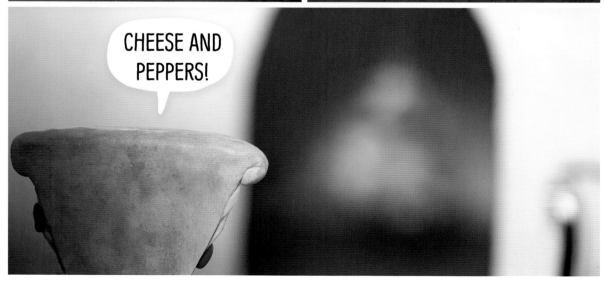

Watch it, Eddie. I can barely move with all my gear on.

Welcome to the party, Roni!

You scared the yeast out of me. Where's everyone else?

Don't know.

Who cares? We're getting paid by the hour.

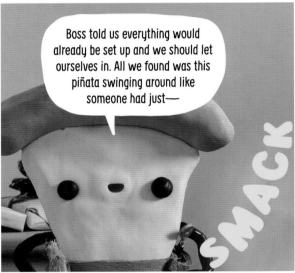

Boss told us everything would already be set up and we should let ourselves in. All we found was this piñata swinging around like someone had just—

SMACK

Maybe Boss got the address wrong?

Nope. It's the right address. This is the house where the *incident* happened.

Get over it, Roni. It comes with the job. See this scar? Kid hated mushrooms and plucked one right off of me. You don't see me crying about it.

POP!

AHHHHHHH!

IT BURNS!

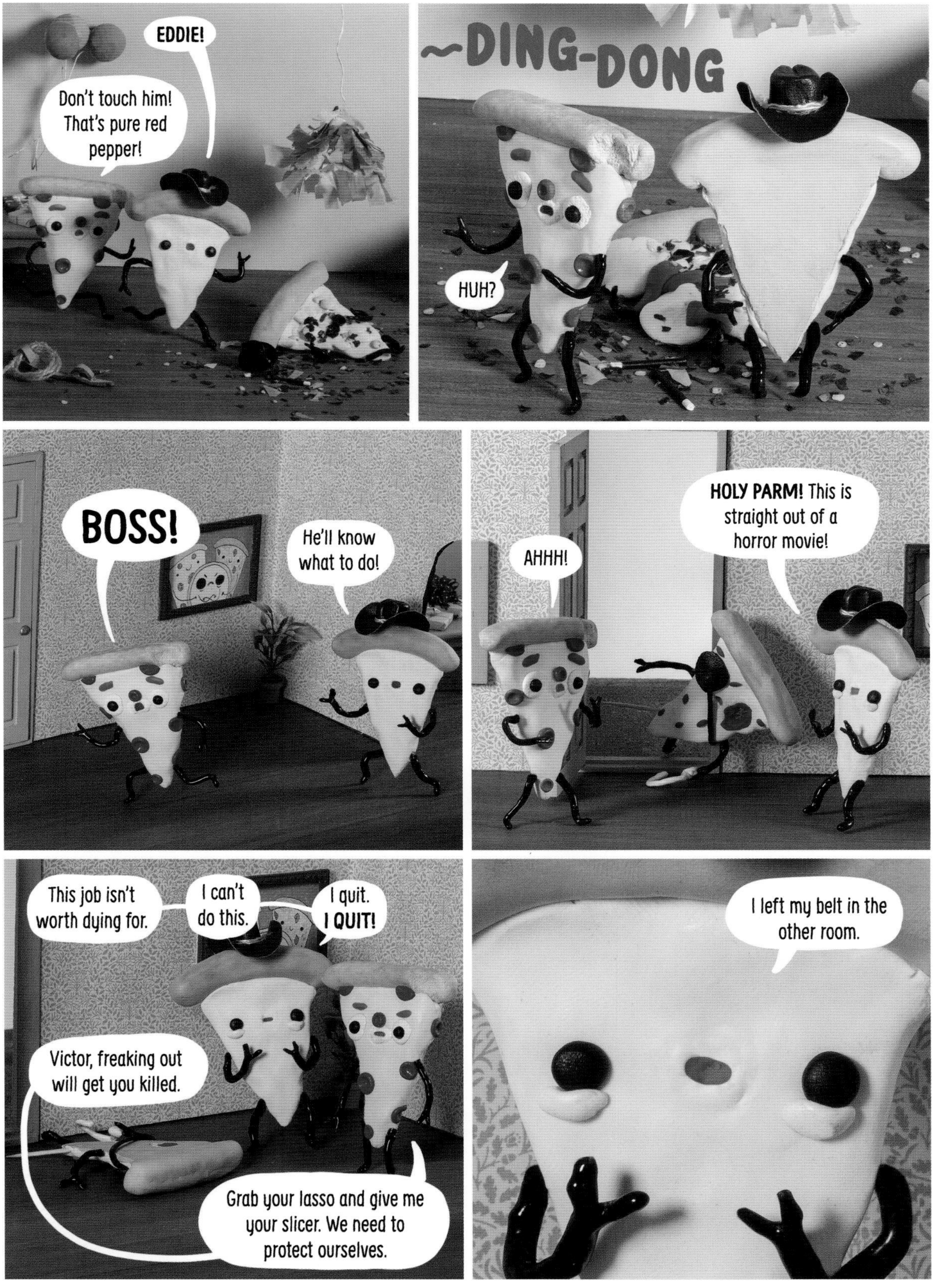
EDDIE!
Don't touch him! That's pure red pepper!
~DING-DONG
HUH?
BOSS!
He'll know what to do!
AHHH!
HOLY PARM! This is straight out of a horror movie!
This job isn't worth dying for.
I can't do this.
I quit. I QUIT!
Victor, freaking out will get you killed.
Grab your lasso and give me your slicer. We need to protect ourselves.
I left my belt in the other room.

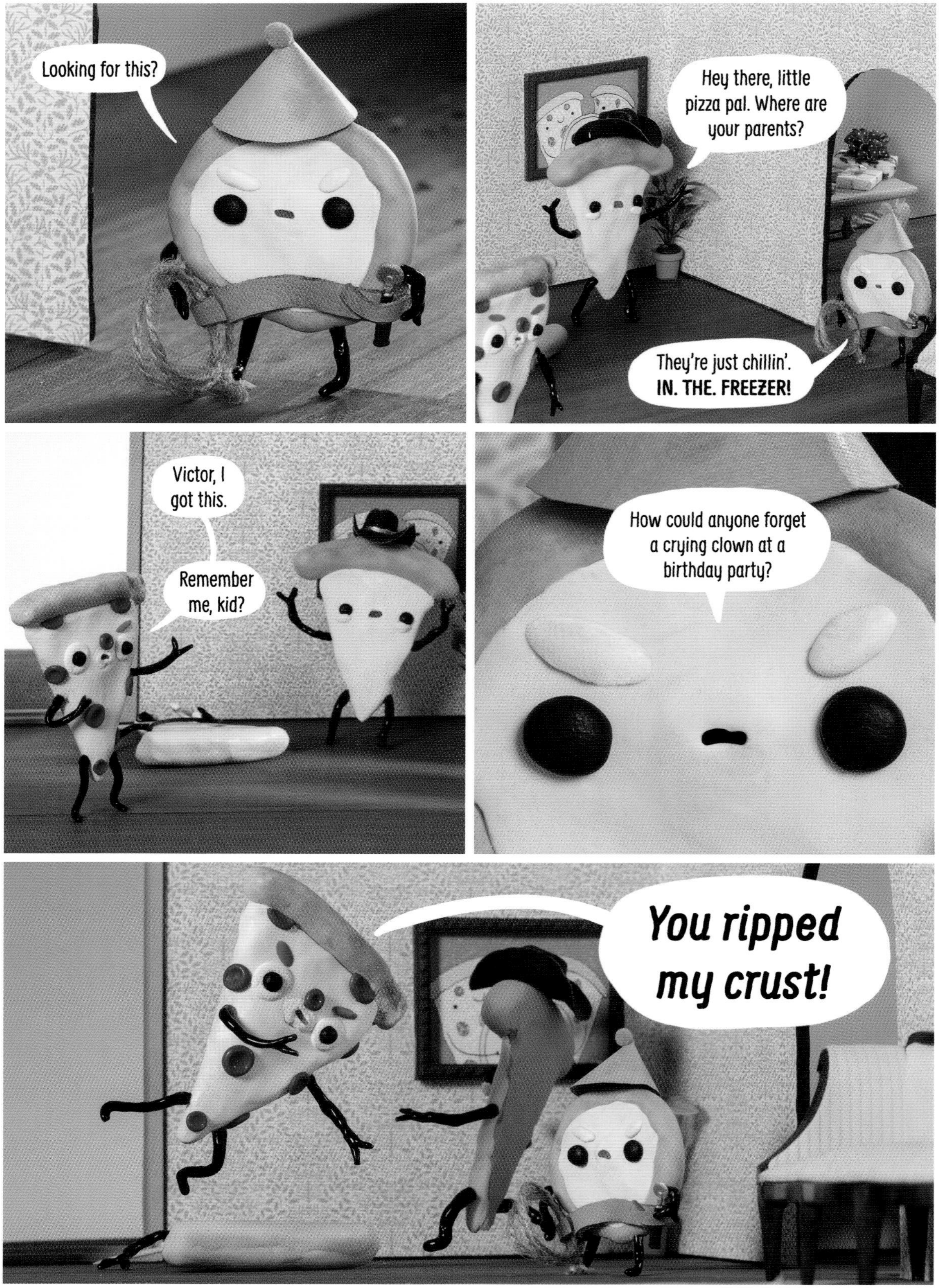
Looking for this?
Hey there, little pizza pal. Where are your parents?
They're just chillin'. **IN. THE. FREEZER!**
Victor, I got this.
Remember me, kid?
How could anyone forget a crying clown at a birthday party?
You ripped my crust!

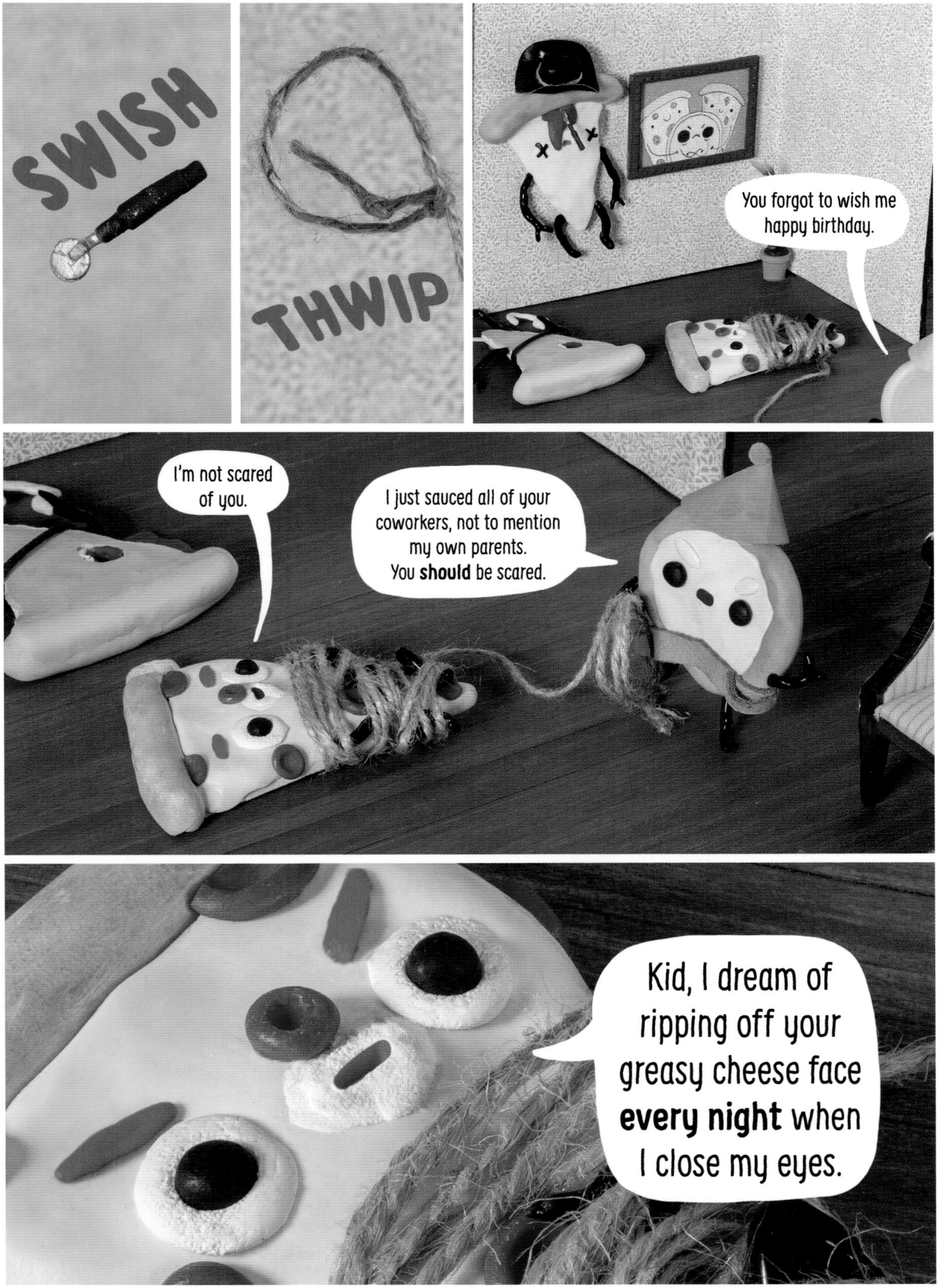
SWISH
THWIP
You forgot to wish me happy birthday.
I'm not scared of you.
I just sauced all of your coworkers, not to mention my own parents. You **should** be scared.
Kid, I dream of ripping off your greasy cheese face **every night** when I close my eyes.

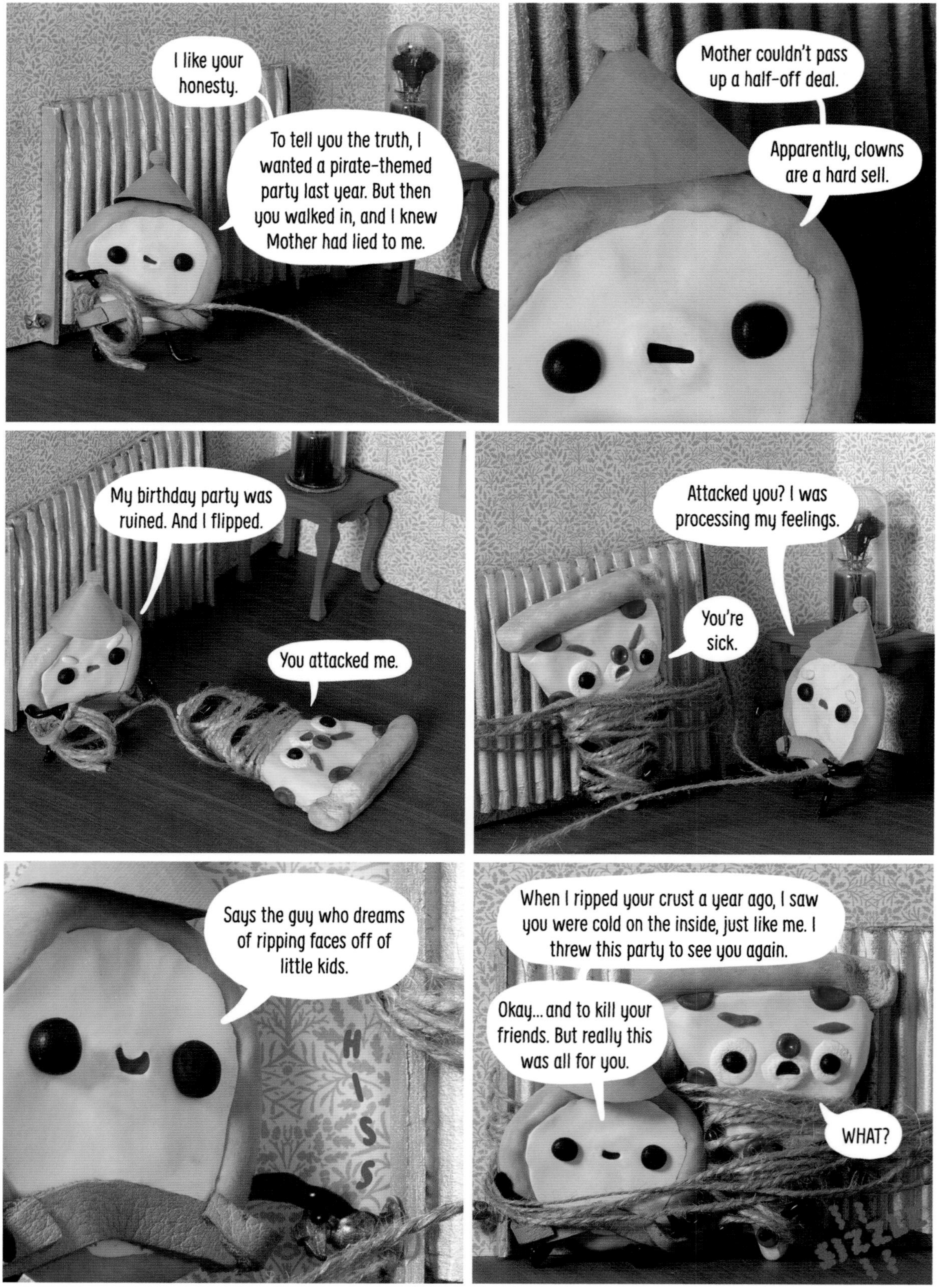
I like your honesty.
To tell you the truth, I wanted a pirate-themed party last year. But then you walked in, and I knew Mother had lied to me.
Mother couldn't pass up a half-off deal.
Apparently, clowns are a hard sell.
My birthday party was ruined. And I flipped.
You attacked me.
Attacked you? I was processing my feelings.
You're sick.
Says the guy who dreams of ripping faces off of little kids.
HISS
When I ripped your crust a year ago, I saw you were cold on the inside, just like me. I threw this party to see you again.
Okay... and to kill your friends. But really this was all for you.
WHAT?
SIZZLE

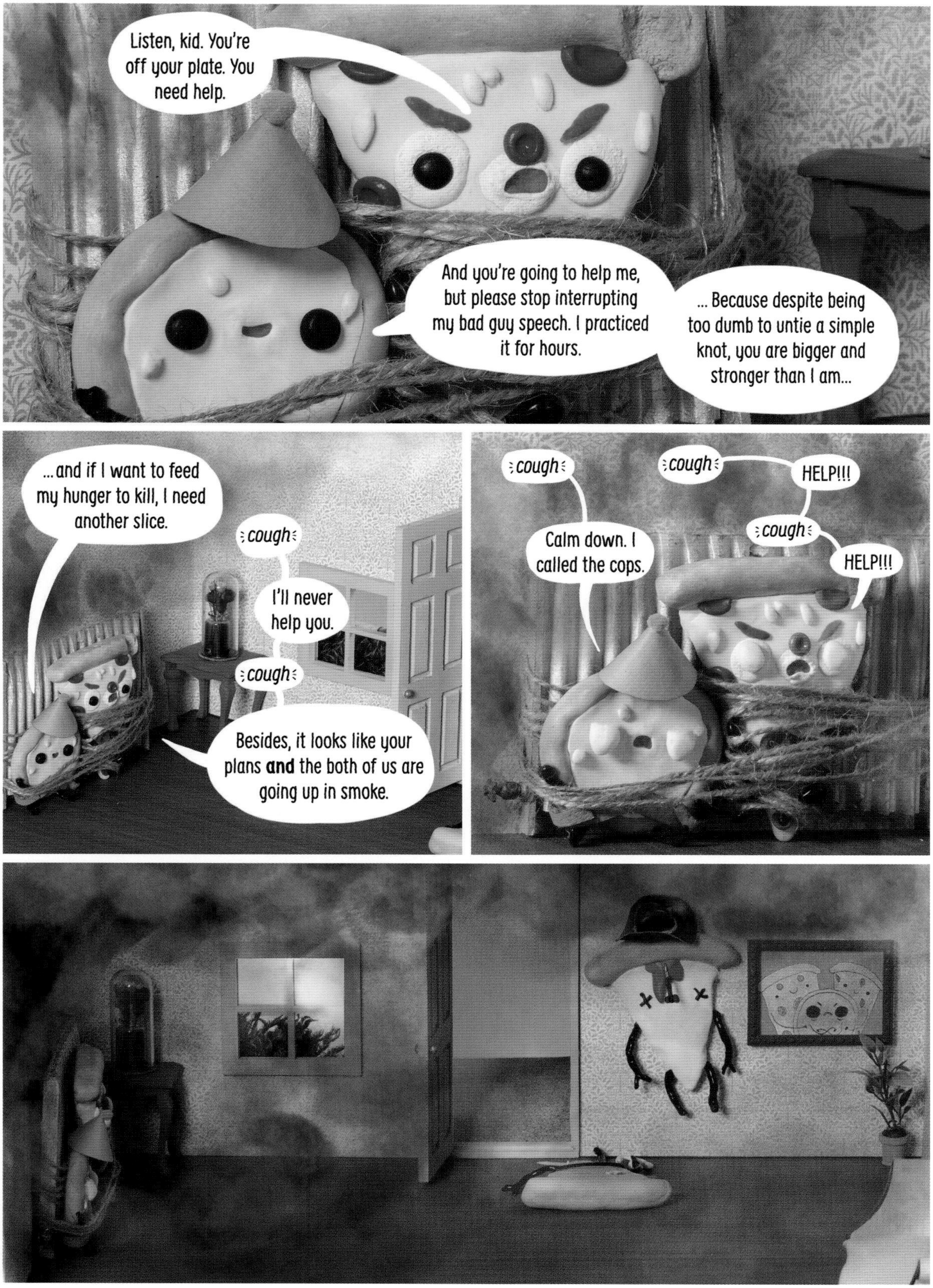
Listen, kid. You're off your plate. You need help.
And you're going to help me, but please stop interrupting my bad guy speech. I practiced it for hours.
... Because despite being too dumb to untie a simple knot, you are bigger and stronger than I am...
... and if I want to feed my hunger to kill, I need another slice.
cough
I'll never help you.
cough
Besides, it looks like your plans **and** the both of us are going up in smoke.
cough
Calm down. I called the cops.
cough
HELP!!!
cough
HELP!!!

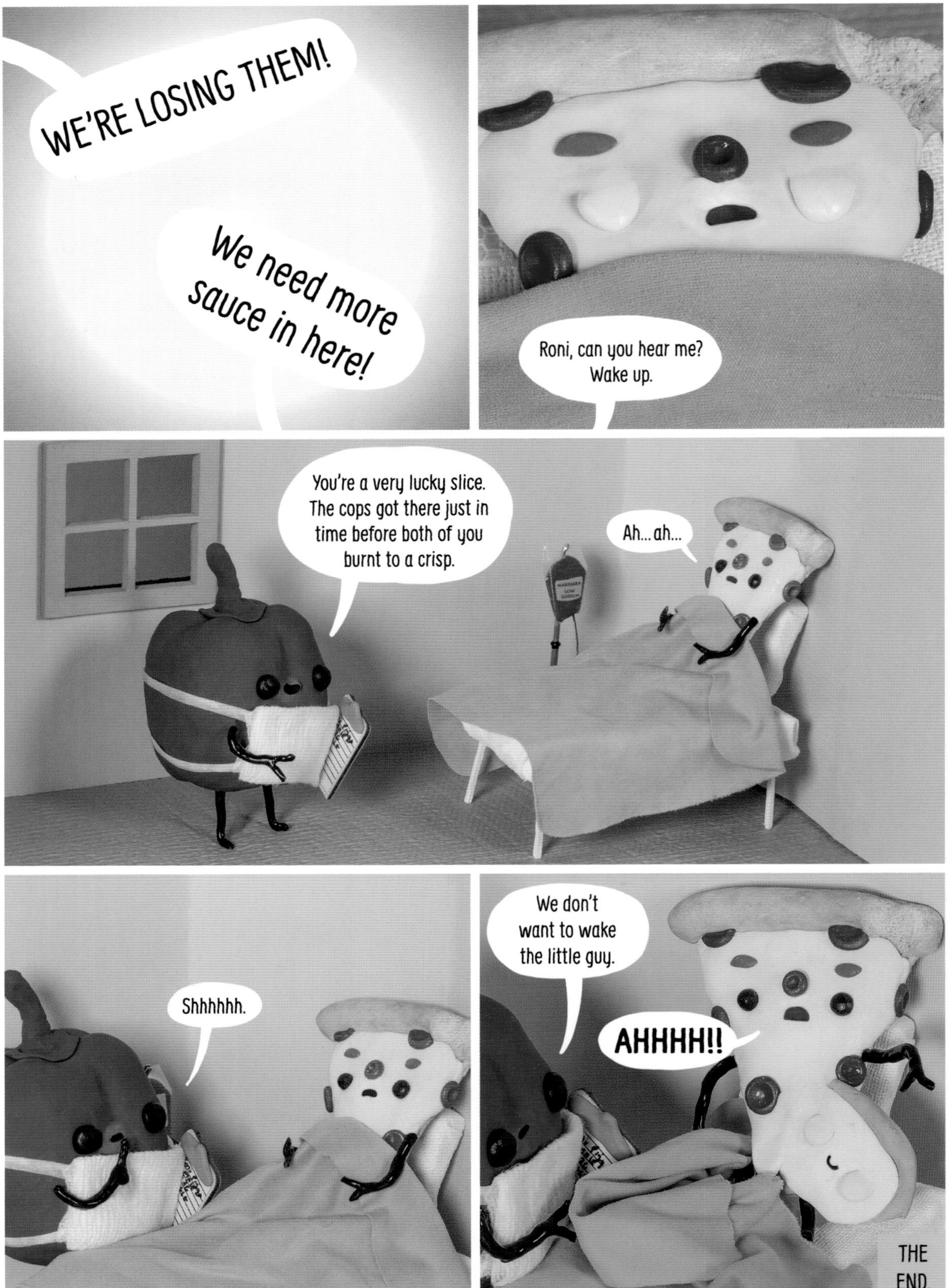
WE'RE LOSING THEM!
We need more sauce in here!
Roni, can you hear me? Wake up.
You're a very lucky slice. The cops got there just in time before both of you burnt to a crisp.
Ah... ah...
MARINARA LOW SODIUM
Shhhhhh.
We don't want to wake the little guy.
AHHHH!!
THE END.

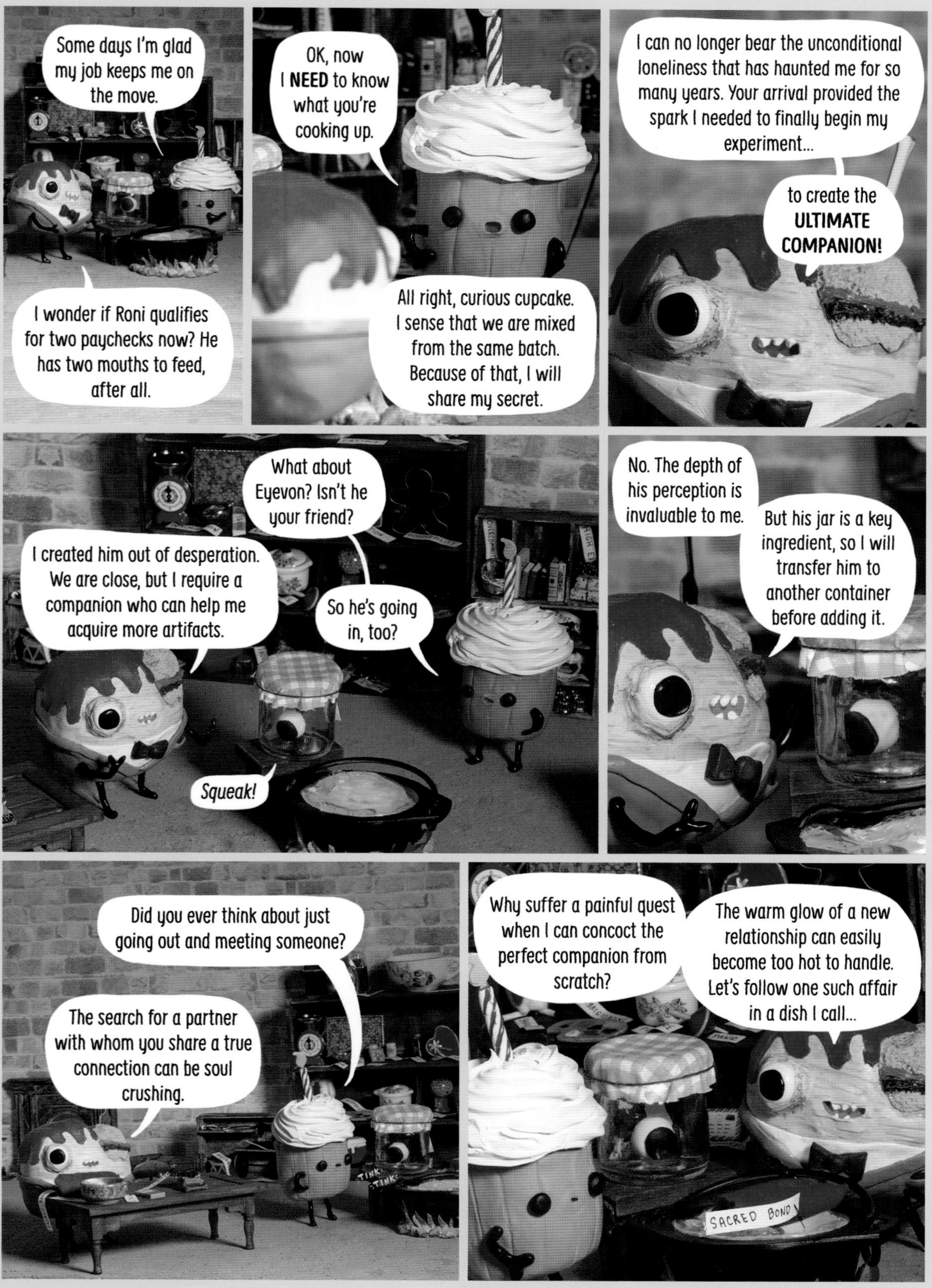
Some days I'm glad my job keeps me on the move.
I wonder if Roni qualifies for two paychecks now? He has two mouths to feed, after all.
OK, now I **NEED** to know what you're cooking up.
All right, curious cupcake. I sense that we are mixed from the same batch. Because of that, I will share my secret.
I can no longer bear the unconditional loneliness that has haunted me for so many years. Your arrival provided the spark I needed to finally begin my experiment...
to create the **ULTIMATE COMPANION!**
What about Eyevon? Isn't he your friend?
I created him out of desperation. We are close, but I require a companion who can help me acquire more artifacts.
So he's going in, too?
Squeak!
No. The depth of his perception is invaluable to me.
But his jar is a key ingredient, so I will transfer him to another container before adding it.
Did you ever think about just going out and meeting someone?
The search for a partner with whom you share a true connection can be soul crushing.
TINK TINK
Why suffer a painful quest when I can concoct the perfect companion from scratch?
The warm glow of a new relationship can easily become too hot to handle. Let's follow one such affair in a dish I call...
SACRED BOND

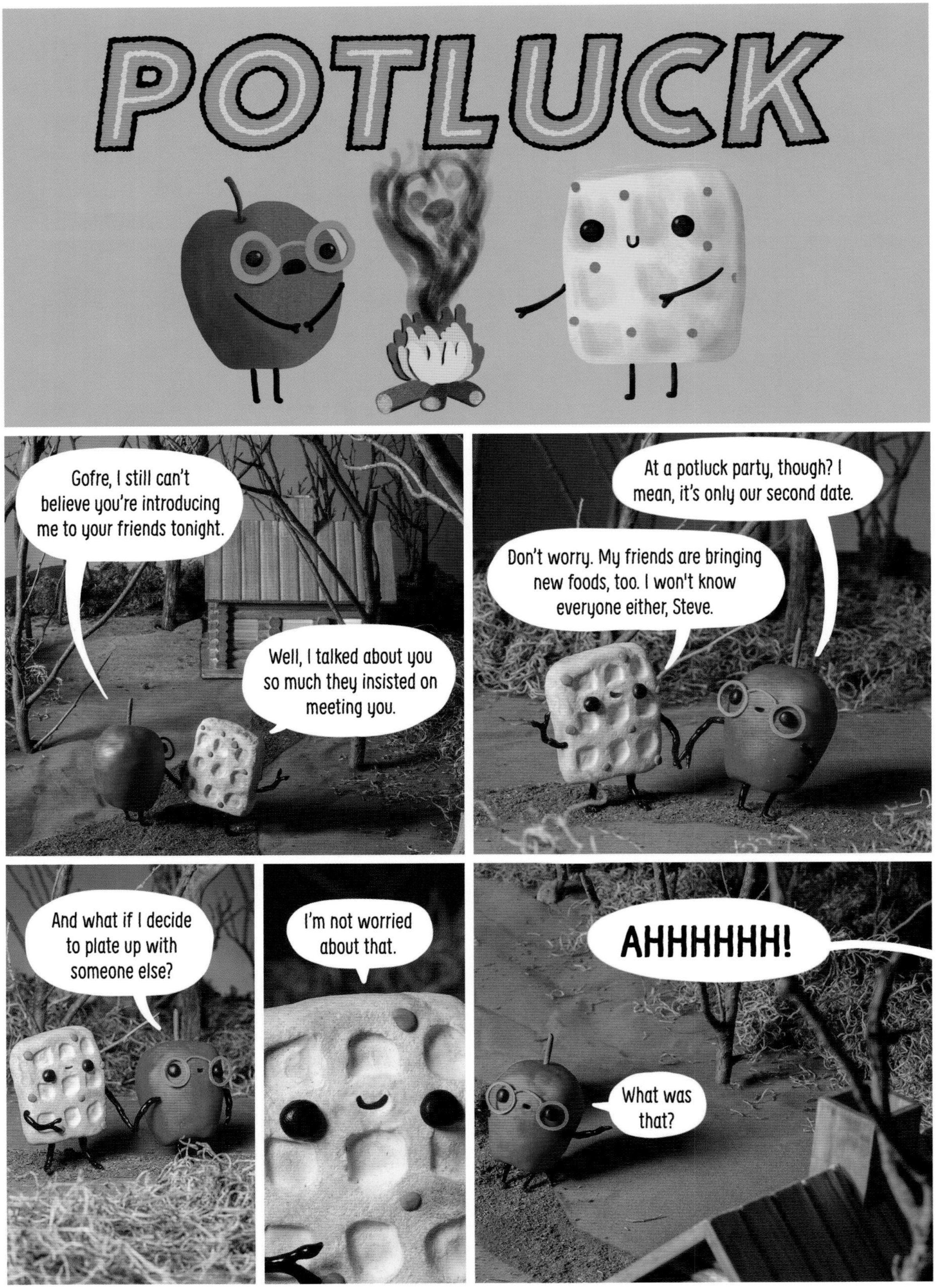
POTLUCK
Gofre, I still can't believe you're introducing me to your friends tonight.
Well, I talked about you so much they insisted on meeting you.
At a potluck party, though? I mean, it's only our second date.
Don't worry. My friends are bringing new foods, too. I won't know everyone either, Steve.
And what if I decide to plate up with someone else?
I'm not worried about that.
AHHHHHH!
What was that?

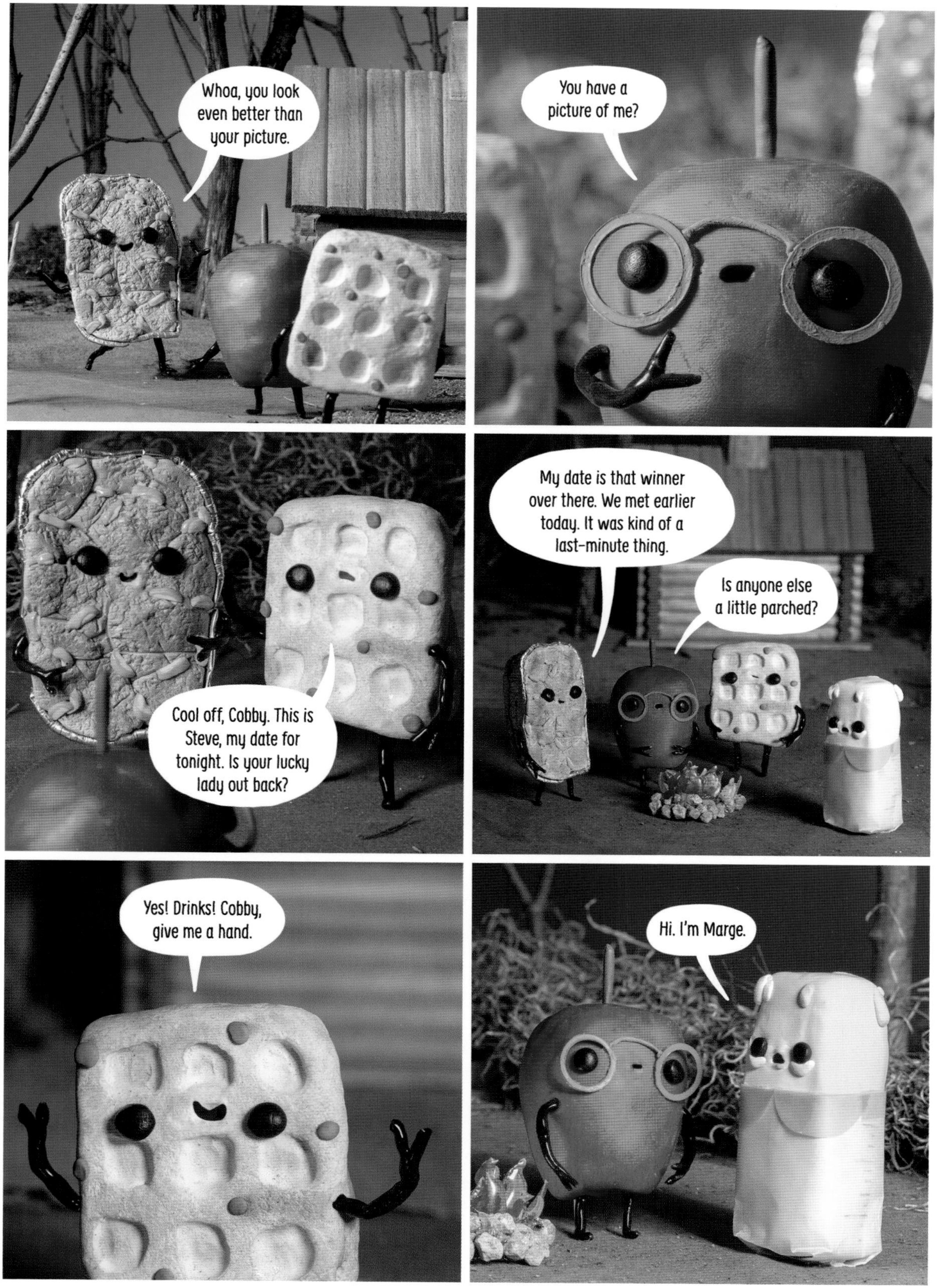
Whoa, you look even better than your picture.
You have a picture of me?
Cool off, Cobby. This is Steve, my date for tonight. Is your lucky lady out back?
My date is that winner over there. We met earlier today. It was kind of a last-minute thing.
Is anyone else a little parched?
Yes! Drinks! Cobby, give me a hand.
Hi. I'm Marge.

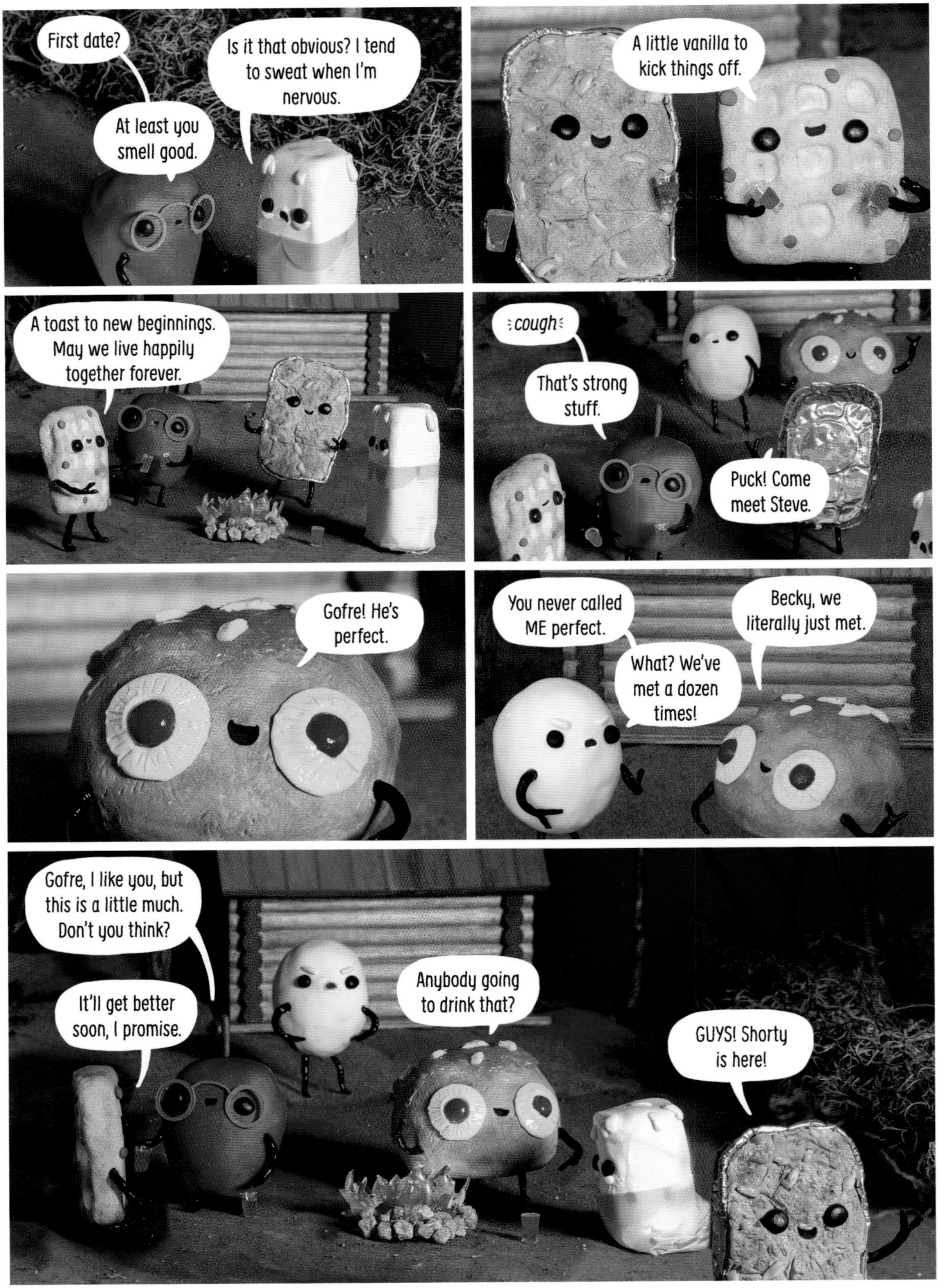
First date?
At least you smell good.
Is it that obvious? I tend to sweat when I'm nervous.
A little vanilla to kick things off.
A toast to new beginnings. May we live happily together forever.
cough
That's strong stuff.
Puck! Come meet Steve.
Gofre! He's perfect.
You never called ME perfect.
What? We've met a dozen times!
Becky, we literally just met.
Gofre, I like you, but this is a little much. Don't you think?
It'll get better soon, I promise.
Anybody going to drink that?
GUYS! Shorty is here!

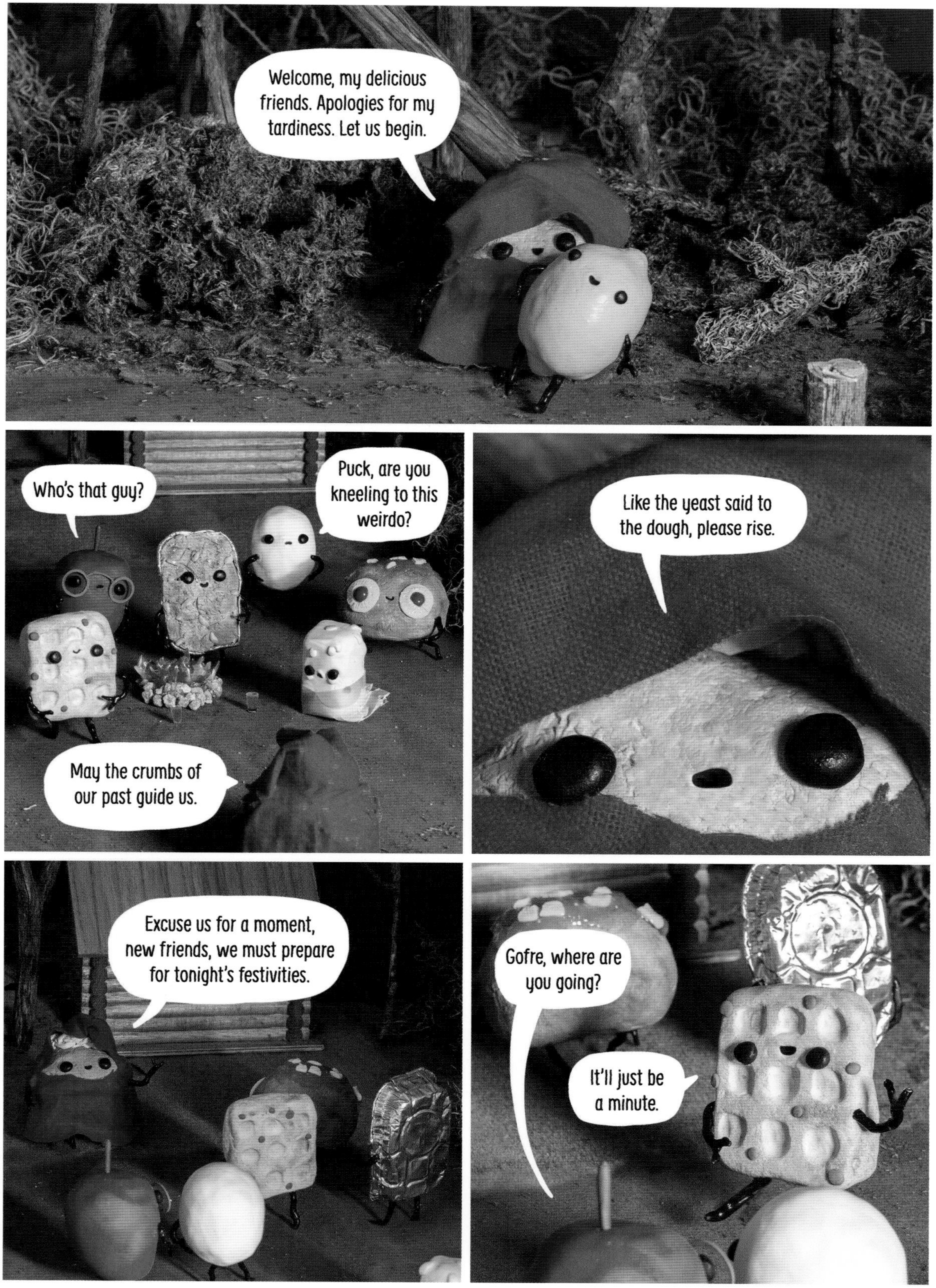
Welcome, my delicious friends. Apologies for my tardiness. Let us begin.
Who's that guy?
Puck, are you kneeling to this weirdo?
May the crumbs of our past guide us.
Like the yeast said to the dough, please rise.
Excuse us for a moment, new friends, we must prepare for tonight's festivities.
Gofre, where are you going?
It'll just be a minute.

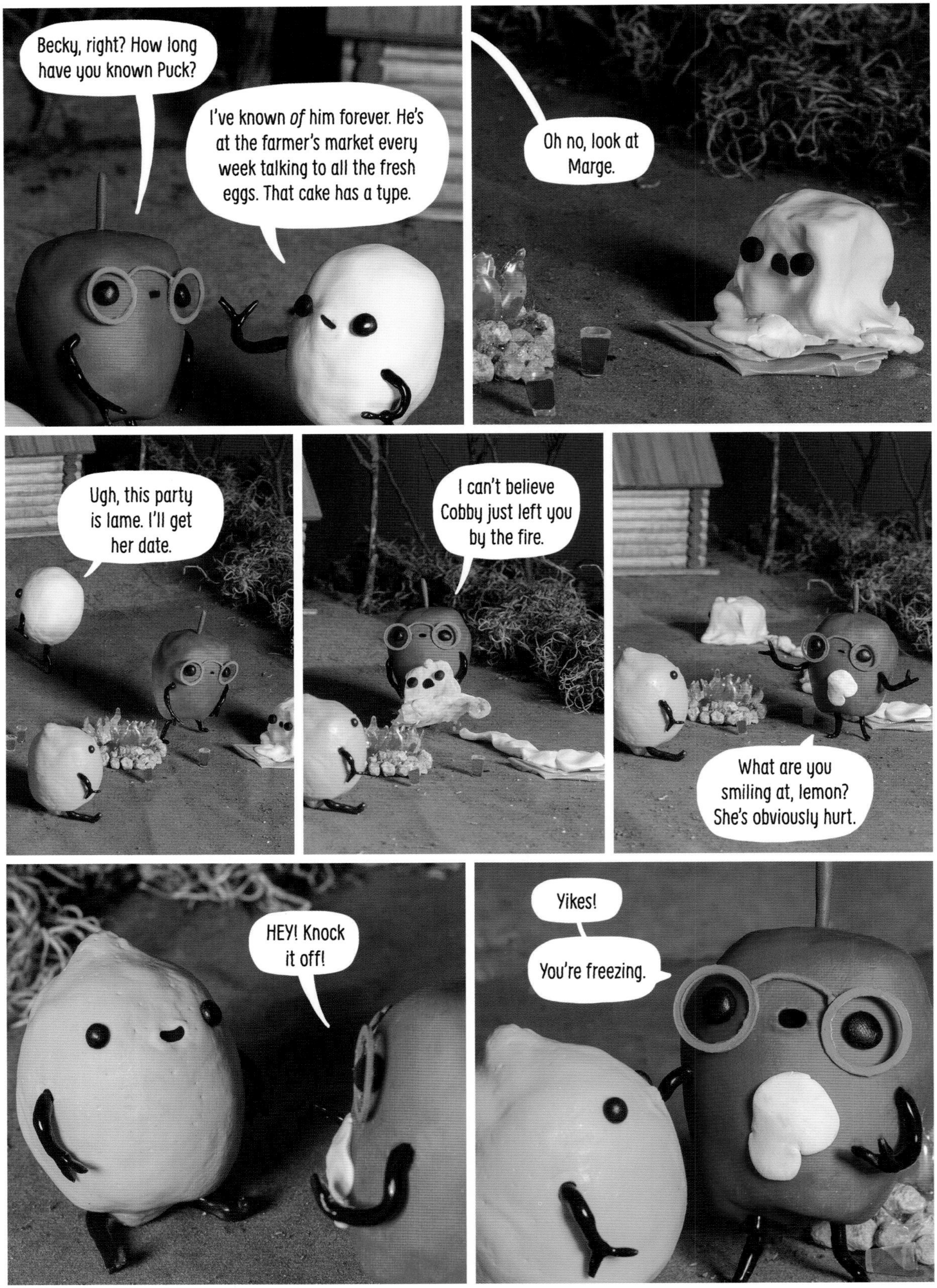

Becky, right? How long have you known Puck?
I've known *of* him forever. He's at the farmer's market every week talking to all the fresh eggs. That cake has a type.
Oh no, look at Marge.
Ugh, this party is lame. I'll get her date.
I can't believe Cobby just left you by the fire.
What are you smiling at, lemon? She's obviously hurt.
HEY! Knock it off!
Yikes!
You're freezing.

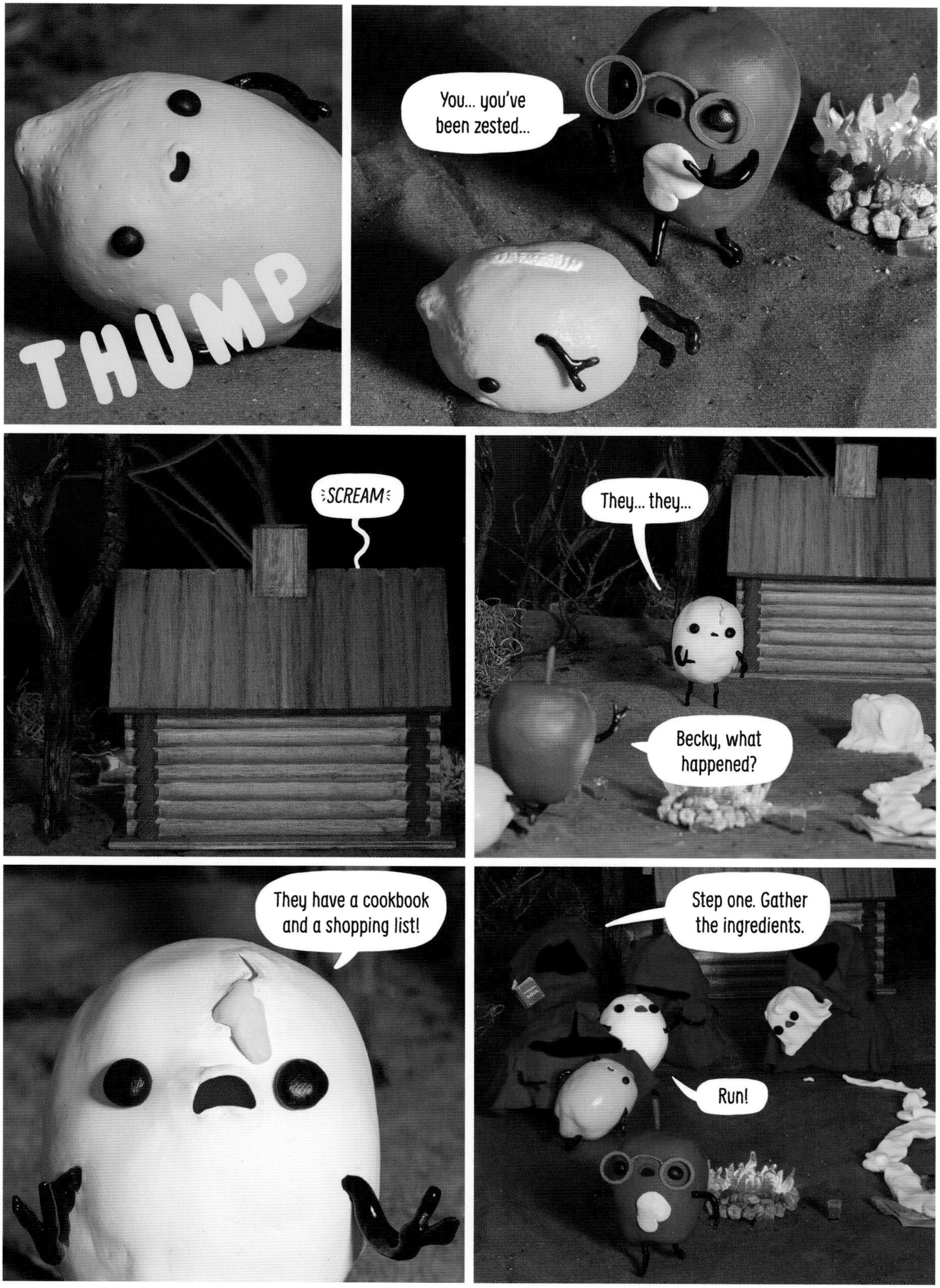
THUMP
You... you've been zested...
SCREAM
They... they...
Becky, what happened?
They have a cookbook and a shopping list!
Step one. Gather the ingredients.
Run!

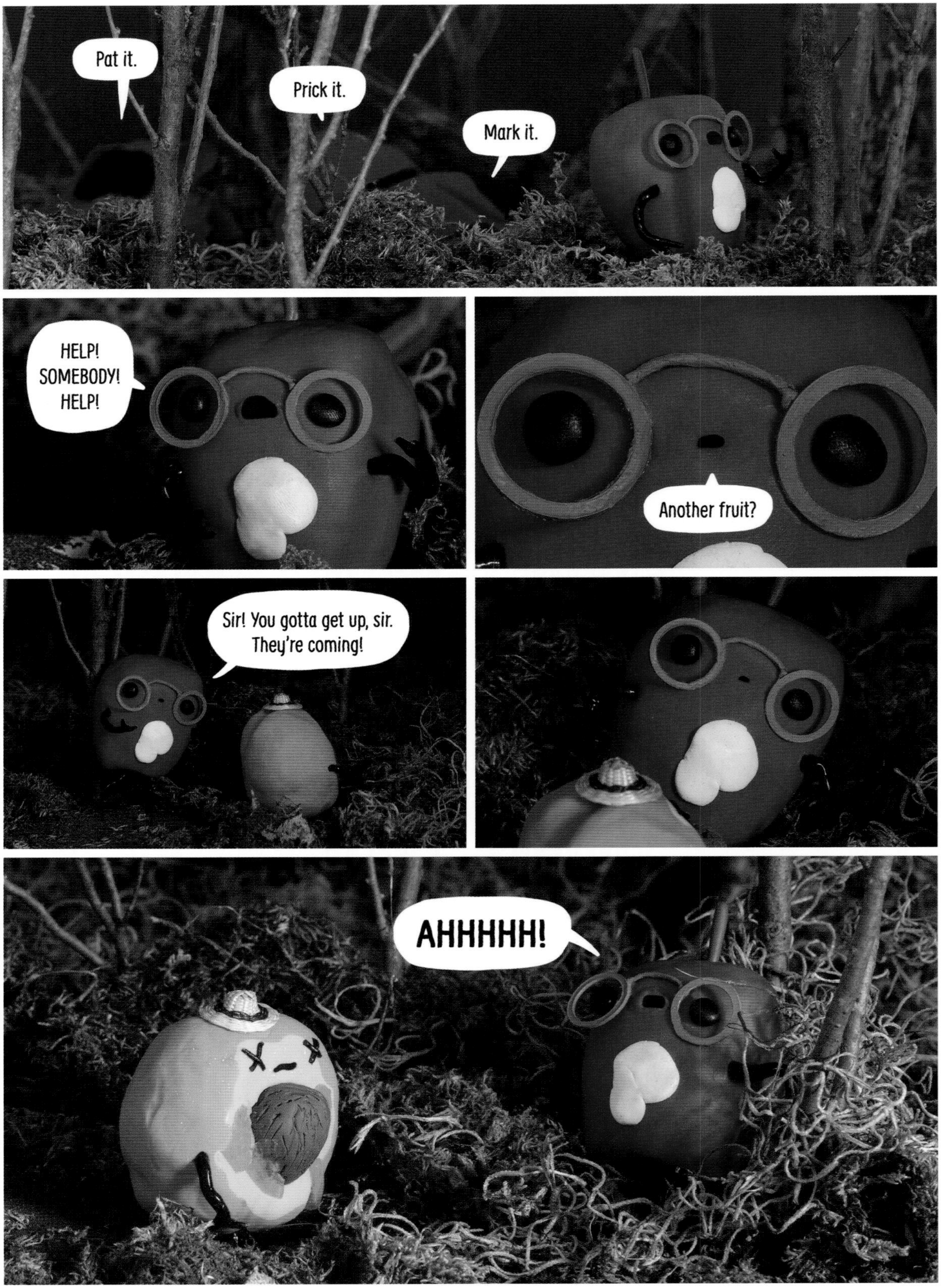
Pat it.
Prick it.
Mark it.
HELP! SOMEBODY! HELP!
Another fruit?
Sir! You gotta get up, sir. They're coming!
AHHHHH!

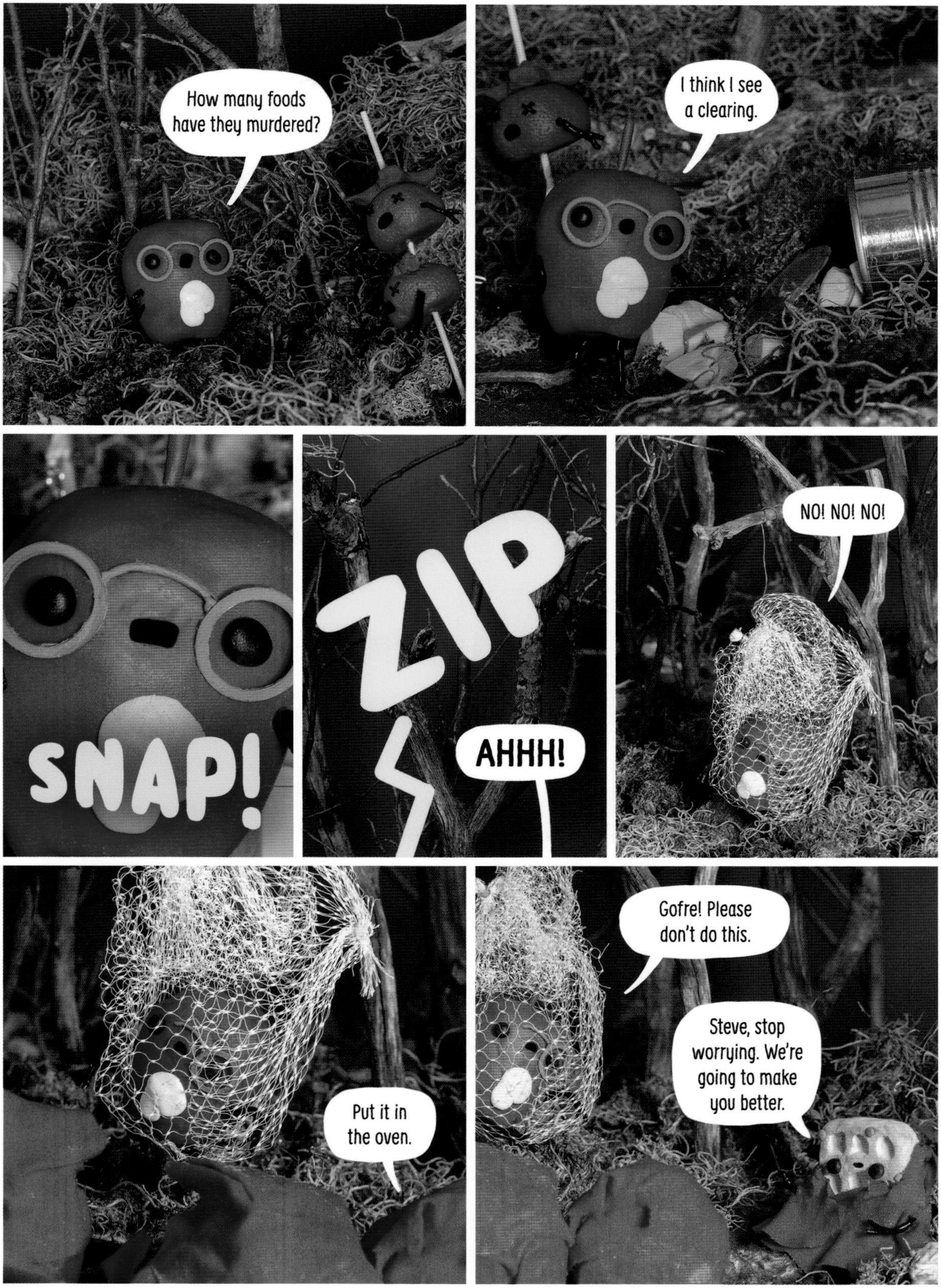
How many foods have they murdered?
I think I see a clearing.
SNAP!
ZIP
AHHH!
NO! NO! NO!
Put it in the oven.
Gofre! Please don't do this.
Steve, stop worrying. We're going to make you better.

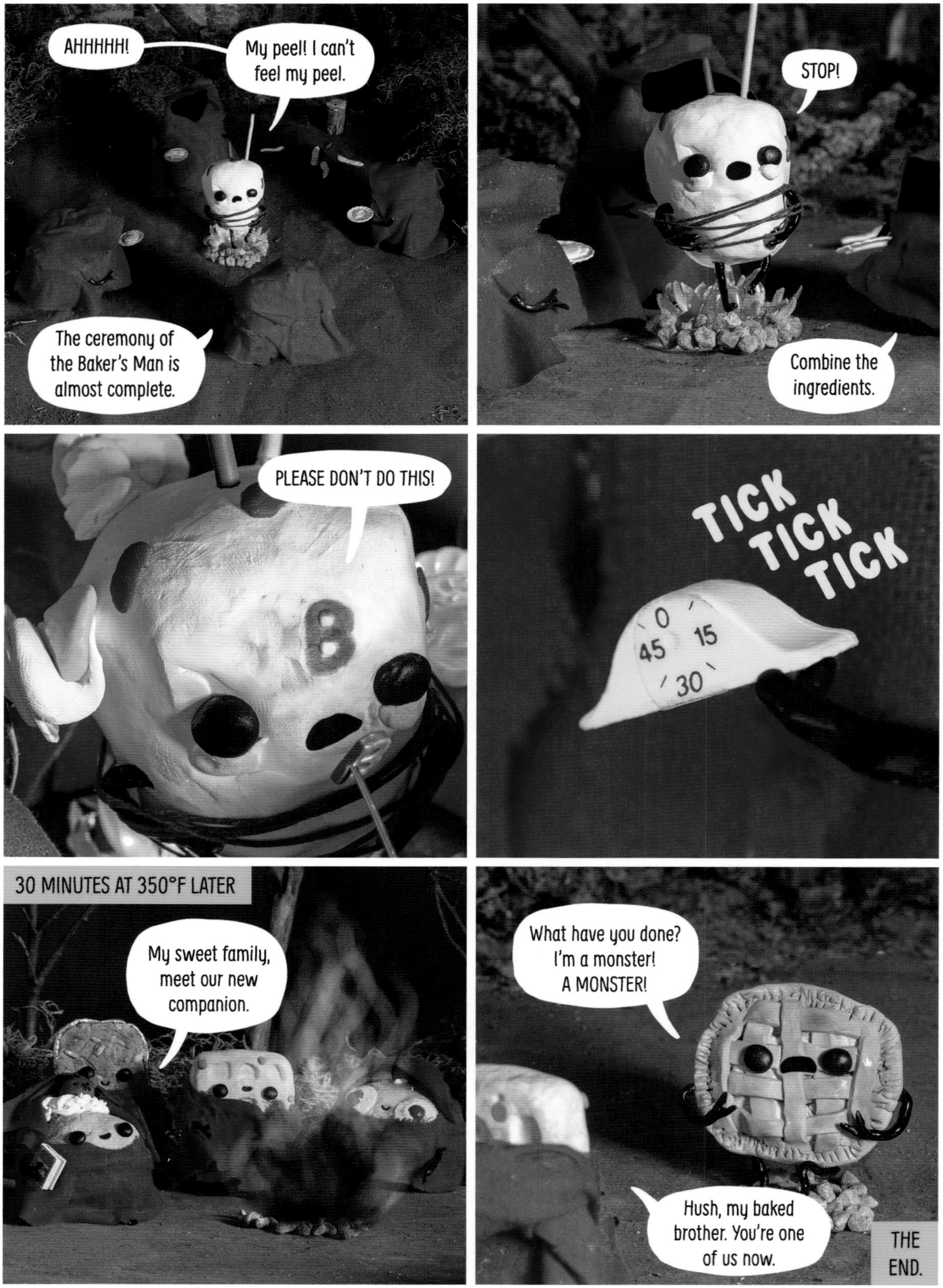
AHHHHH!
My peel! I can't feel my peel.
The ceremony of the Baker's Man is almost complete.
STOP!
Combine the ingredients.
PLEASE DON'T DO THIS!
B
TICK
TICK
TICK
0
15
30
45
30 MINUTES AT 350°F LATER
My sweet family, meet our new companion.
What have you done? I'm a monster! A MONSTER!
Hush, my baked brother. You're one of us now.
THE END.

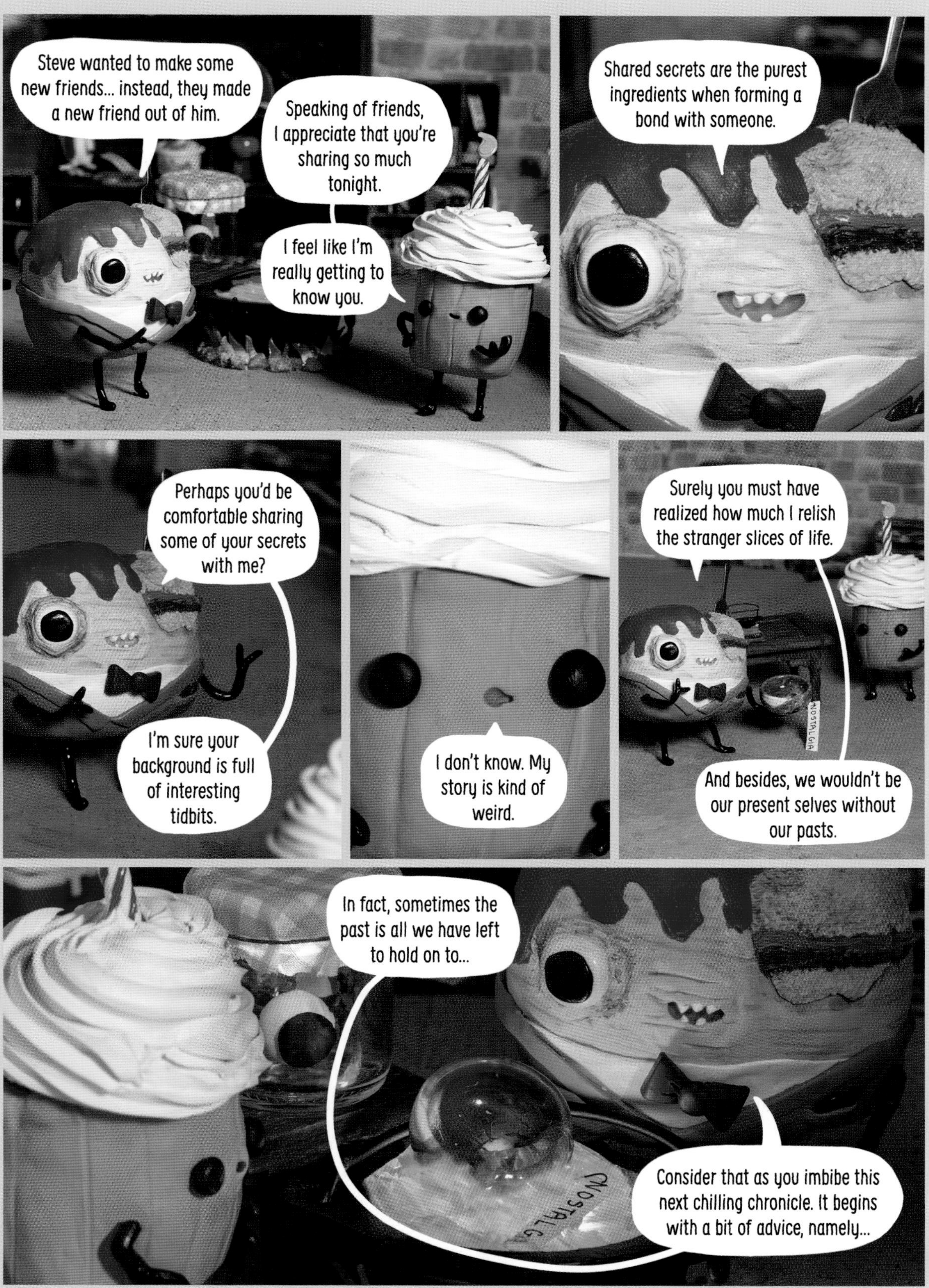
Steve wanted to make some new friends... instead, they made a new friend out of him.
Speaking of friends, I appreciate that you're sharing so much tonight.
I feel like I'm really getting to know you.
Shared secrets are the purest ingredients when forming a bond with someone.
Perhaps you'd be comfortable sharing some of your secrets with me?
I'm sure your background is full of interesting tidbits.
I don't know. My story is kind of weird.
Surely you must have realized how much I relish the stranger slices of life.
NOSTALGIA
And besides, we wouldn't be our present selves without our pasts.
In fact, sometimes the past is all we have left to hold on to...
NOSTALG
Consider that as you imbibe this next chilling chronicle. It begins with a bit of advice, namely...

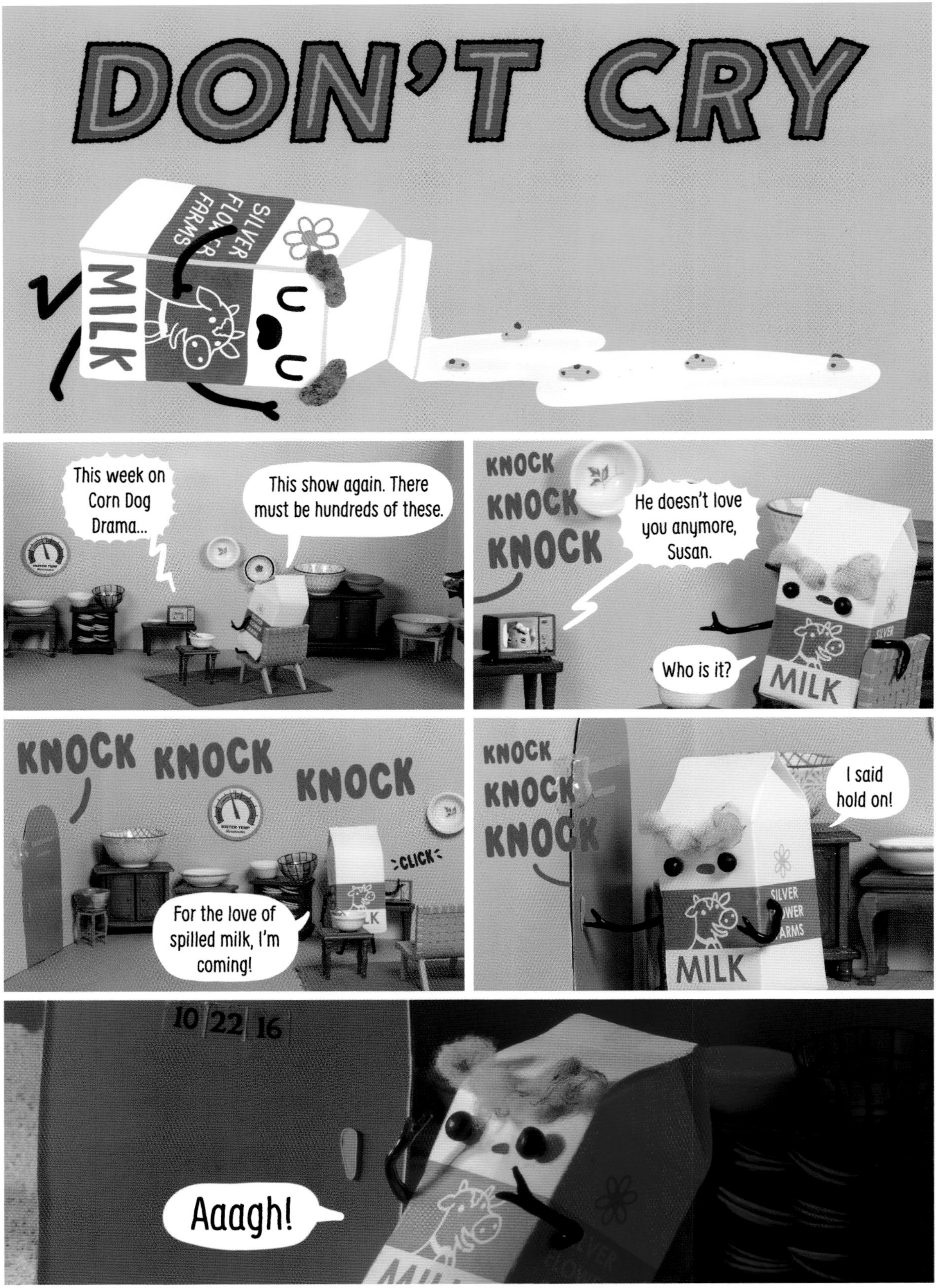
DON'T CRY
SILVER FLOWER FARMS
MILK
This week on Corn Dog Drama...
This show again. There must be hundreds of these.
KNOCK
KNOCK
KNOCK
He doesn't love you anymore, Susan.
Who is it?
KNOCK KNOCK KNOCK
CLICK
For the love of spilled milk, I'm coming!
KNOCK
KNOCK
KNOCK
I said hold on!
10 22 16
Aaagh!

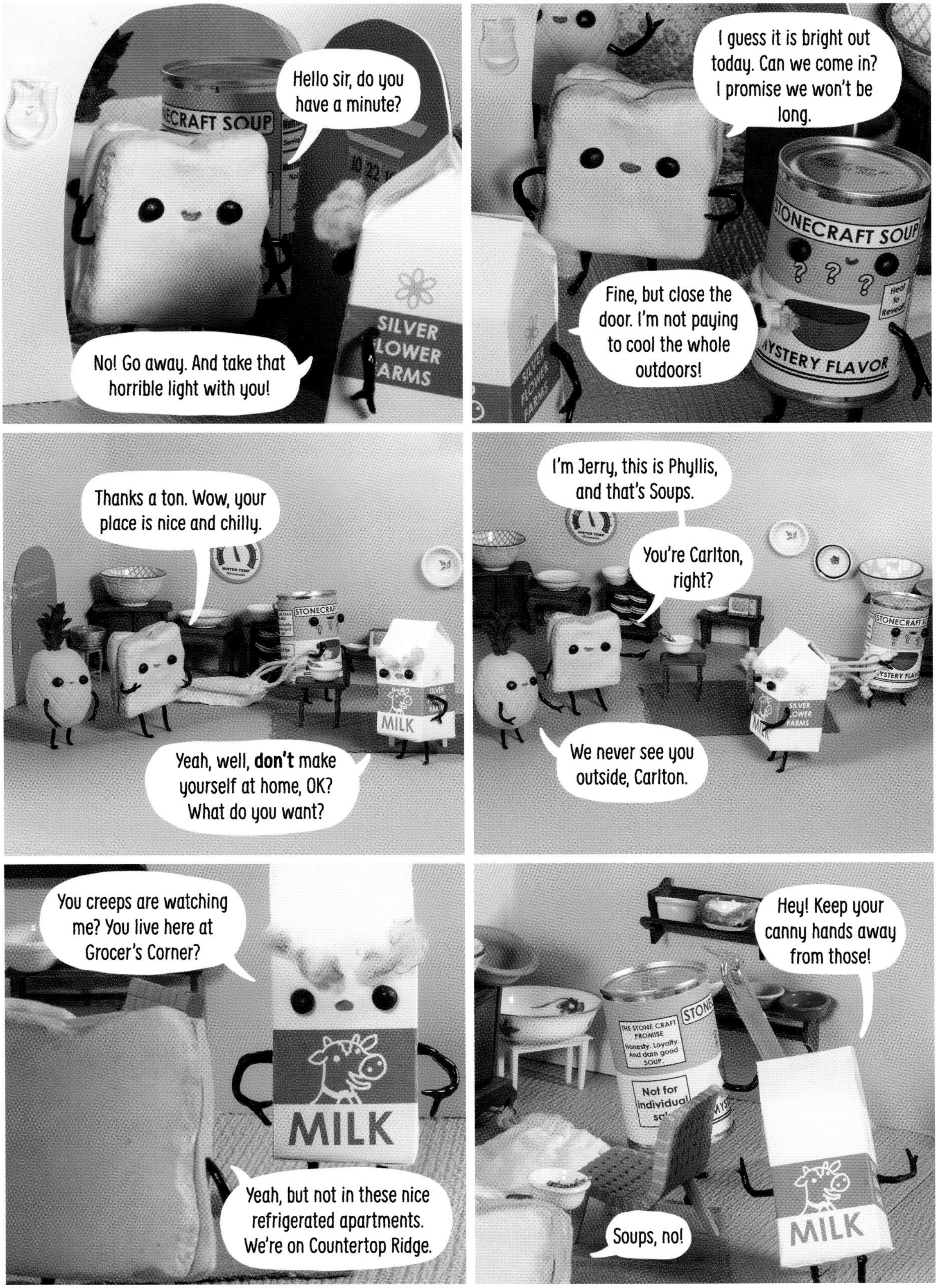
Hello sir, do you have a minute?
No! Go away. And take that horrible light with you!
I guess it is bright out today. Can we come in? I promise we won't be long.
Fine, but close the door. I'm not paying to cool the whole outdoors!
Thanks a ton. Wow, your place is nice and chilly.
Yeah, well, **don't** make yourself at home, OK? What do you want?
I'm Jerry, this is Phyllis, and that's Soups.
You're Carlton, right?
We never see you outside, Carlton.
You creeps are watching me? You live here at Grocer's Corner?
Yeah, but not in these nice refrigerated apartments. We're on Countertop Ridge.
Hey! Keep your canny hands away from those!
Soups, no!

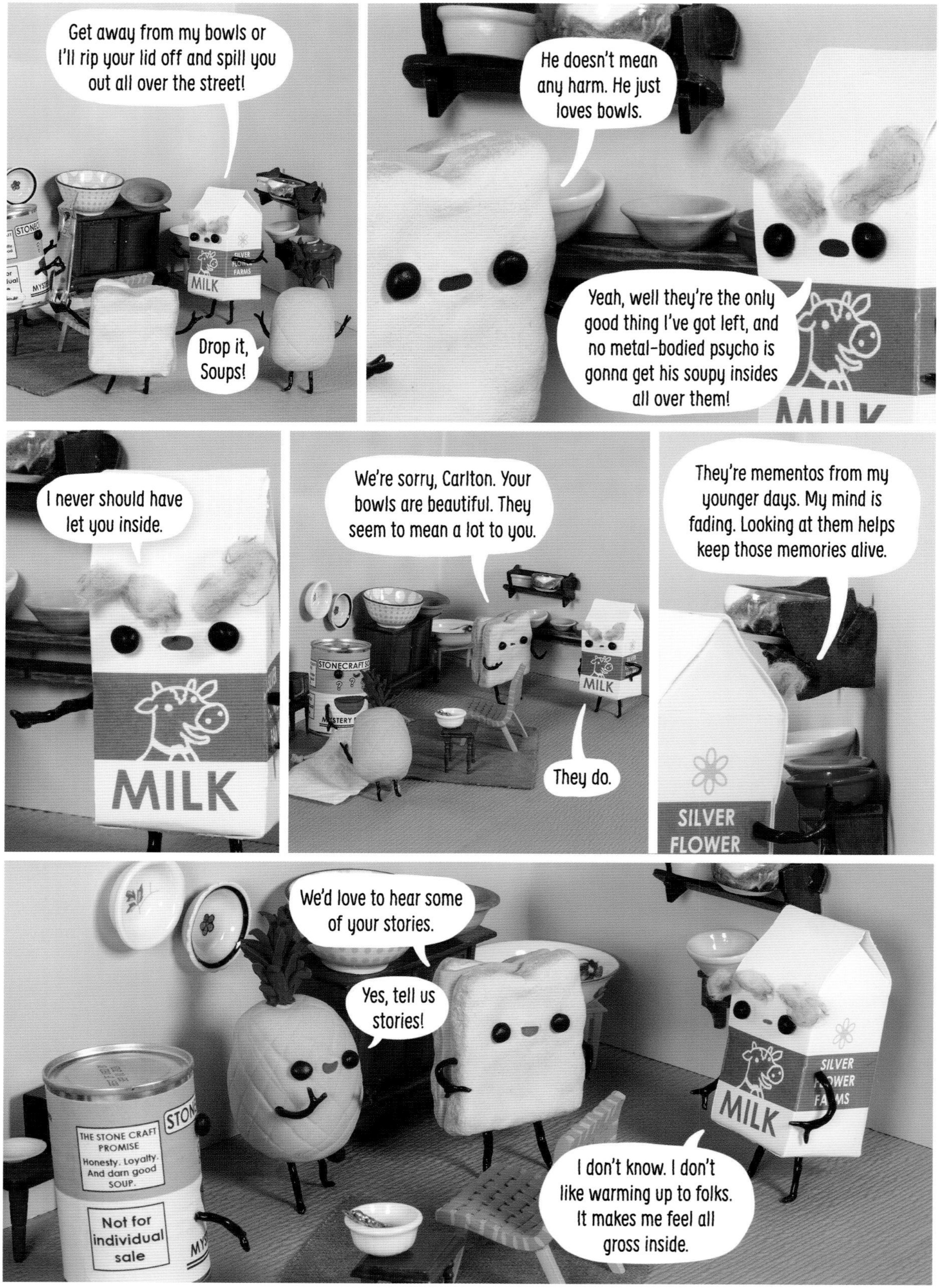
Get away from my bowls or I'll rip your lid off and spill you out all over the street!
Drop it, Soups!
He doesn't mean any harm. He just loves bowls.
Yeah, well they're the only good thing I've got left, and no metal-bodied psycho is gonna get his soupy insides all over them!
I never should have let you inside.
MILK
We're sorry, Carlton. Your bowls are beautiful. They seem to mean a lot to you.
They do.
They're mementos from my younger days. My mind is fading. Looking at them helps keep those memories alive.
SILVER FLOWER
We'd love to hear some of your stories.
Yes, tell us stories!
THE STONE CRAFT PROMISE
Honesty. Loyalty. And darn good SOUP.
Not for individual sale
MILK
I don't know. I don't like warming up to folks. It makes me feel all gross inside.

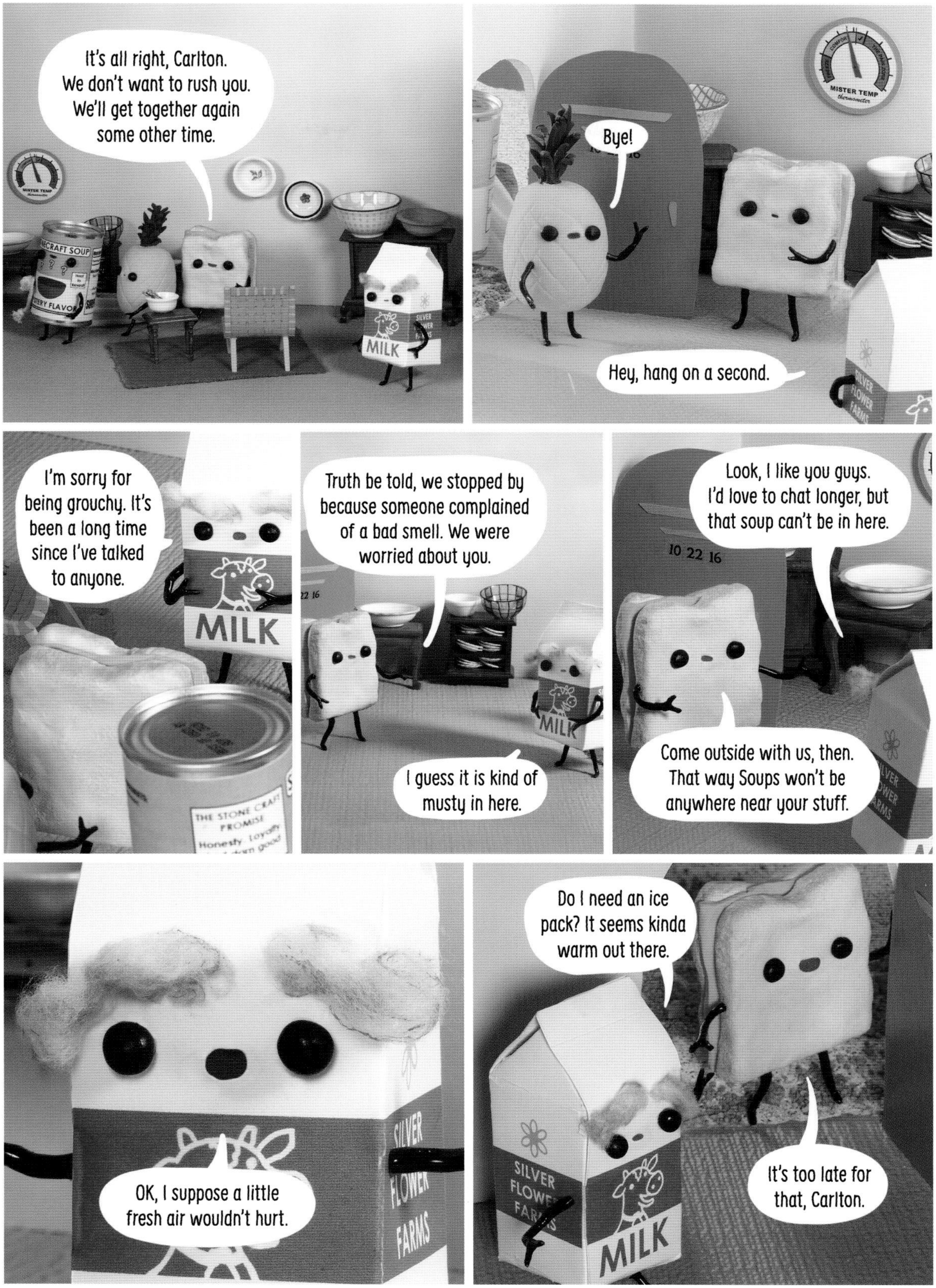
It's all right, Carlton. We don't want to rush you. We'll get together again some other time.
Bye!
Hey, hang on a second.
I'm sorry for being grouchy. It's been a long time since I've talked to anyone.
Truth be told, we stopped by because someone complained of a bad smell. We were worried about you.
I guess it is kind of musty in here.
Look, I like you guys. I'd love to chat longer, but that soup can't be in here.
Come outside with us, then. That way Soups won't be anywhere near your stuff.
OK, I suppose a little fresh air wouldn't hurt.
Do I need an ice pack? It seems kinda warm out there.
It's too late for that, Carlton.

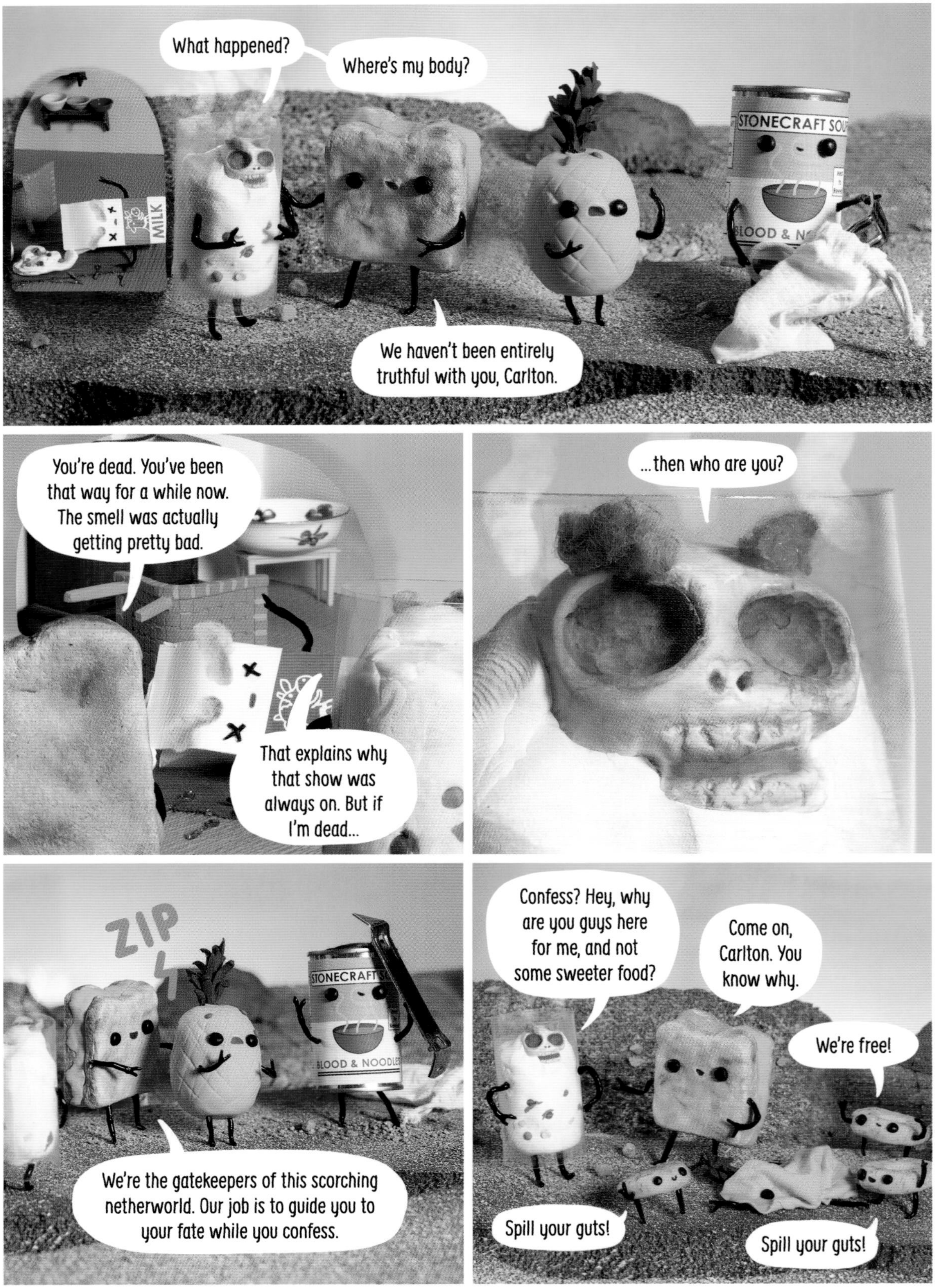
What happened?
Where's my body?
MILK
We haven't been entirely truthful with you, Carlton.
You're dead. You've been that way for a while now. The smell was actually getting pretty bad.
That explains why that show was always on. But if I'm dead...
...then who are you?
ZIP
We're the gatekeepers of this scorching netherworld. Our job is to guide you to your fate while you confess.
Confess? Hey, why are you guys here for me, and not some sweeter food?
Come on, Carlton. You know why.
We're free!
Spill your guts!
Spill your guts!

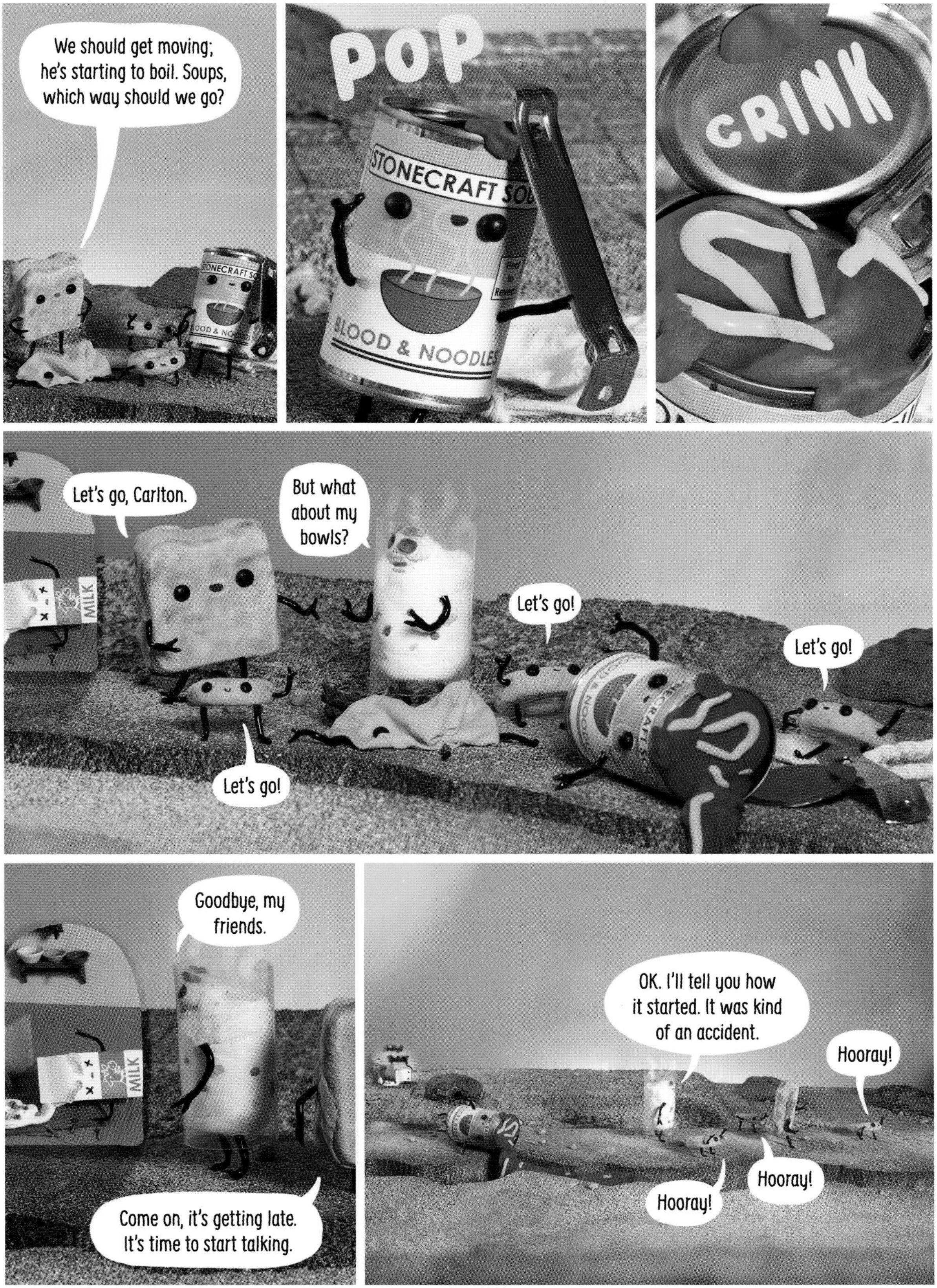
We should get moving; he's starting to boil. Soups, which way should we go?
POP
STONECRAFT SOU
BLOOD & NOODLES
CRINK
Let's go, Carlton.
But what about my bowls?
MILK
Let's go!
Let's go!
Let's go!
Goodbye, my friends.
Come on, it's getting late. It's time to start talking.
OK. I'll tell you how it started. It was kind of an accident.
Hooray!
Hooray!
Hooray!

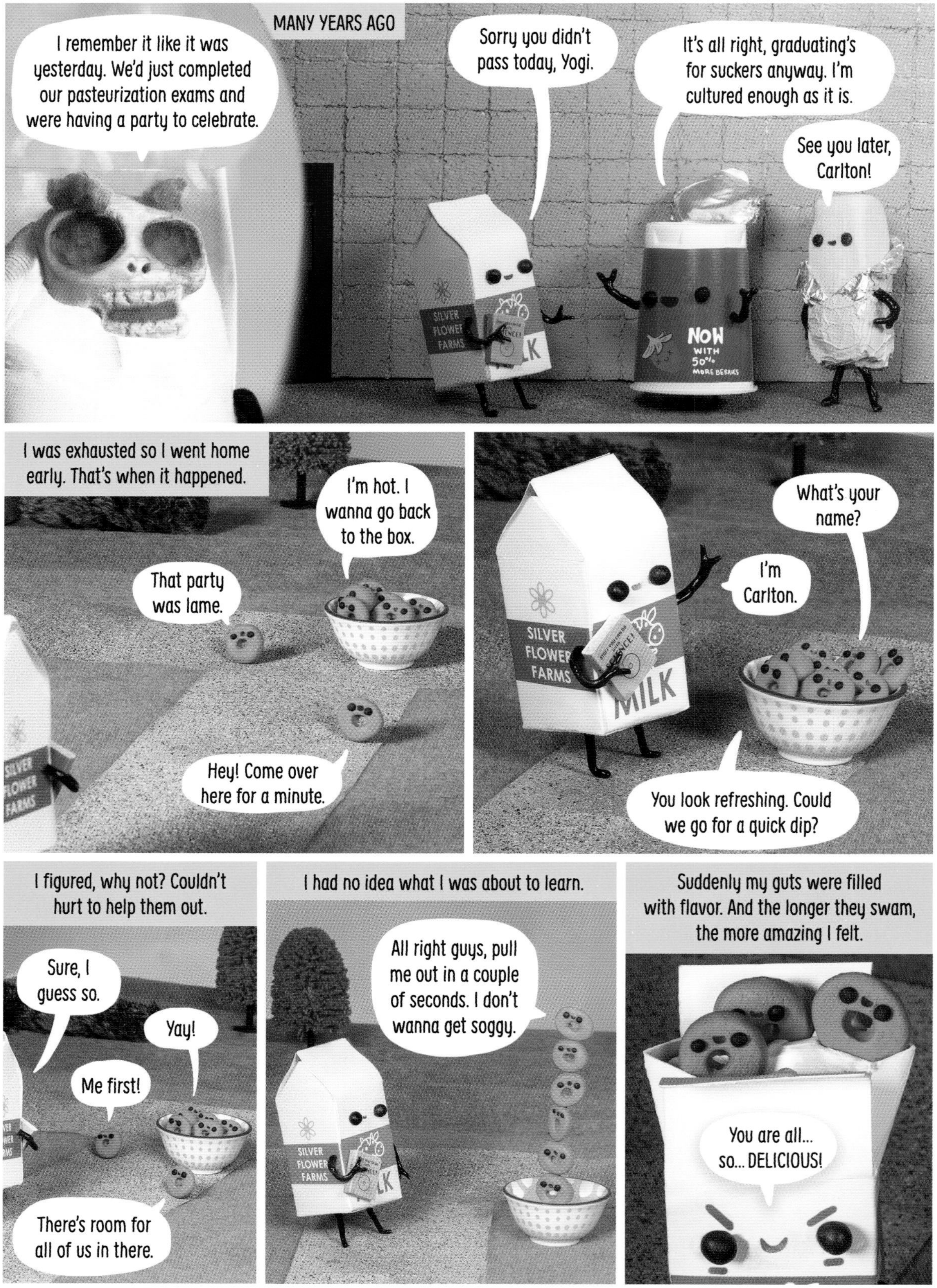

MANY YEARS AGO
I remember it like it was yesterday. We'd just completed our pasteurization exams and were having a party to celebrate.
Sorry you didn't pass today, Yogi.
It's all right, graduating's for suckers anyway. I'm cultured enough as it is.
See you later, Carlton!
SILVER FLOWER FARMS
MILK
NOW WITH 50% MORE BERRIES
I was exhausted so I went home early. That's when it happened.
I'm hot. I wanna go back to the box.
That party was lame.
Hey! Come over here for a minute.
SILVER FLOWER FARMS
What's your name?
I'm Carlton.
You look refreshing. Could we go for a quick dip?
SILVER FLOWER FARMS
MILK
I figured, why not? Couldn't hurt to help them out.
Sure, I guess so.
Yay!
Me first!
There's room for all of us in there.
I had no idea what I was about to learn.
All right guys, pull me out in a couple of seconds. I don't wanna get soggy.
SILVER FLOWER FARMS
Suddenly my guts were filled with flavor. And the longer they swam, the more amazing I felt.
You are all... so... DELICIOUS!

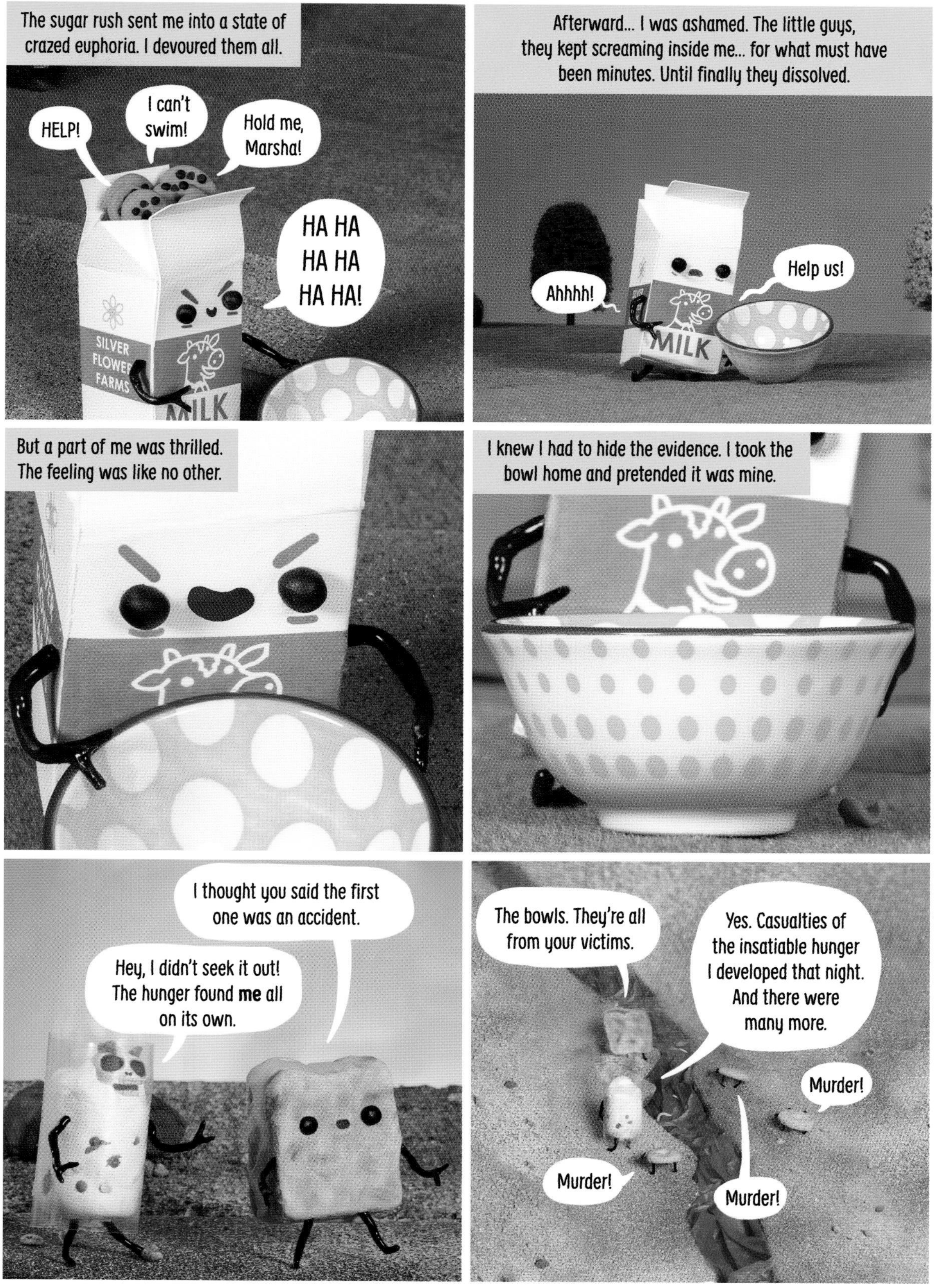
The sugar rush sent me into a state of crazed euphoria. I devoured them all.
HELP!
I can't swim!
Hold me, Marsha!
HA HA HA HA HA HA!
SILVER FLOWER FARMS
MILK
Afterward... I was ashamed. The little guys, they kept screaming inside me... for what must have been minutes. Until finally they dissolved.
Ahhhh!
Help us!
MILK
But a part of me was thrilled. The feeling was like no other.
I knew I had to hide the evidence. I took the bowl home and pretended it was mine.
I thought you said the first one was an accident.
Hey, I didn't seek it out! The hunger found **me** all on its own.
The bowls. They're all from your victims.
Yes. Casualties of the insatiable hunger I developed that night. And there were many more.
Murder!
Murder!
Murder!

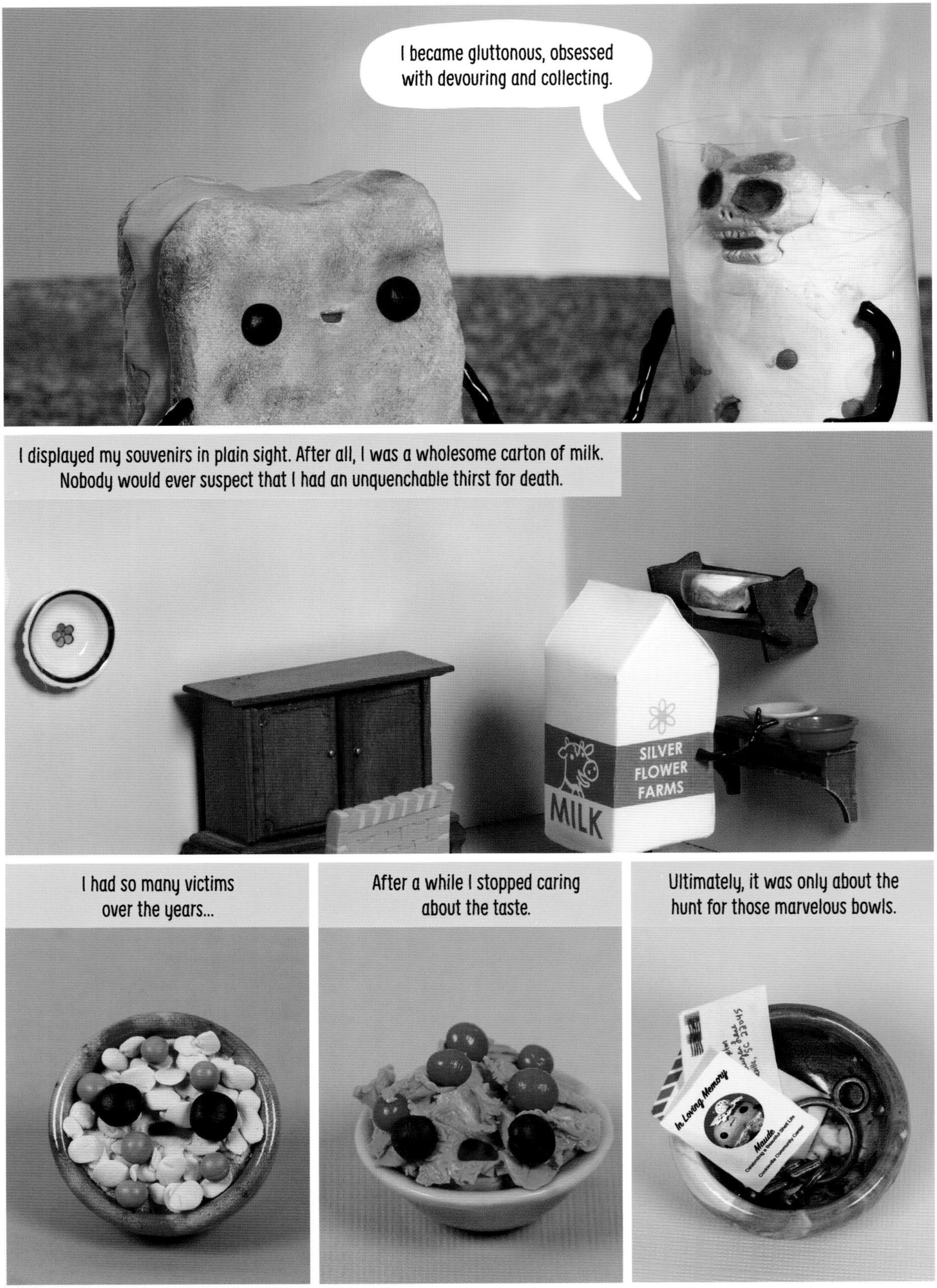
I became gluttonous, obsessed with devouring and collecting.
I displayed my souvenirs in plain sight. After all, I was a wholesome carton of milk. Nobody would ever suspect that I had an unquenchable thirst for death.
SILVER FLOWER FARMS
MILK
I had so many victims over the years...
After a while I stopped caring about the taste.
Ultimately, it was only about the hunt for those marvelous bowls.
In Loving Memory
Maude

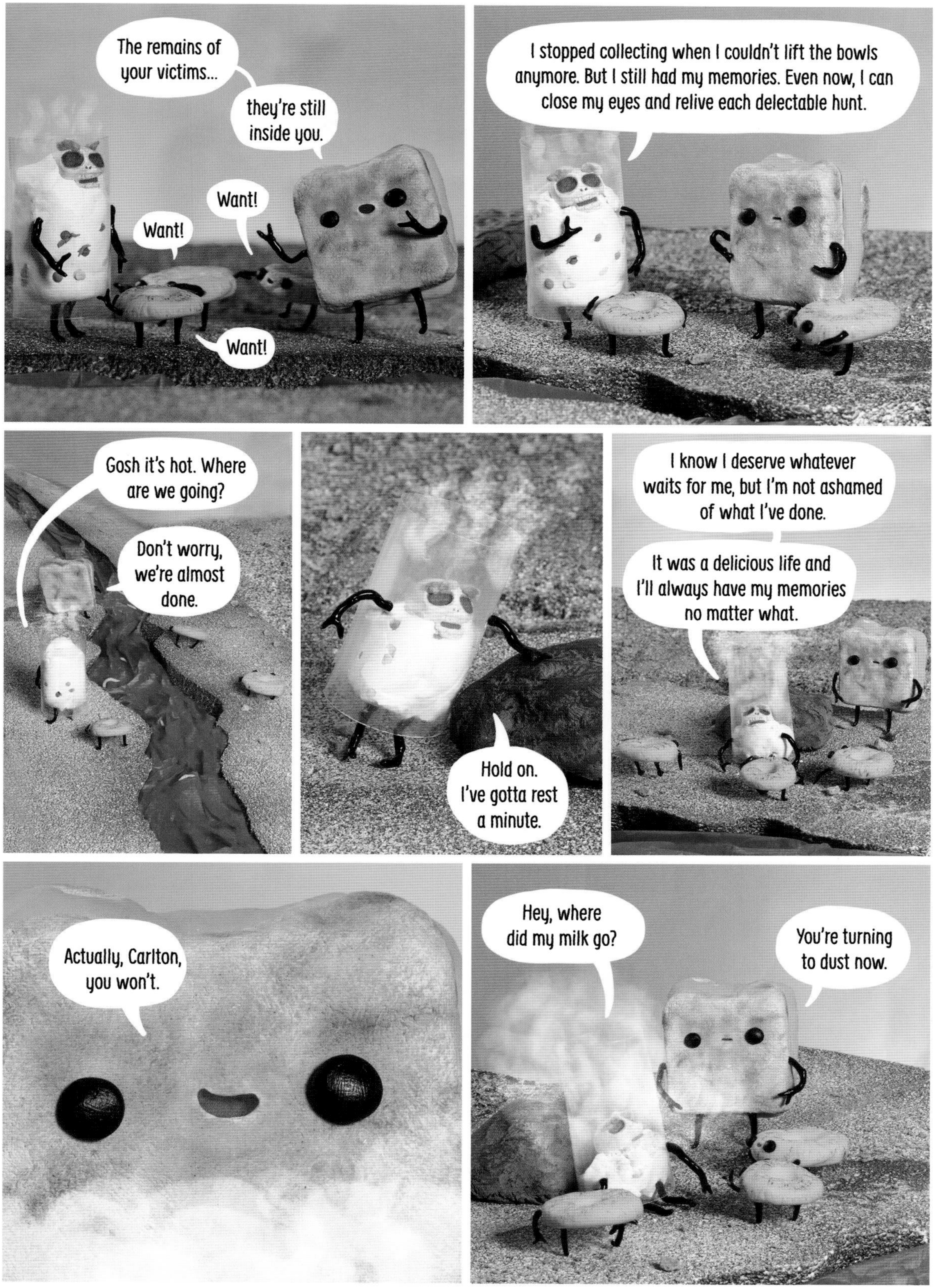
The remains of your victims...
they're still inside you.
Want!
Want!
Want!
I stopped collecting when I couldn't lift the bowls anymore. But I still had my memories. Even now, I can close my eyes and relive each delectable hunt.
Gosh it's hot. Where are we going?
Don't worry, we're almost done.
Hold on. I've gotta rest a minute.
I know I deserve whatever waits for me, but I'm not ashamed of what I've done.
It was a delicious life and I'll always have my memories no matter what.
Actually, Carlton, you won't.
Hey, where did my milk go?
You're turning to dust now.

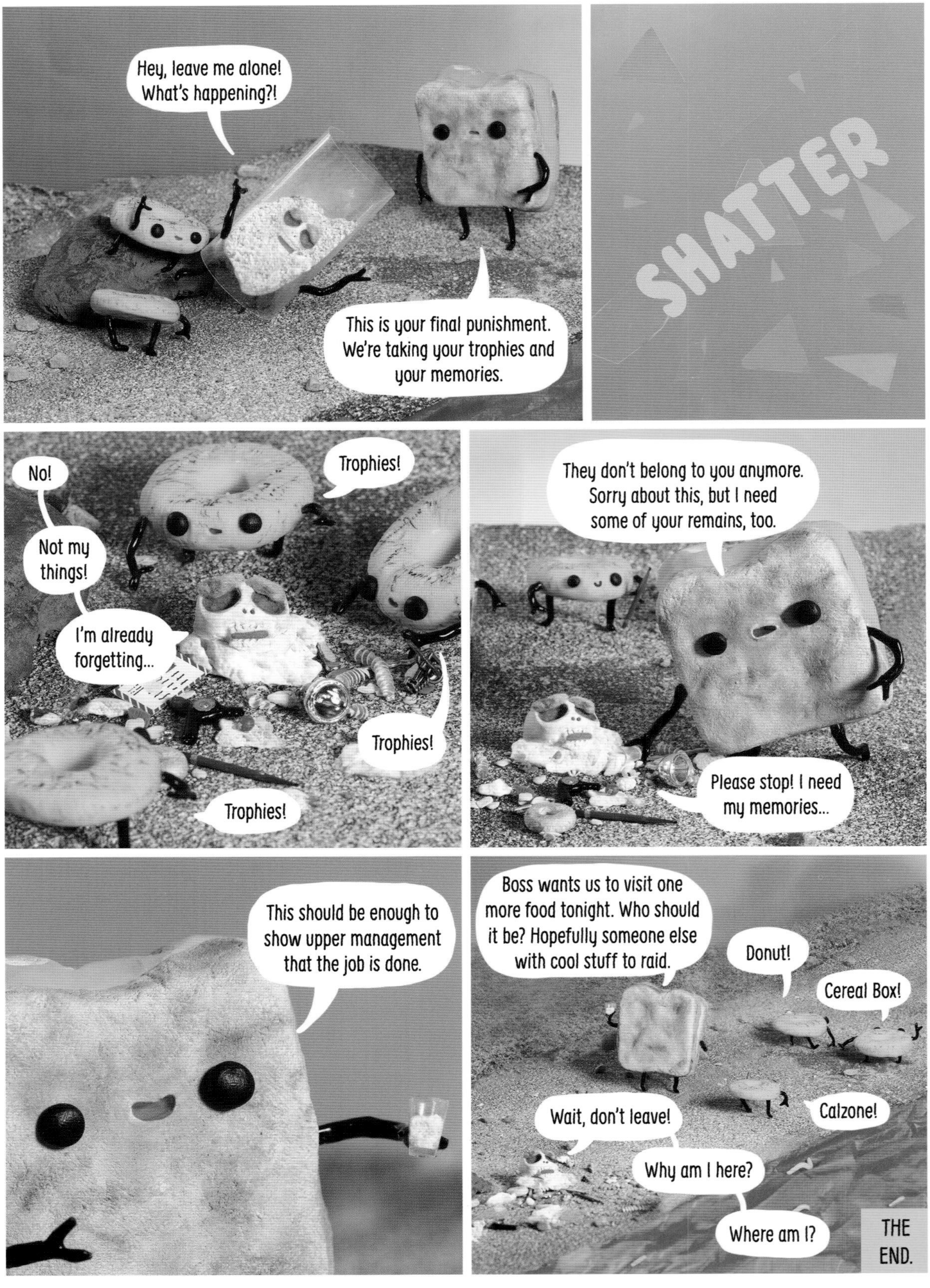
Hey, leave me alone! What's happening?!
This is your final punishment. We're taking your trophies and your memories.
SHATTER
No!
Not my things!
I'm already forgetting...
Trophies!
Trophies!
Trophies!
They don't belong to you anymore. Sorry about this, but I need some of your remains, too.
Please stop! I need my memories...
This should be enough to show upper management that the job is done.
Boss wants us to visit one more food tonight. Who should it be? Hopefully someone else with cool stuff to raid.
Donut!
Cereal Box!
Calzone!
Wait, don't leave!
Why am I here?
Where am I?
THE END.

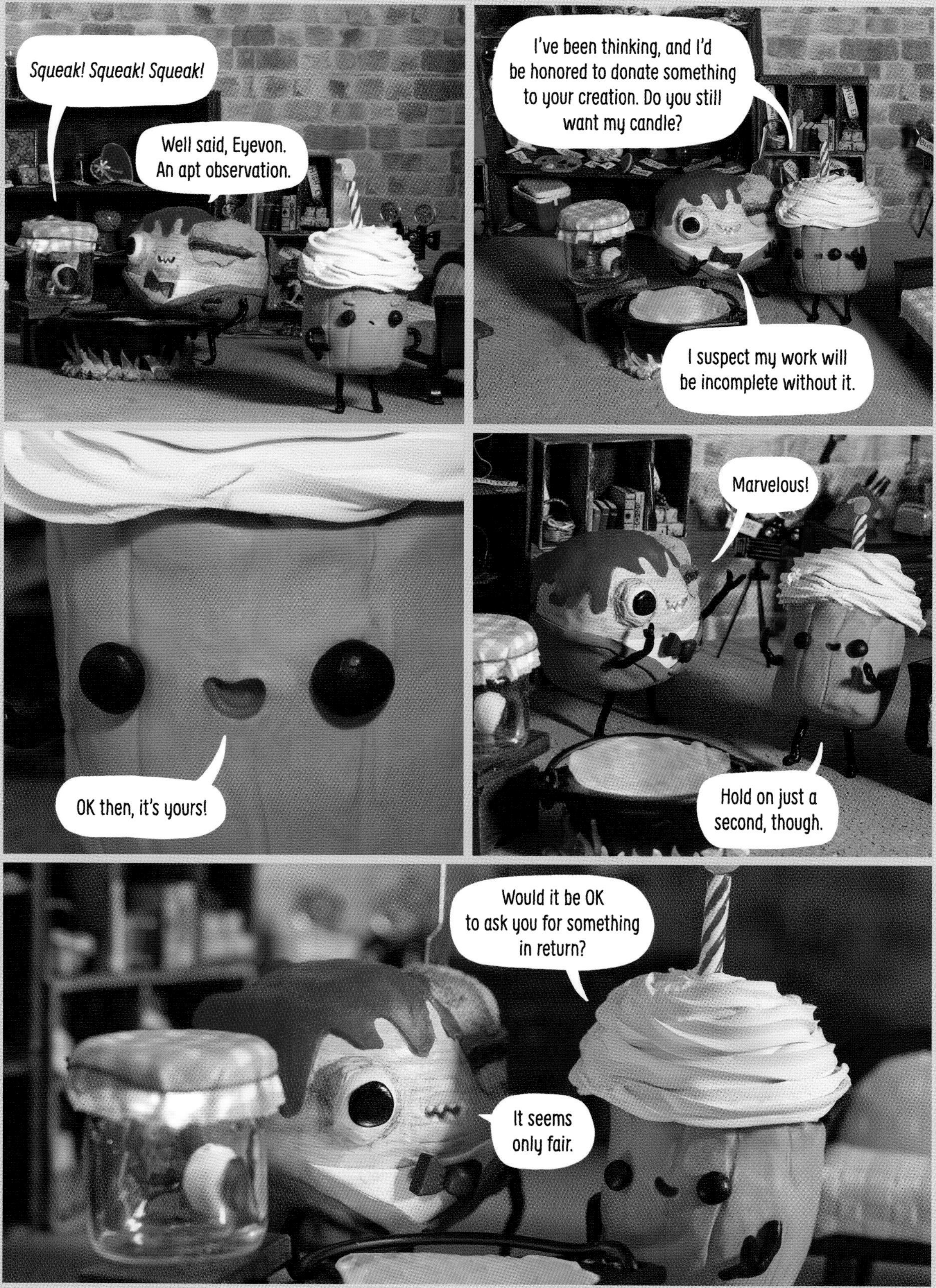

Squeak! Squeak! Squeak!
Well said, Eyevon. An apt observation.
I've been thinking, and I'd be honored to donate something to your creation. Do you still want my candle?
I suspect my work will be incomplete without it.
OK then, it's yours!
Marvelous!
Hold on just a second, though.
Would it be OK to ask you for something in return?
It seems only fair.

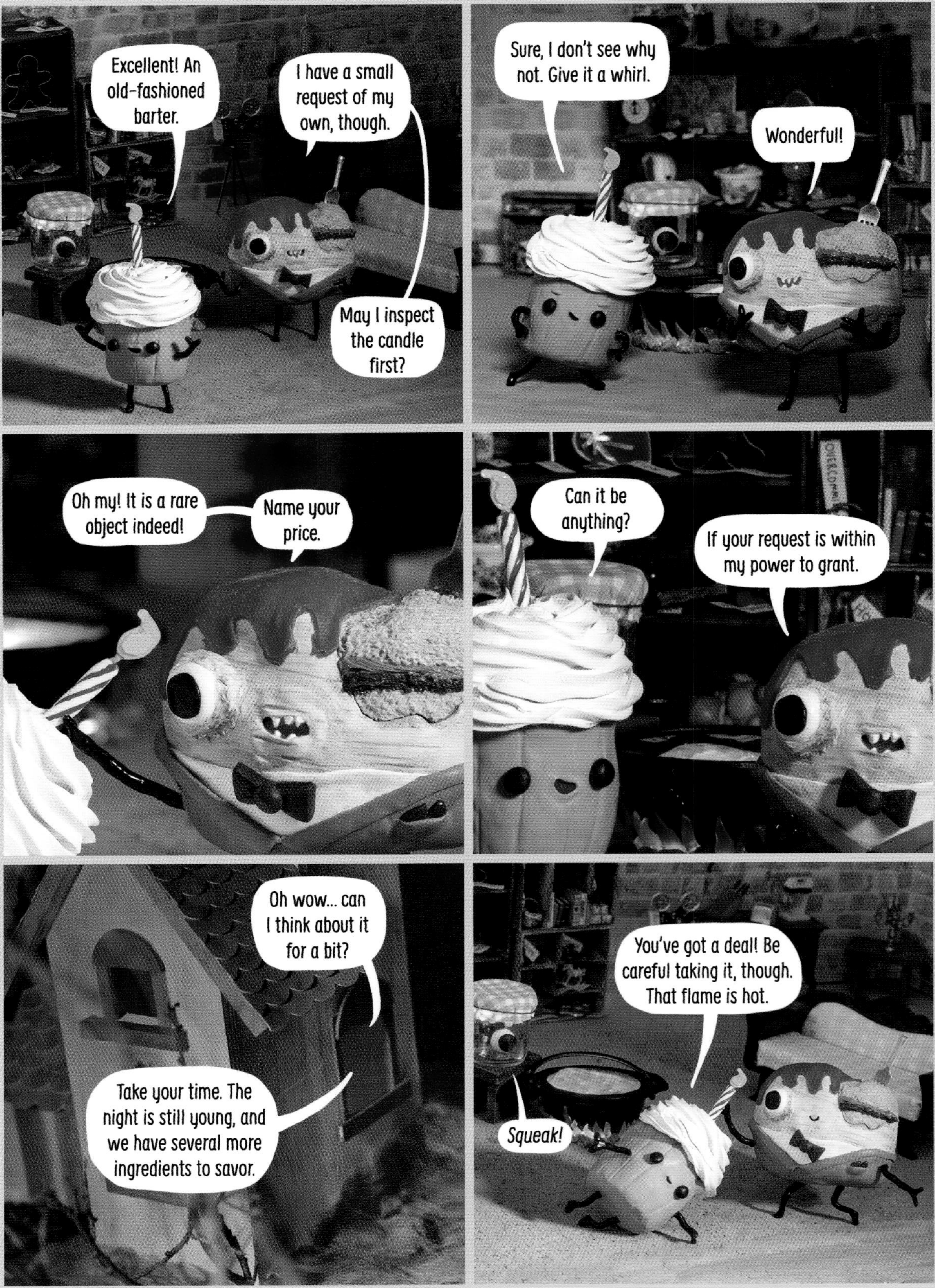
Excellent! An old-fashioned barter.
I have a small request of my own, though.
May I inspect the candle first?
Sure, I don't see why not. Give it a whirl.
Wonderful!
Oh my! It is a rare object indeed!
Name your price.
Can it be anything?
If your request is within my power to grant.
Oh wow... can I think about it for a bit?
Take your time. The night is still young, and we have several more ingredients to savor.
You've got a deal! Be careful taking it, though. That flame is hot.
Squeak!

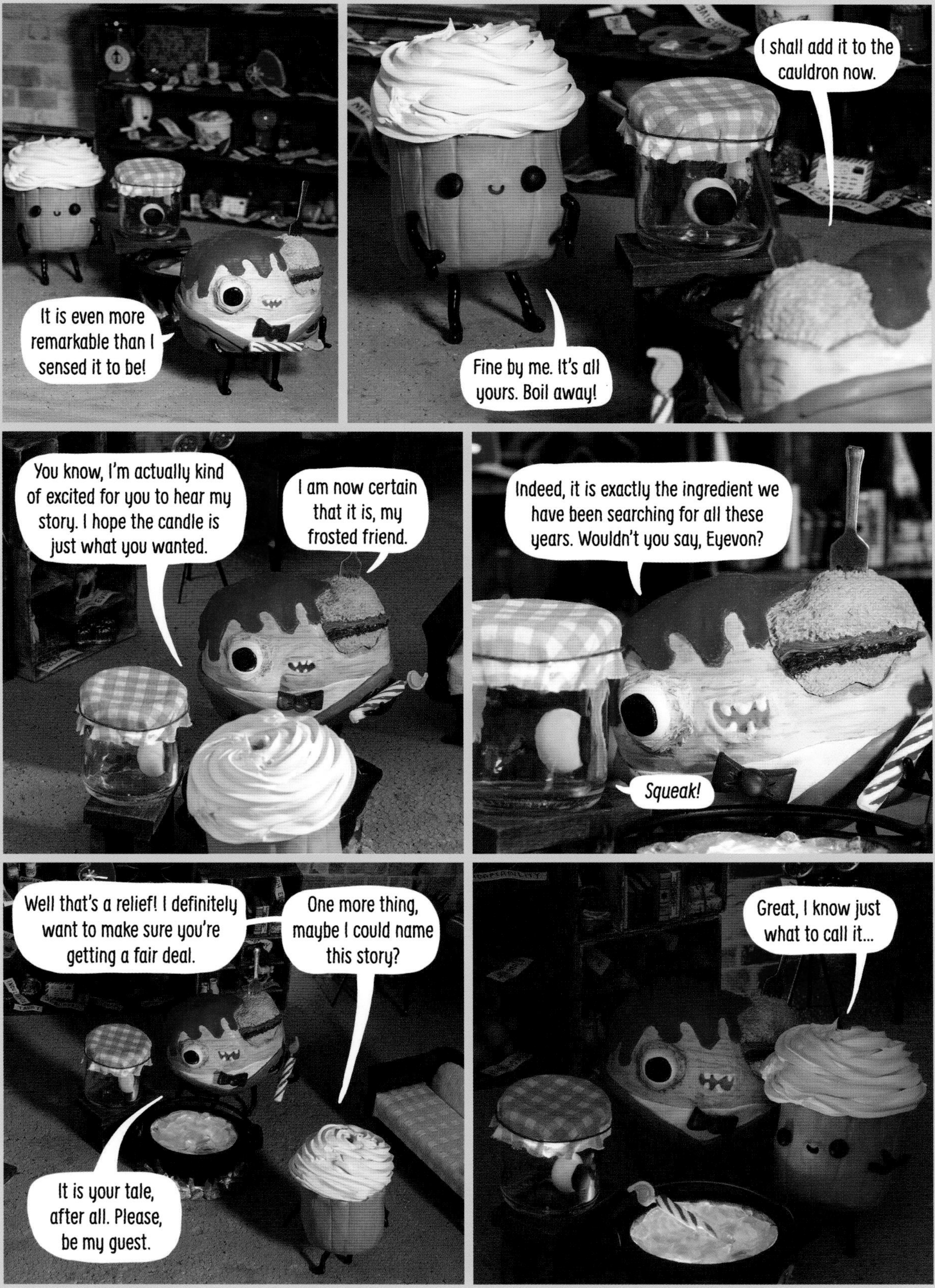

It is even more remarkable than I sensed it to be!
I shall add it to the cauldron now.
Fine by me. It's all yours. Boil away!
You know, I'm actually kind of excited for you to hear my story. I hope the candle is just what you wanted.
I am now certain that it is, my frosted friend.
Indeed, it is exactly the ingredient we have been searching for all these years. Wouldn't you say, Eyevon?
Squeak!
Well that's a relief! I definitely want to make sure you're getting a fair deal.
One more thing, maybe I could name this story?
It is your tale, after all. Please, be my guest.
Great, I know just what to call it...

DESSERTS

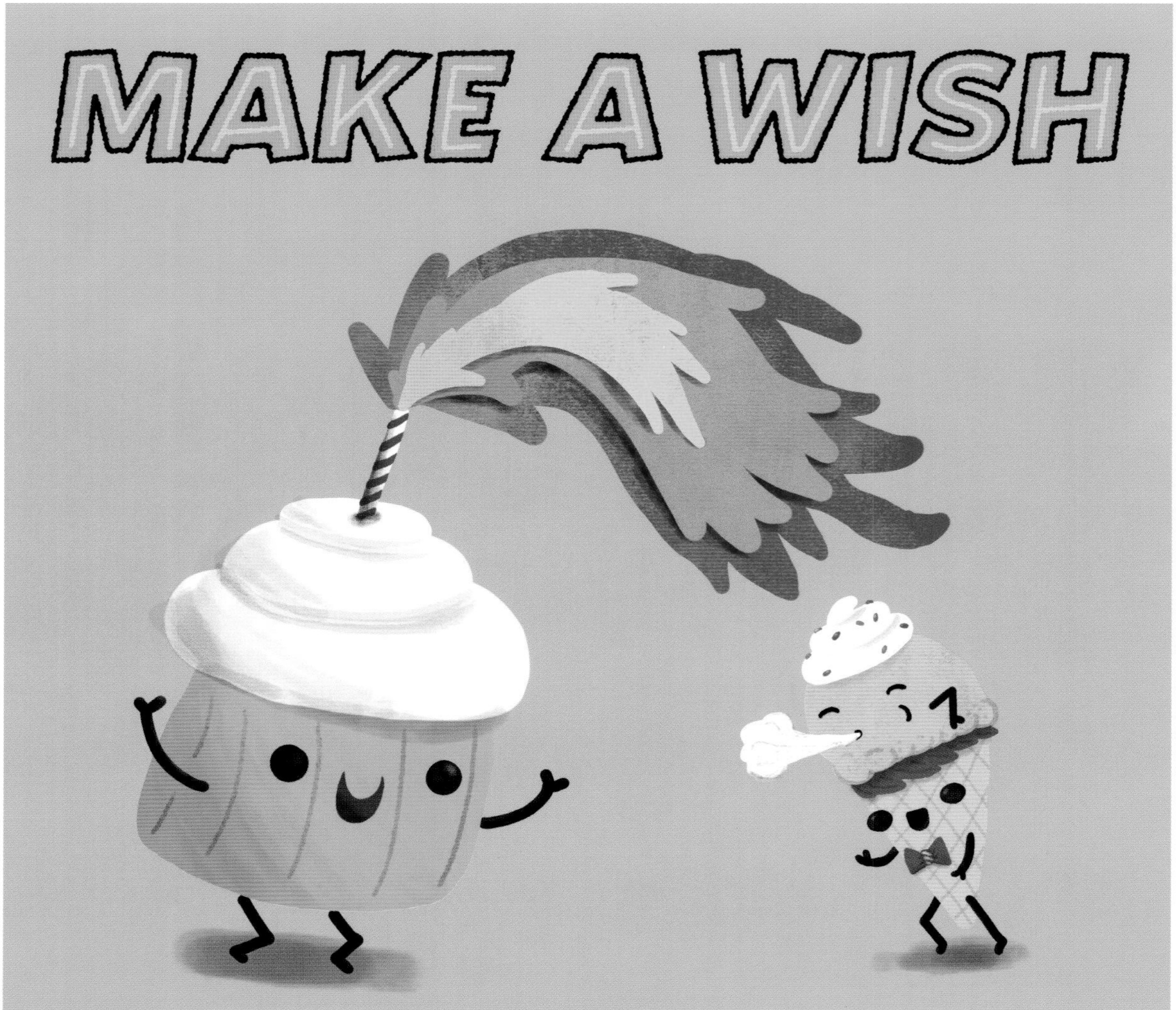
MAKE A WISH

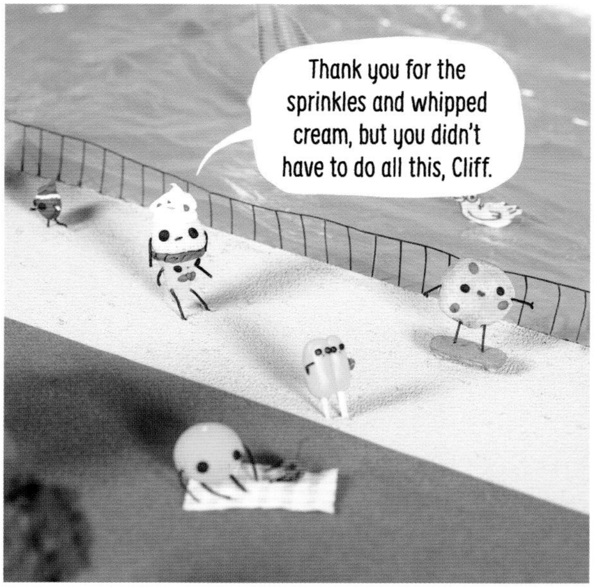
Thank you for the sprinkles and whipped cream, but you didn't have to do all this, Cliff.

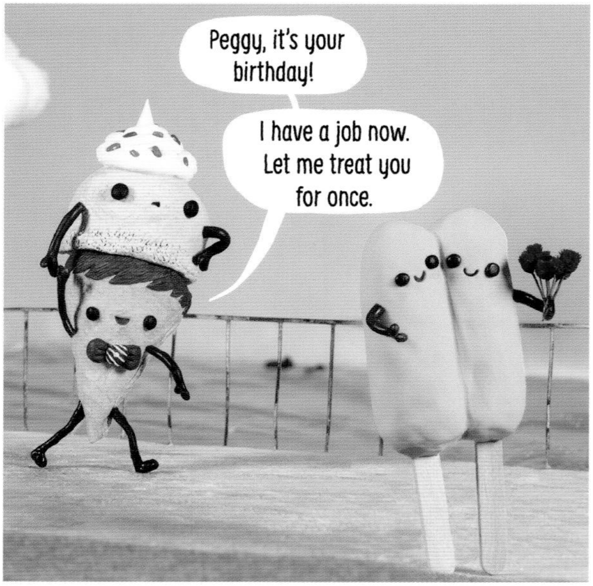
Peggy, it's your birthday!
I have a job now. Let me treat you for once.

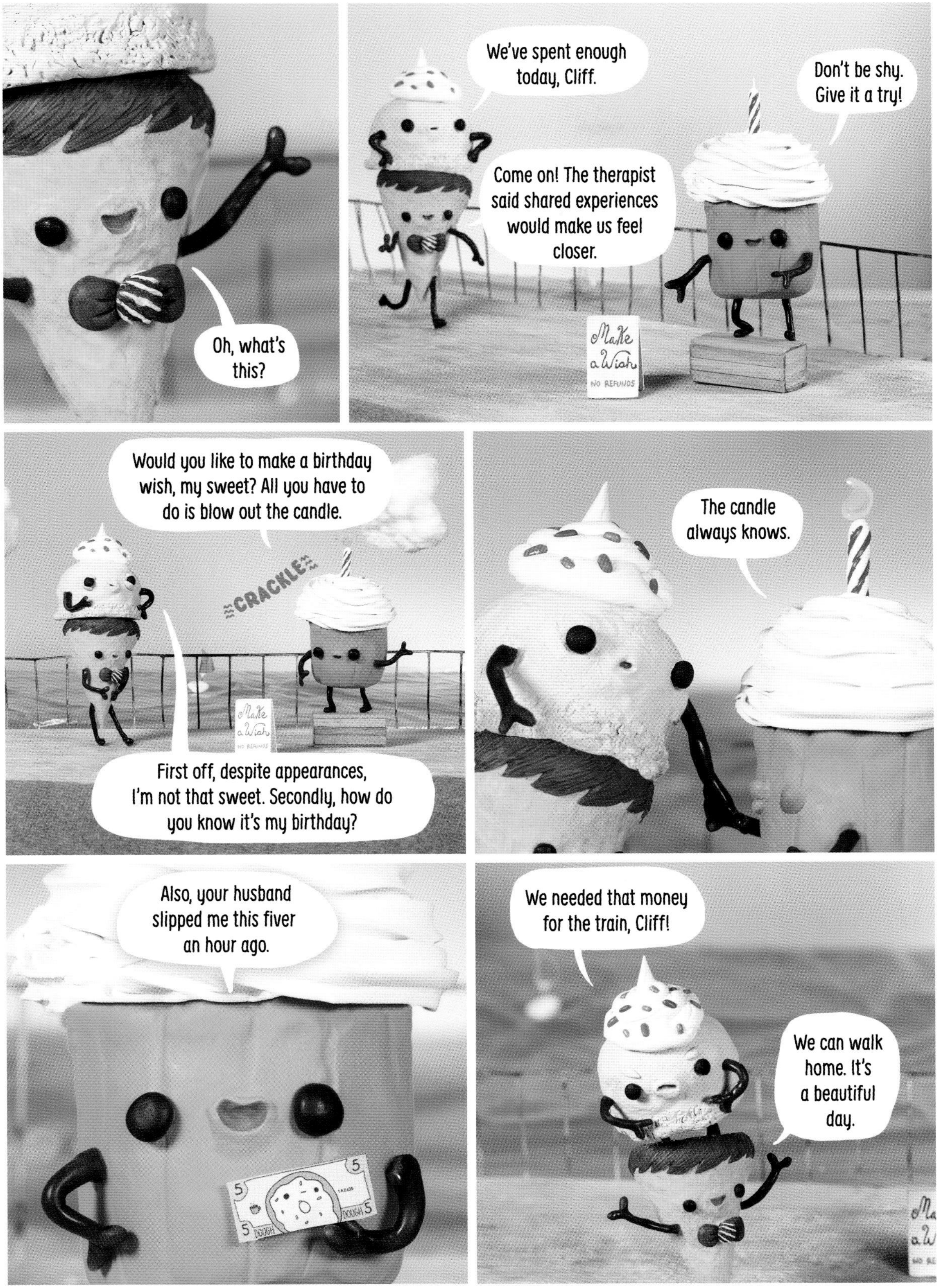
Oh, what's this?
We've spent enough today, Cliff.
Come on! The therapist said shared experiences would make us feel closer.
Don't be shy. Give it a try!
Make a Wish
NO REFUNDS
Would you like to make a birthday wish, my sweet? All you have to do is blow out the candle.
CRACKLE
First off, despite appearances, I'm not that sweet. Secondly, how do you know it's my birthday?
The candle always knows.
Also, your husband slipped me this fiver an hour ago.
5
DOUGH
We needed that money for the train, Cliff!
We can walk home. It's a beautiful day.

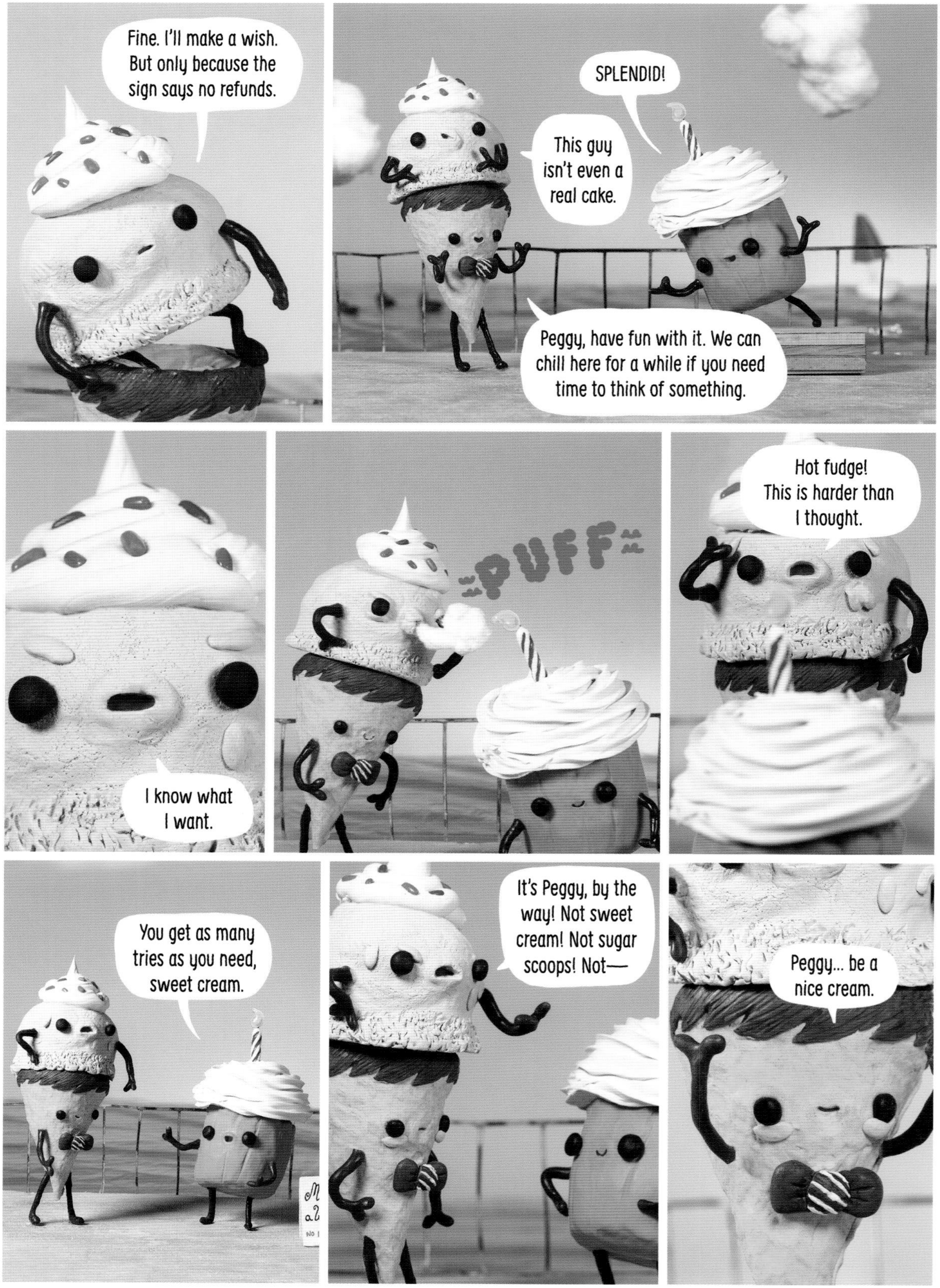
Fine. I'll make a wish. But only because the sign says no refunds.
SPLENDID!
This guy isn't even a real cake.
Peggy, have fun with it. We can chill here for a while if you need time to think of something.
I know what I want.
PUFF
Hot fudge! This is harder than I thought.
You get as many tries as you need, sweet cream.
It's Peggy, by the way! Not sweet cream! Not sugar scoops! Not—
Peggy... be a nice cream.

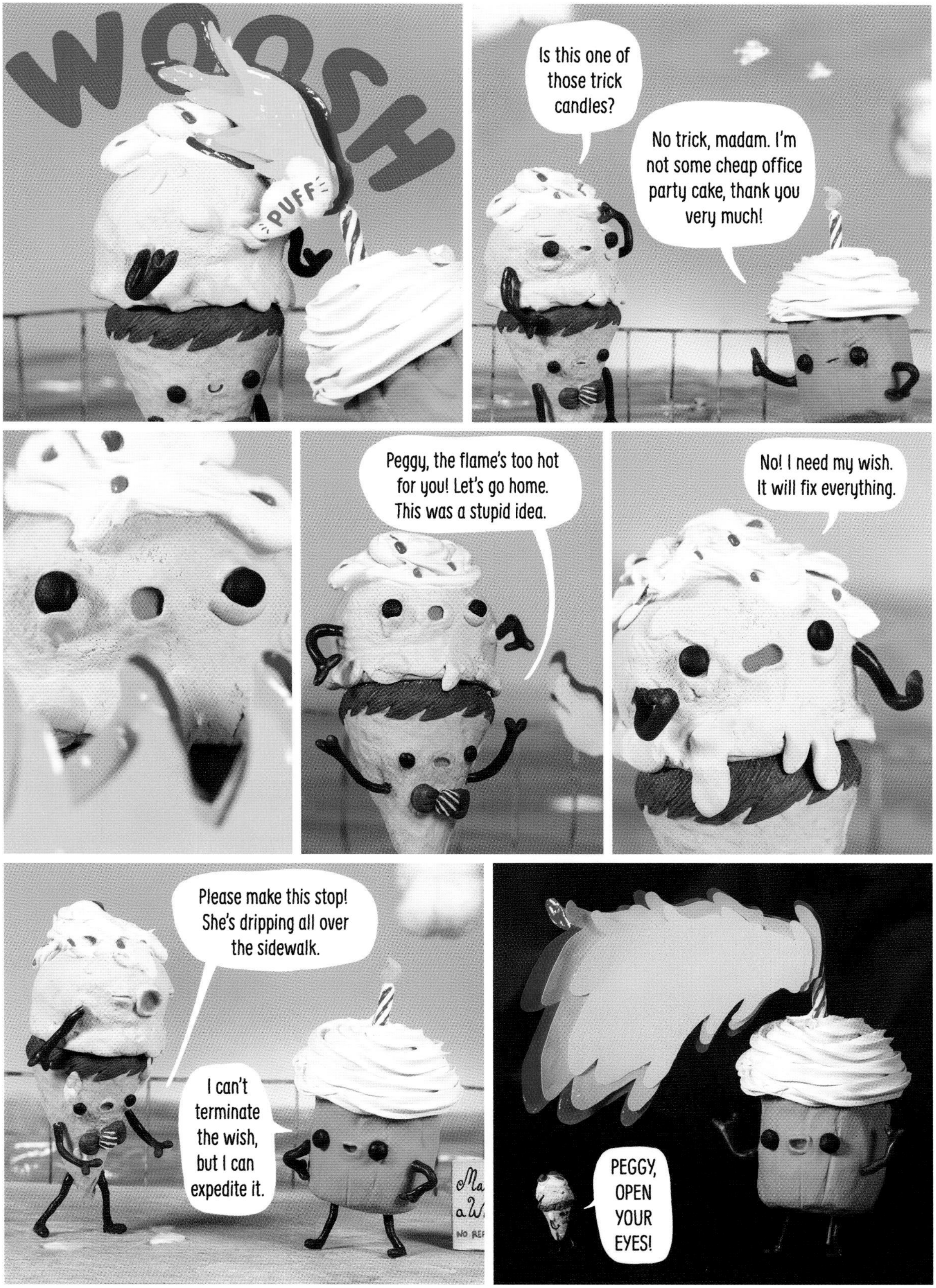
WOOSH
PUFF
Is this one of those trick candles?
No trick, madam. I'm not some cheap office party cake, thank you very much!
Peggy, the flame's too hot for you! Let's go home. This was a stupid idea.
No! I need my wish. It will fix everything.
Please make this stop! She's dripping all over the sidewalk.
I can't terminate the wish, but I can expedite it.
PEGGY, OPEN YOUR EYES!

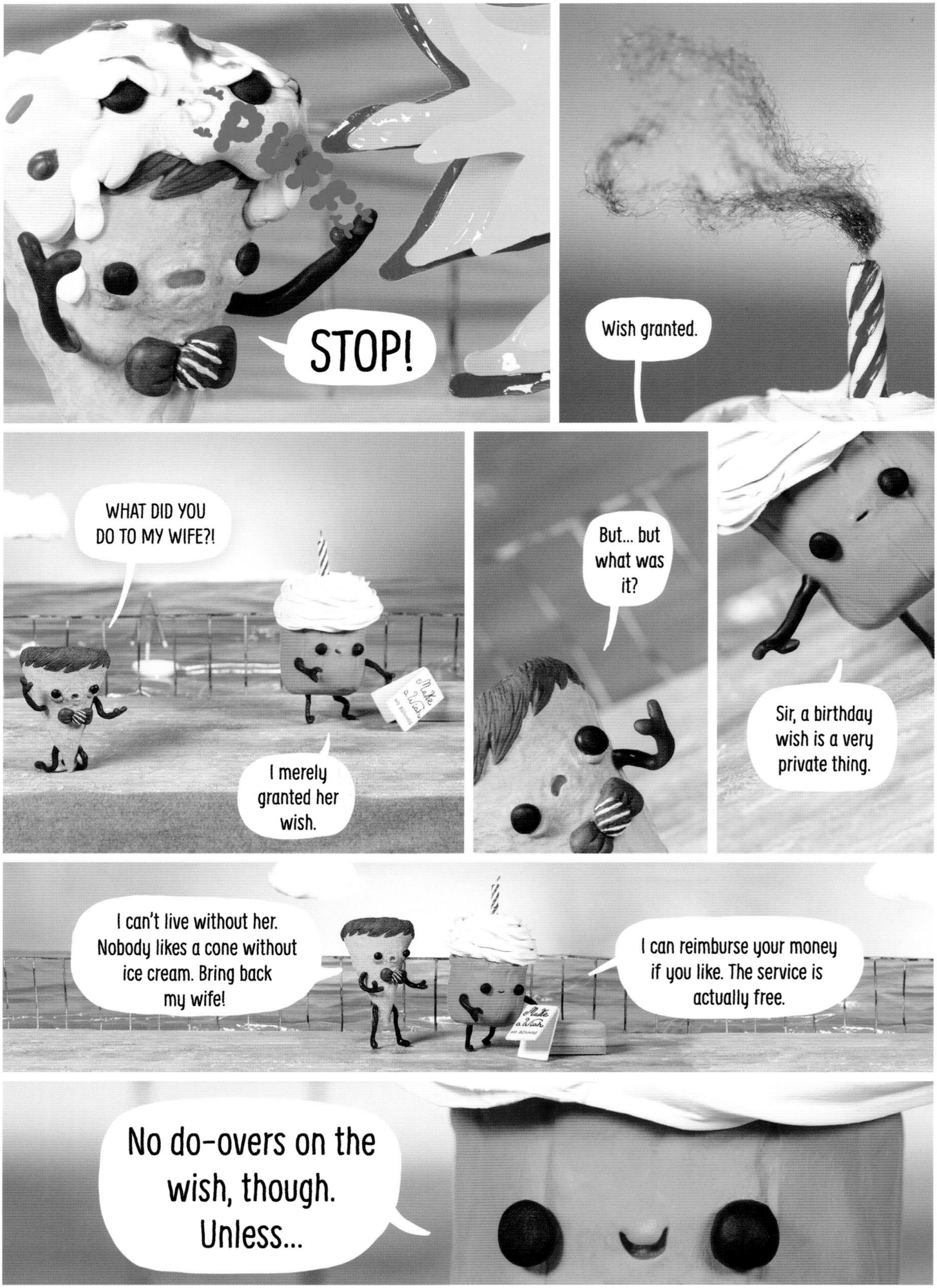
PUFF
STOP!
Wish granted.
WHAT DID YOU DO TO MY WIFE?!
I merely granted her wish.
But... but what was it?
Sir, a birthday wish is a very private thing.
I can't live without her. Nobody likes a cone without ice cream. Bring back my wife!
I can reimburse your money if you like. The service is actually free.
No do-overs on the wish, though. Unless...

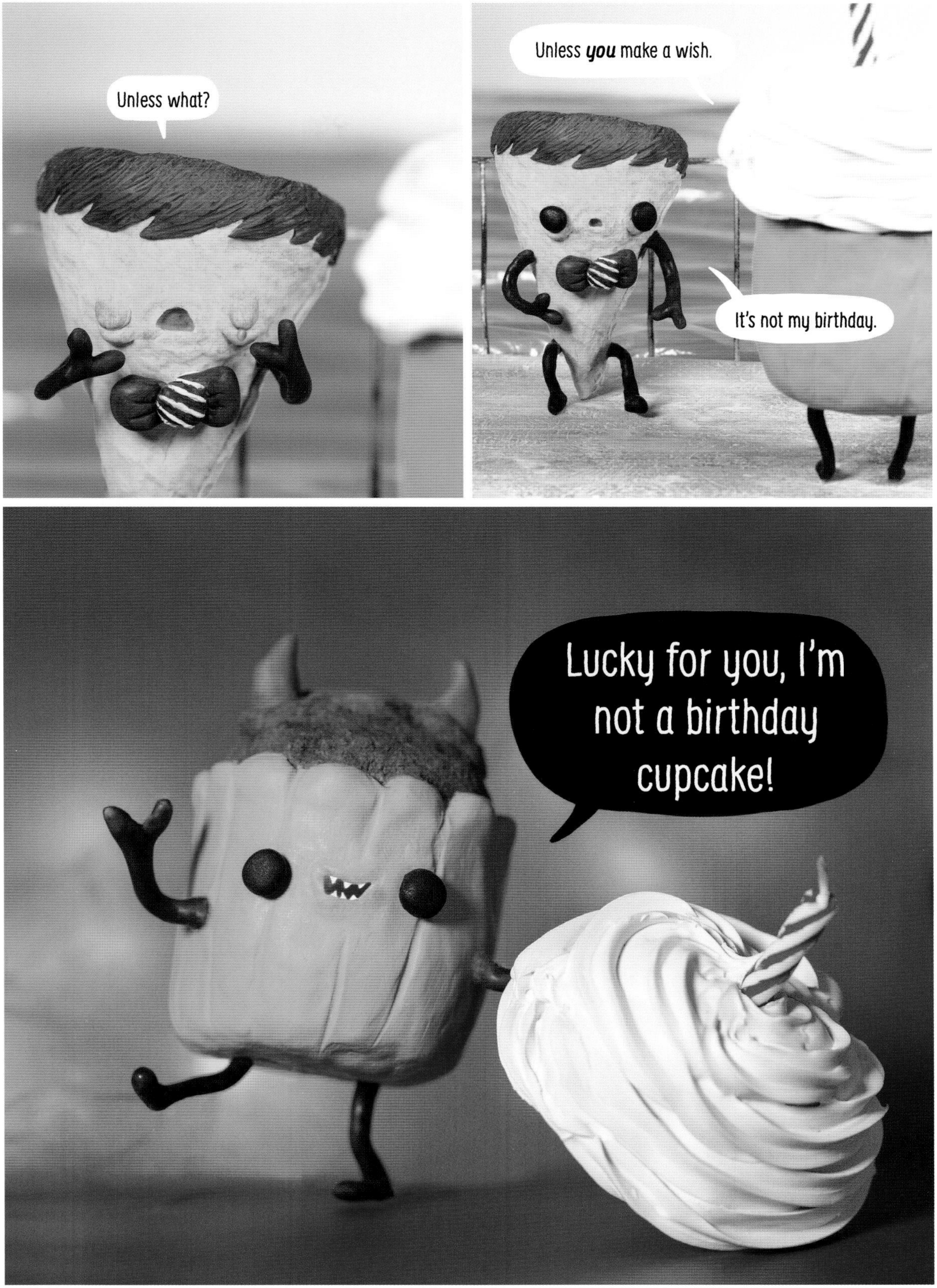
Unless what?
Unless **you** make a wish.
It's not my birthday.
Lucky for you, I'm not a birthday cupcake!

HOLY SCOOP! You're a DEVIL'S FOOD CAKE!

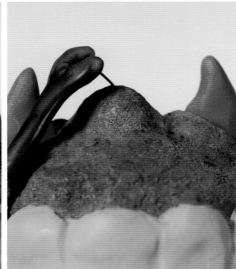

Well? Do you accept my offer?

I need her. I'll take the wish.

SNAP

Can I say my wish out loud so there won't be any misinterpretations?

Certainly!

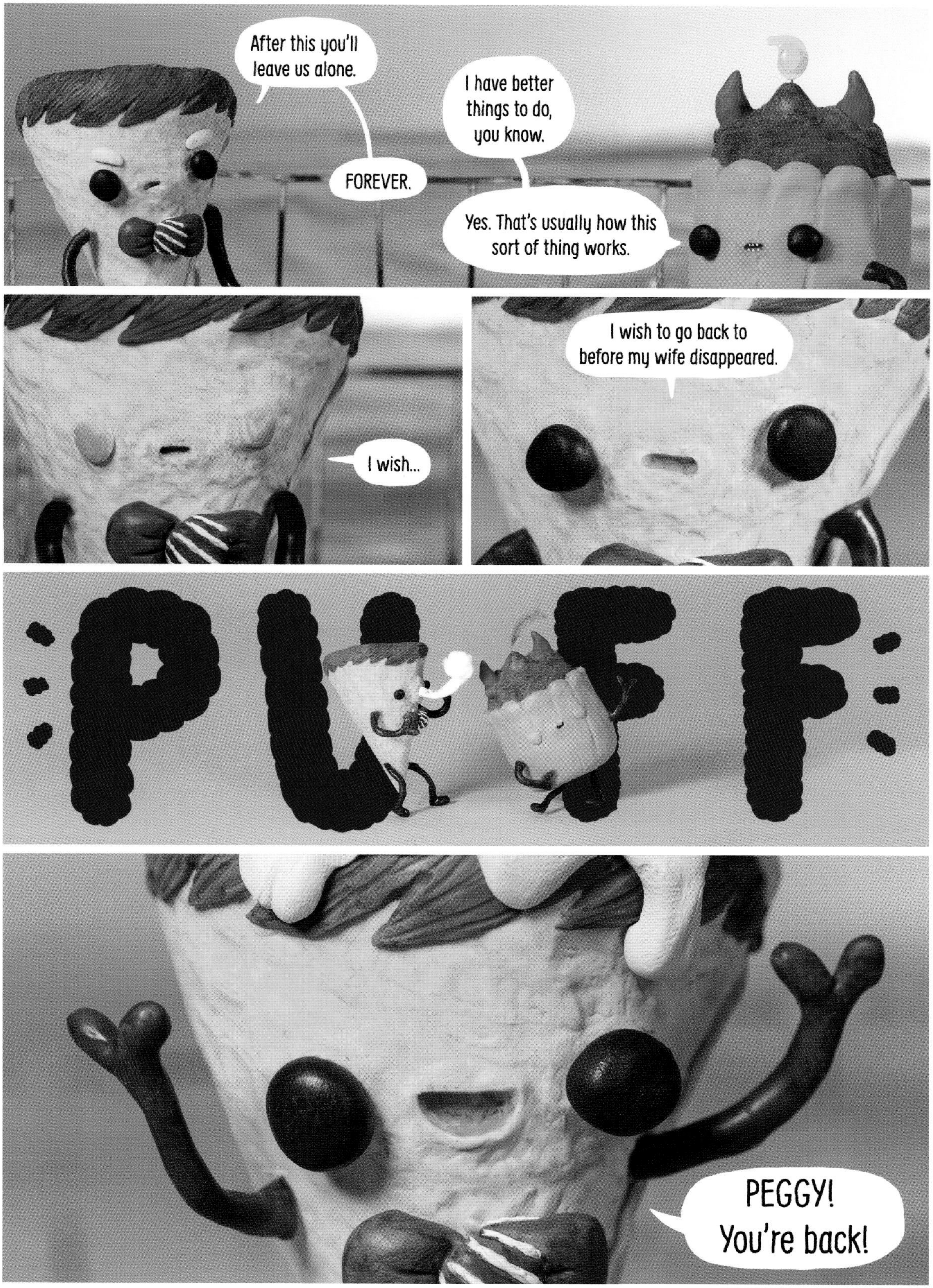
After this you'll leave us alone.
FOREVER.
I have better things to do, you know.
Yes. That's usually how this sort of thing works.
I wish...
I wish to go back to before my wife disappeared.
PUFF
PEGGY! You're back!

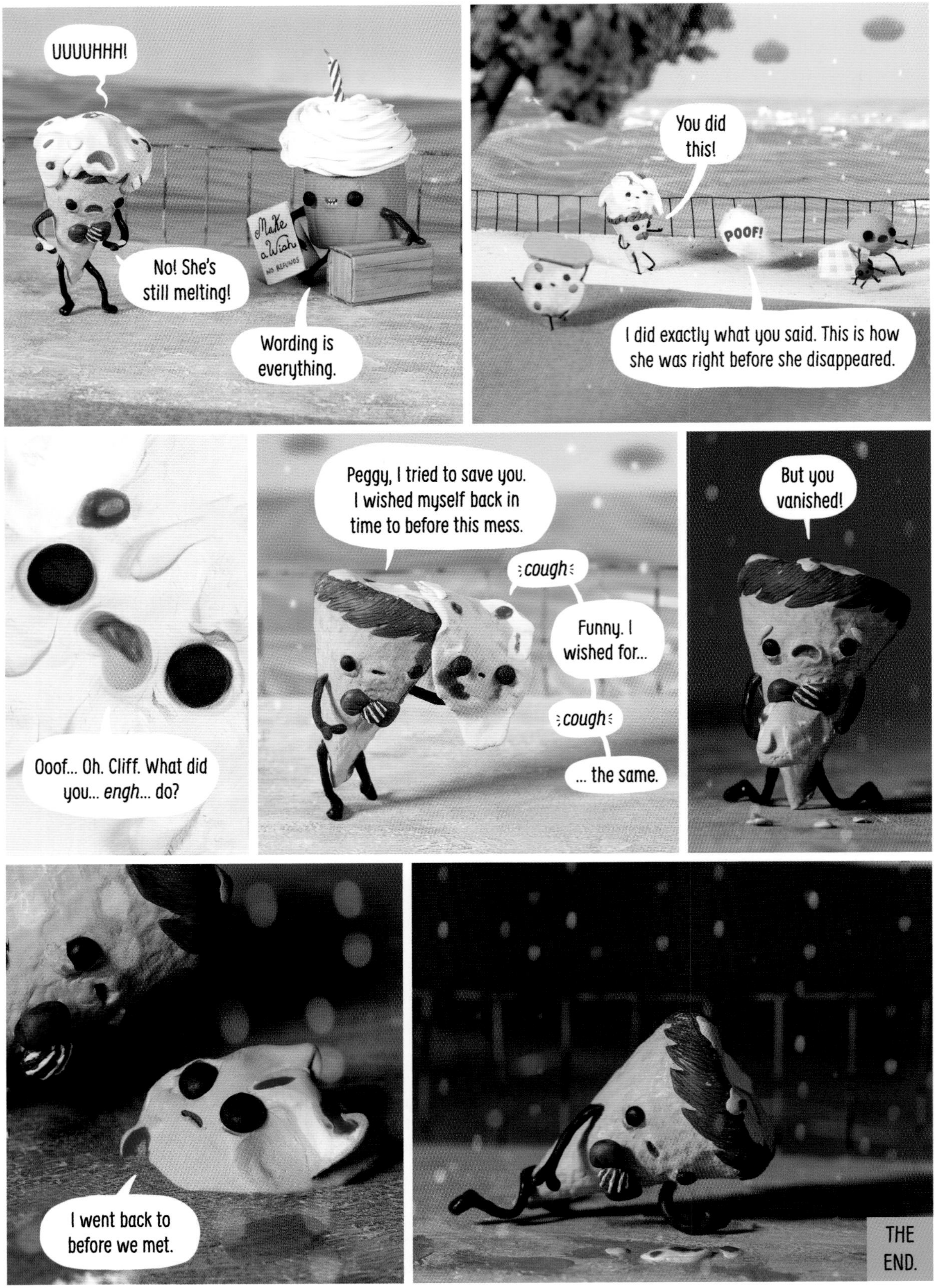
UUUUHHH!
No! She's still melting!
Make a Wish
NO REFUNDS
Wording is everything.
You did this!
POOF!
I did exactly what you said. This is how she was right before she disappeared.
Ooof... Oh. Cliff. What did you... *engh*... do?
Peggy, I tried to save you. I wished myself back in time to before this mess.
cough
Funny. I wished for...
cough
... the same.
But you vanished!
I went back to before we met.
THE END.

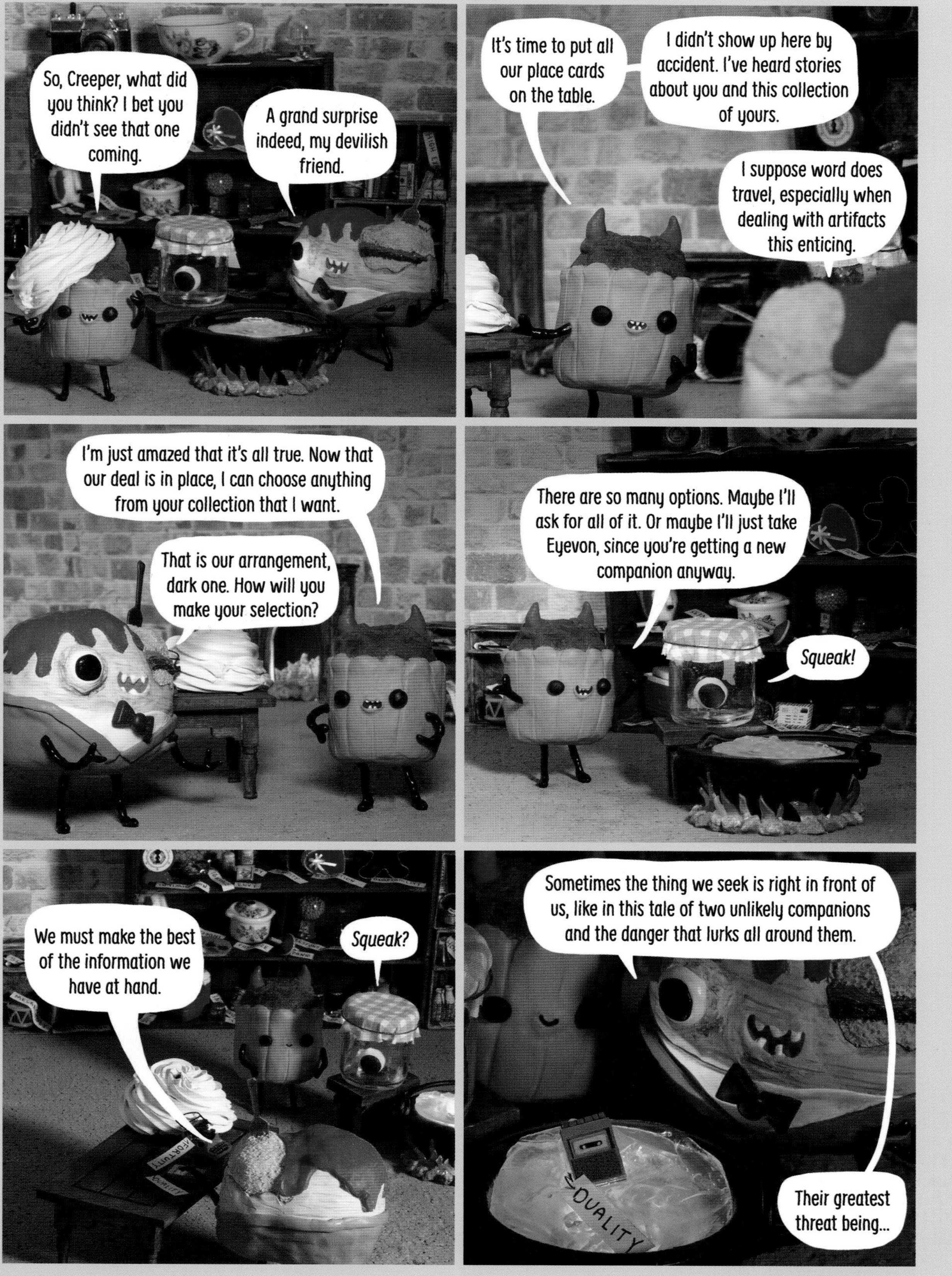

So, Creeper, what did you think? I bet you didn't see that one coming.
A grand surprise indeed, my devilish friend.
It's time to put all our place cards on the table.
I didn't show up here by accident. I've heard stories about you and this collection of yours.
I suppose word does travel, especially when dealing with artifacts this enticing.
I'm just amazed that it's all true. Now that our deal is in place, I can choose anything from your collection that I want.
That is our arrangement, dark one. How will you make your selection?
There are so many options. Maybe I'll ask for all of it. Or maybe I'll just take Eyevon, since you're getting a new companion anyway.
Squeak!
We must make the best of the information we have at hand.
Squeak?
Sometimes the thing we seek is right in front of us, like in this tale of two unlikely companions and the danger that lurks all around them.
Their greatest threat being...
QUALITY

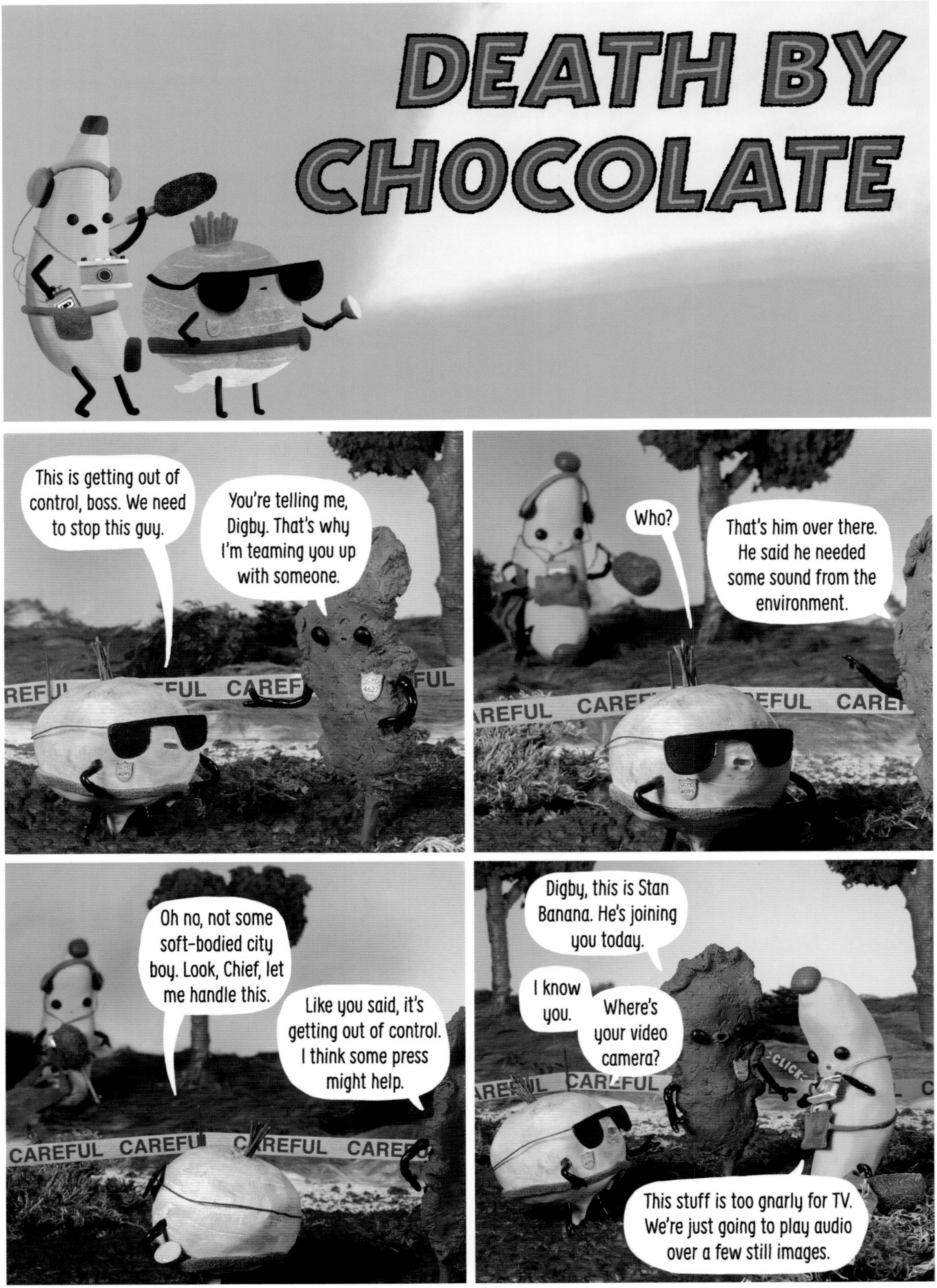
DEATH BY CHOCOLATE
This is getting out of control, boss. We need to stop this guy.
You're telling me, Digby. That's why I'm teaming you up with someone.
Who?
That's him over there. He said he needed some sound from the environment.
Oh no, not some soft-bodied city boy. Look, Chief, let me handle this.
Like you said, it's getting out of control. I think some press might help.
Digby, this is Stan Banana. He's joining you today.
I know you.
Where's your video camera?
CLICK
This stuff is too gnarly for TV. We're just going to play audio over a few still images.

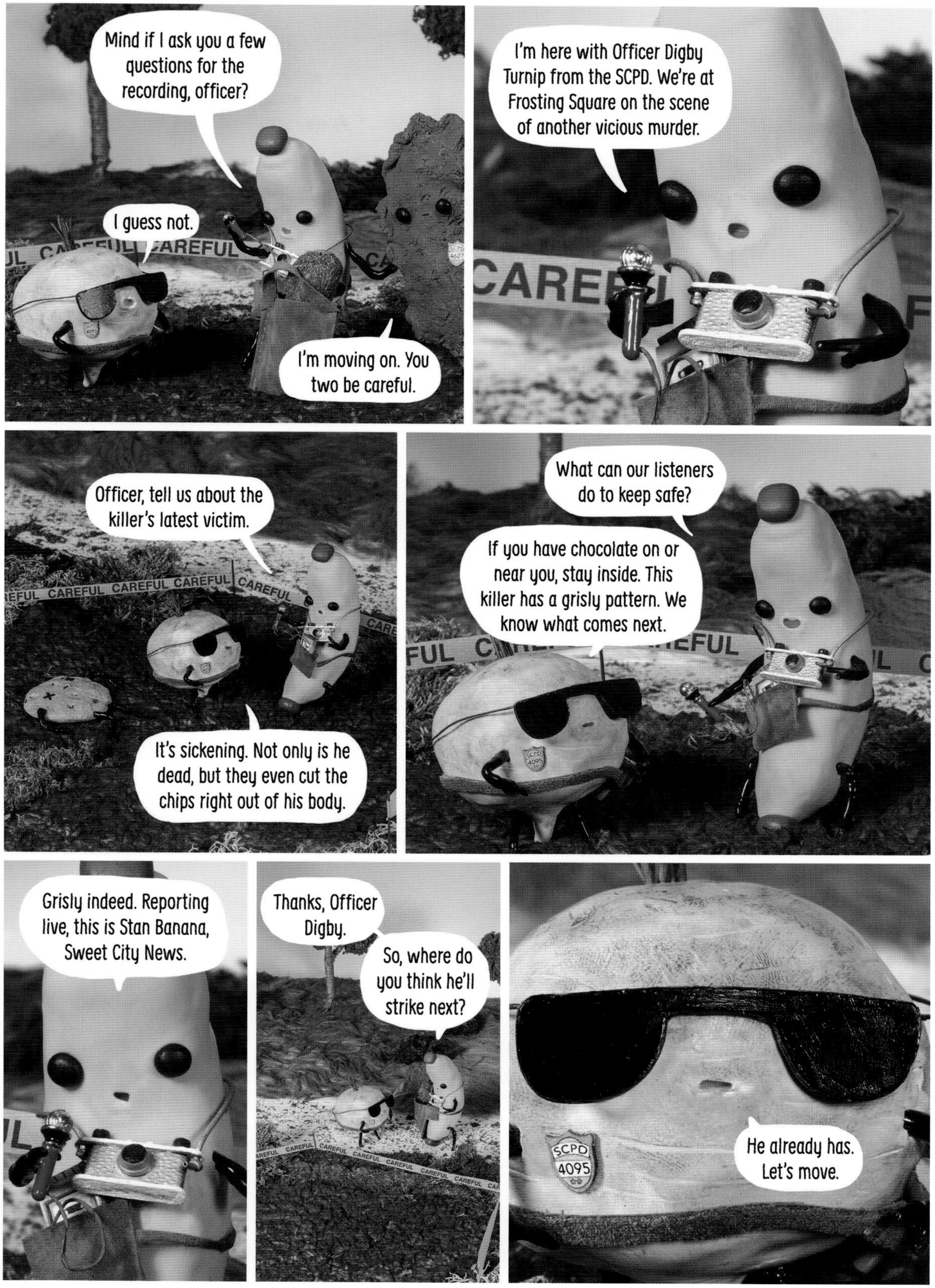
Mind if I ask you a few questions for the recording, officer?
I guess not.
CAREFUL CAREFUL
SCPD 4627
I'm moving on. You two be careful.
I'm here with Officer Digby Turnip from the SCPD. We're at Frosting Square on the scene of another vicious murder.
CAREFUL
Officer, tell us about the killer's latest victim.
CAREFUL CAREFUL CAREFUL CAREFUL
It's sickening. Not only is he dead, but they even cut the chips right out of his body.
What can our listeners do to keep safe?
If you have chocolate on or near you, stay inside. This killer has a grisly pattern. We know what comes next.
SCPD 4095
Grisly indeed. Reporting live, this is Stan Banana, Sweet City News.
Thanks, Officer Digby.
So, where do you think he'll strike next?
SCPD 4095
He already has. Let's move.

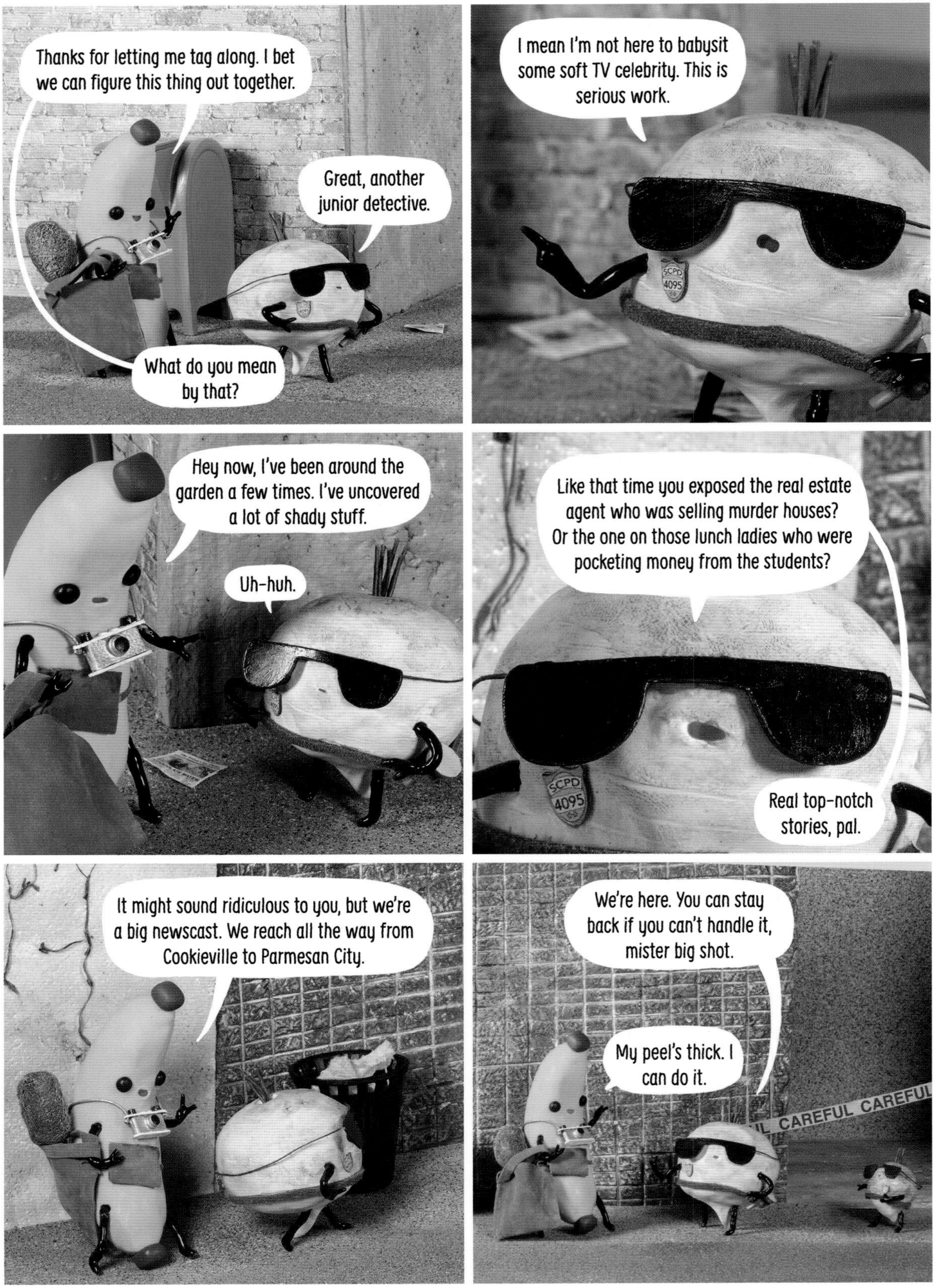
Thanks for letting me tag along. I bet we can figure this thing out together.
Great, another junior detective.
What do you mean by that?
I mean I'm not here to babysit some soft TV celebrity. This is serious work.
SCPD 4095
Hey now, I've been around the garden a few times. I've uncovered a lot of shady stuff.
Uh-huh.
Like that time you exposed the real estate agent who was selling murder houses? Or the one on those lunch ladies who were pocketing money from the students?
Real top-notch stories, pal.
It might sound ridiculous to you, but we're a big newscast. We reach all the way from Cookieville to Parmesan City.
We're here. You can stay back if you can't handle it, mister big shot.
My peel's thick. I can do it.
CAREFUL CAREFUL

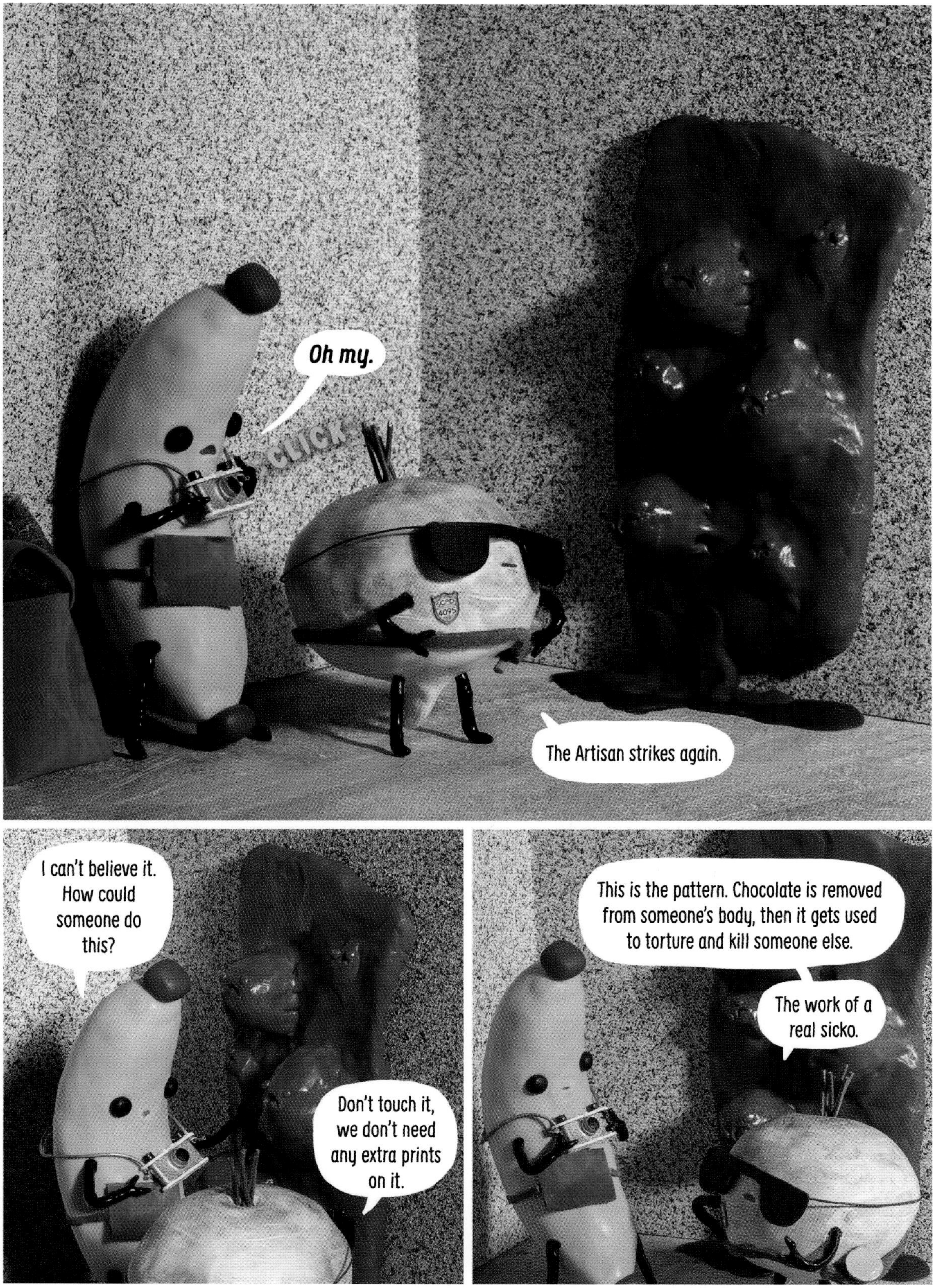
Oh my.
CLICK
The Artisan strikes again.
I can't believe it. How could someone do this?
Don't touch it, we don't need any extra prints on it.
This is the pattern. Chocolate is removed from someone's body, then it gets used to torture and kill someone else.
The work of a real sicko.

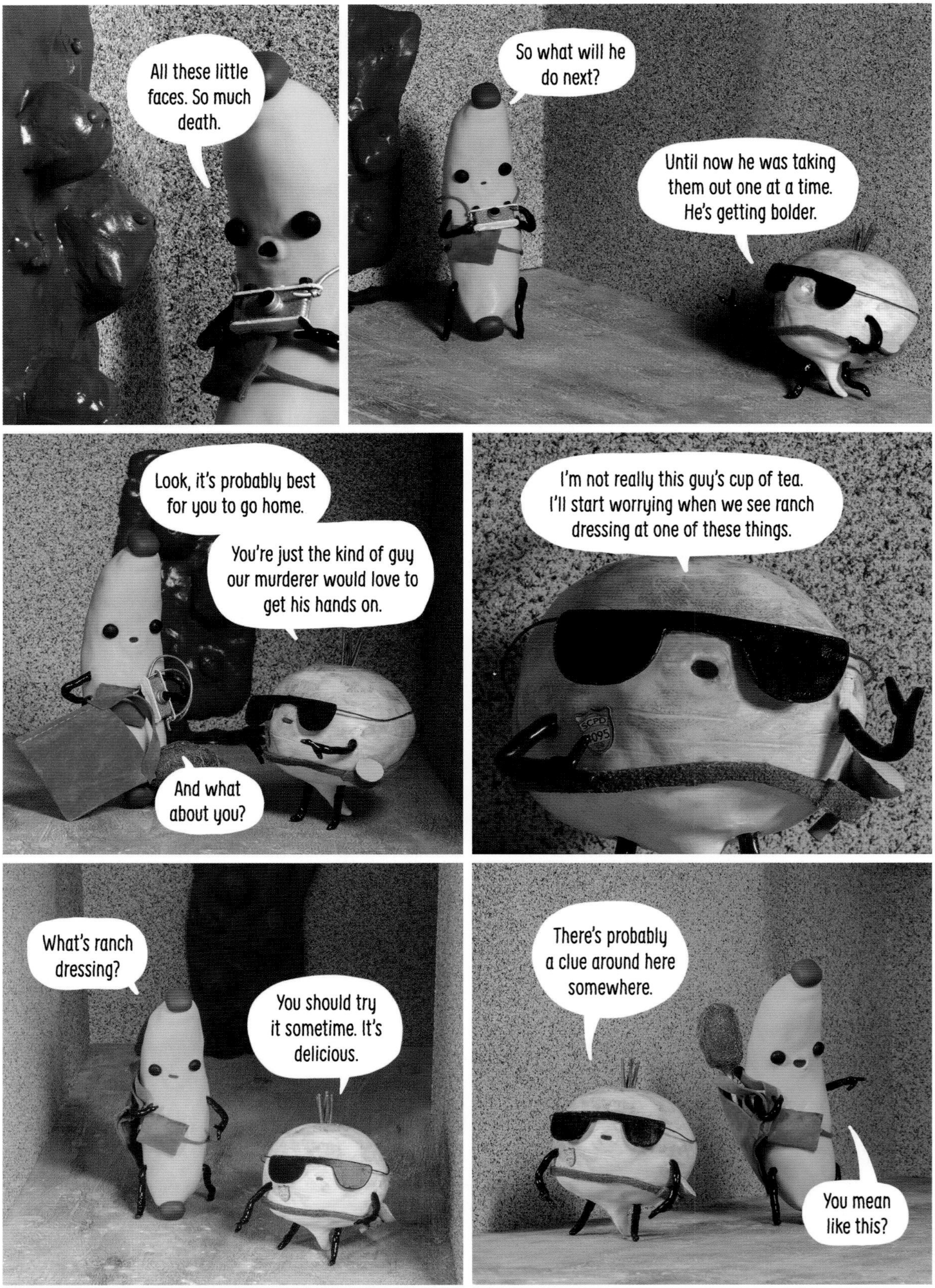
All these little faces. So much death.
So what will he do next?
Until now he was taking them out one at a time. He's getting bolder.
Look, it's probably best for you to go home.
You're just the kind of guy our murderer would love to get his hands on.
And what about you?
I'm not really this guy's cup of tea. I'll start worrying when we see ranch dressing at one of these things.
SCPD 8095
What's ranch dressing?
You should try it sometime. It's delicious.
There's probably a clue around here somewhere.
You mean like this?

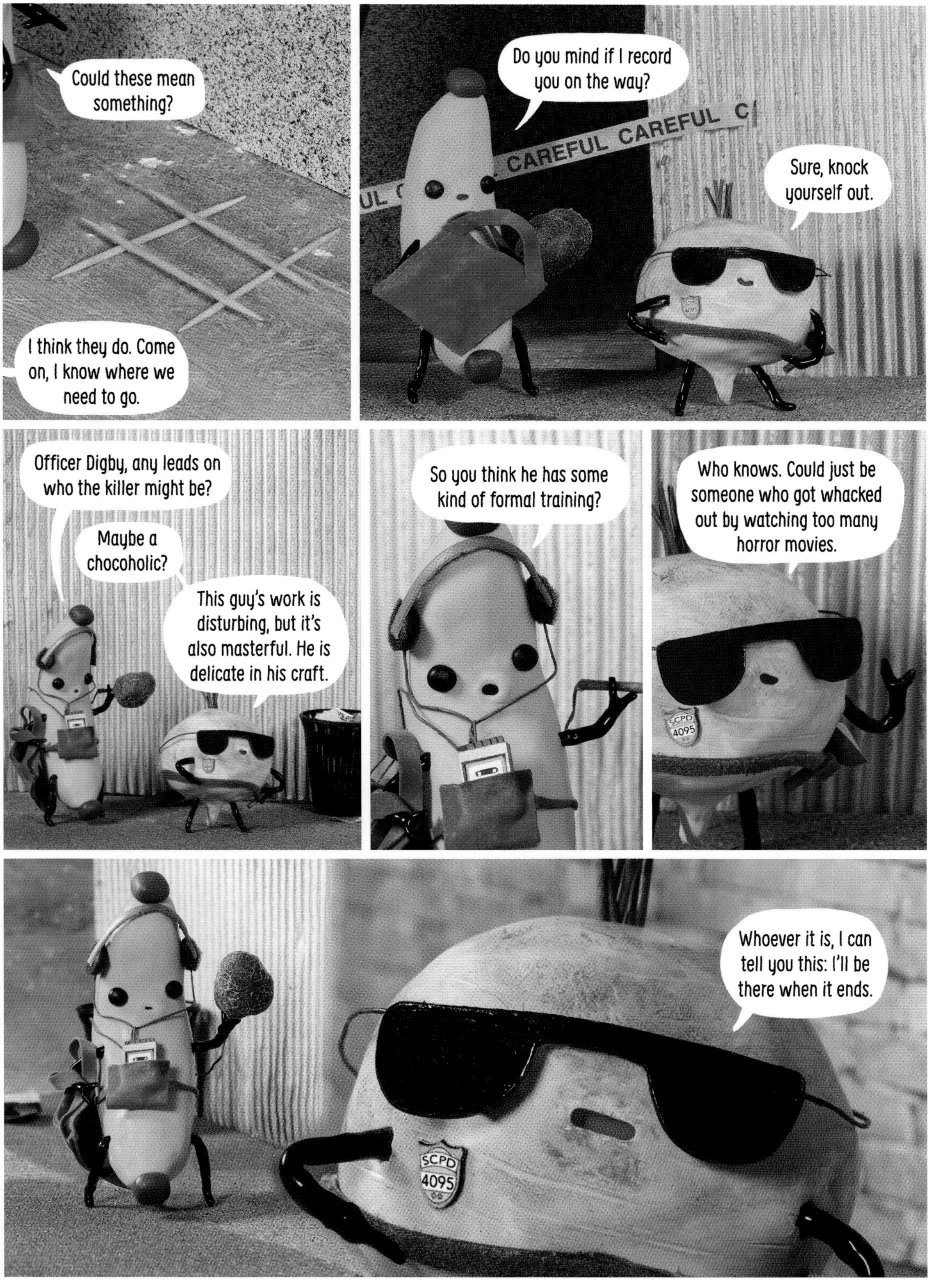
Could these mean something?
I think they do. Come on, I know where we need to go.
Do you mind if I record you on the way?
CAREFUL CAREFUL
Sure, knock yourself out.
Officer Digby, any leads on who the killer might be?
Maybe a chocoholic?
This guy's work is disturbing, but it's also masterful. He is delicate in his craft.
So you think he has some kind of formal training?
Who knows. Could just be someone who got whacked out by watching too many horror movies.
SCPD 4095
Whoever it is, I can tell you this: I'll be there when it ends.
SCPD 4095

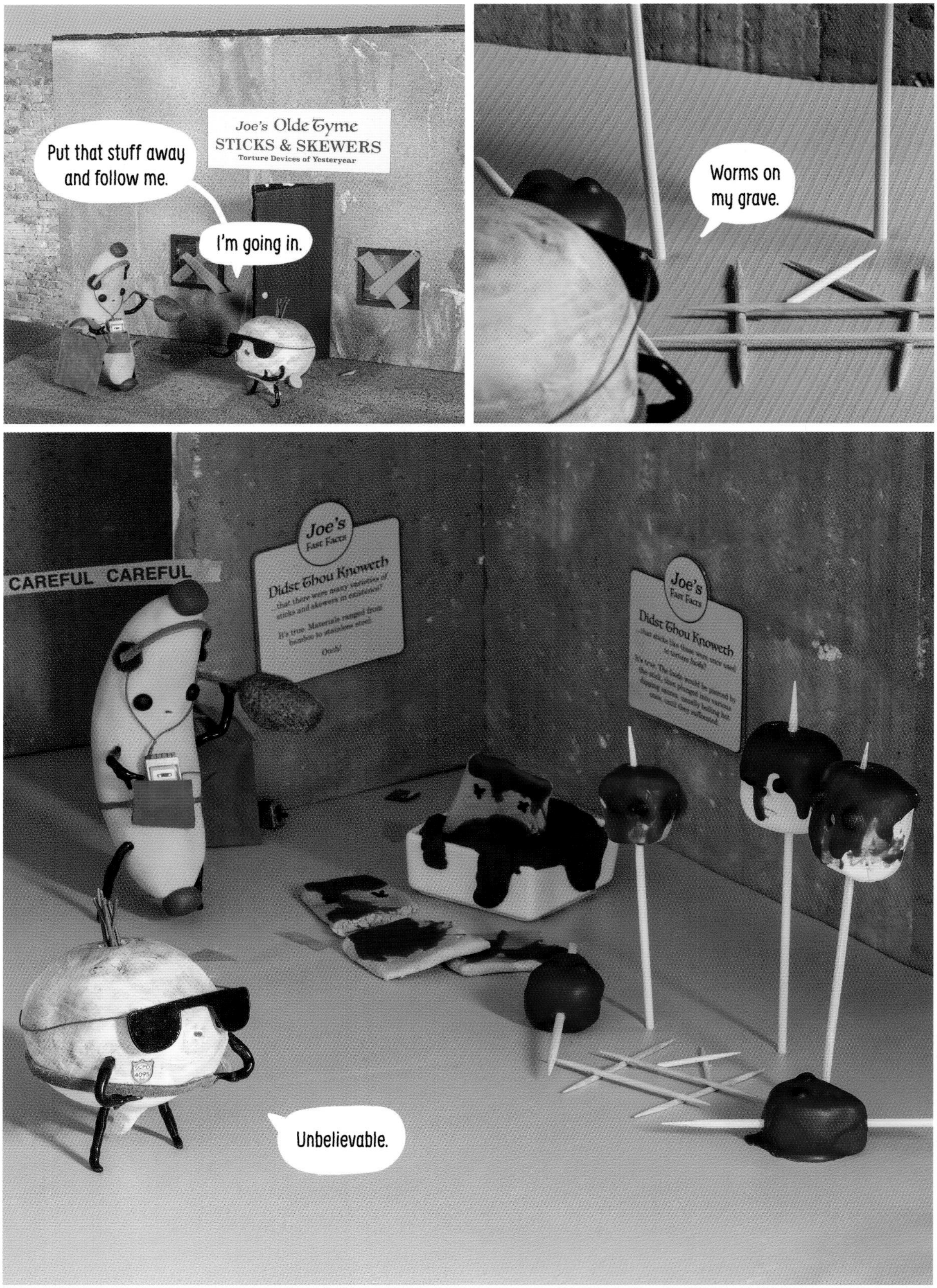
Joe's Olde Tyme
STICKS & SKEWERS
Torture Devices of Yesteryear
Put that stuff away and follow me.
I'm going in.
Worms on my grave.
CAREFUL CAREFUL
Joe's Fast Facts
Didst Thou Knoweth
...that there were many varieties of sticks and skewers in existence?
It's true. Materials ranged from bamboo to stainless steel.
Ouch!
Joe's Fast Facts
Didst Thou Knoweth
Unbelievable.

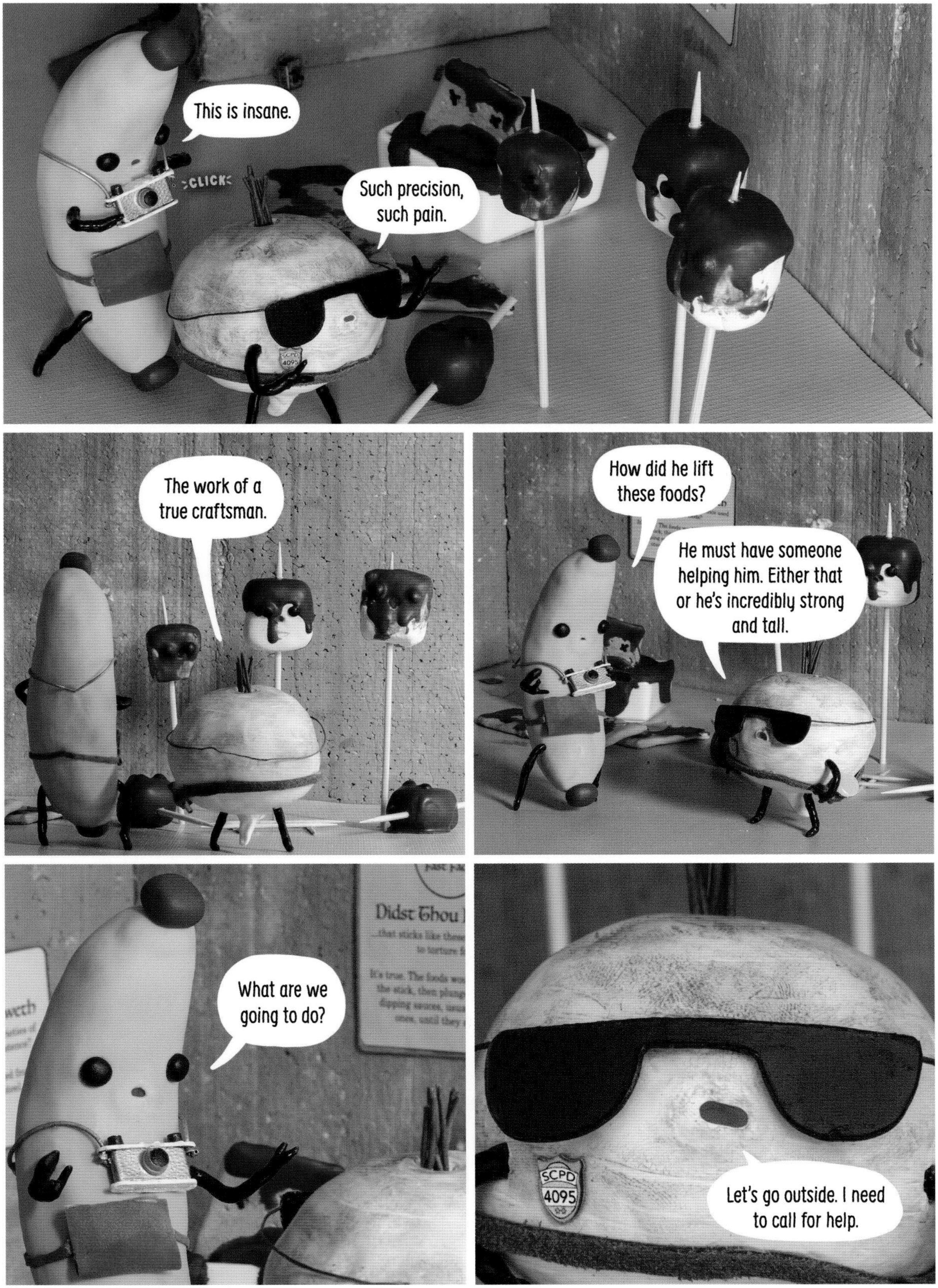
This is insane.
CLICK
Such precision, such pain.
SCPD
4095
The work of a true craftsman.
How did he lift these foods?
He must have someone helping him. Either that or he's incredibly strong and tall.
What are we going to do?
SCPD
4095
Let's go outside. I need to call for help.

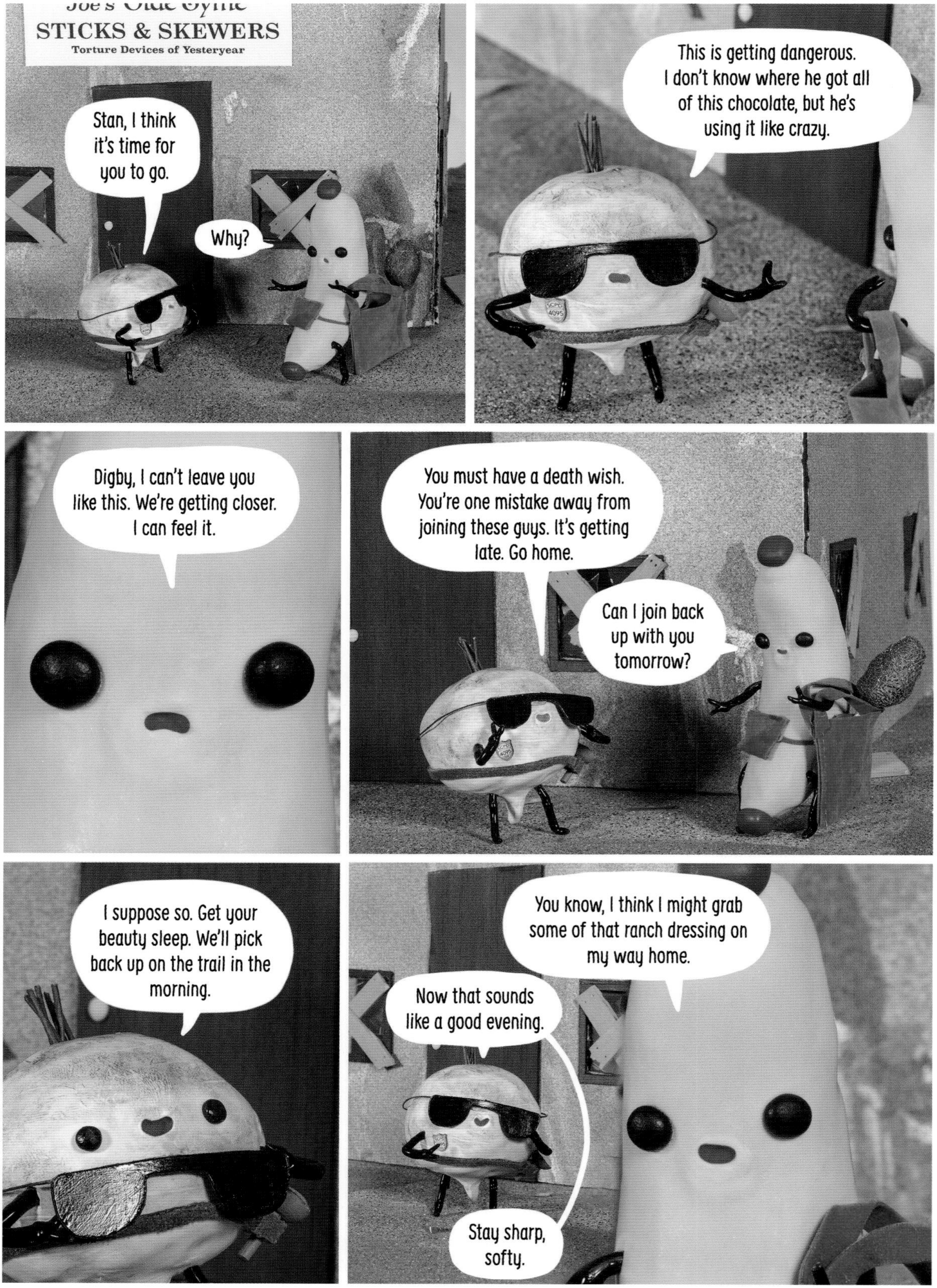
Joe's Olde Tyme
STICKS & SKEWERS
Torture Devices of Yesteryear
Stan, I think it's time for you to go.
Why?
This is getting dangerous. I don't know where he got all of this chocolate, but he's using it like crazy.
Digby, I can't leave you like this. We're getting closer. I can feel it.
You must have a death wish. You're one mistake away from joining these guys. It's getting late. Go home.
Can I join back up with you tomorrow?
I suppose so. Get your beauty sleep. We'll pick back up on the trail in the morning.
You know, I think I might grab some of that ranch dressing on my way home.
Now that sounds like a good evening.
Stay sharp, softy.

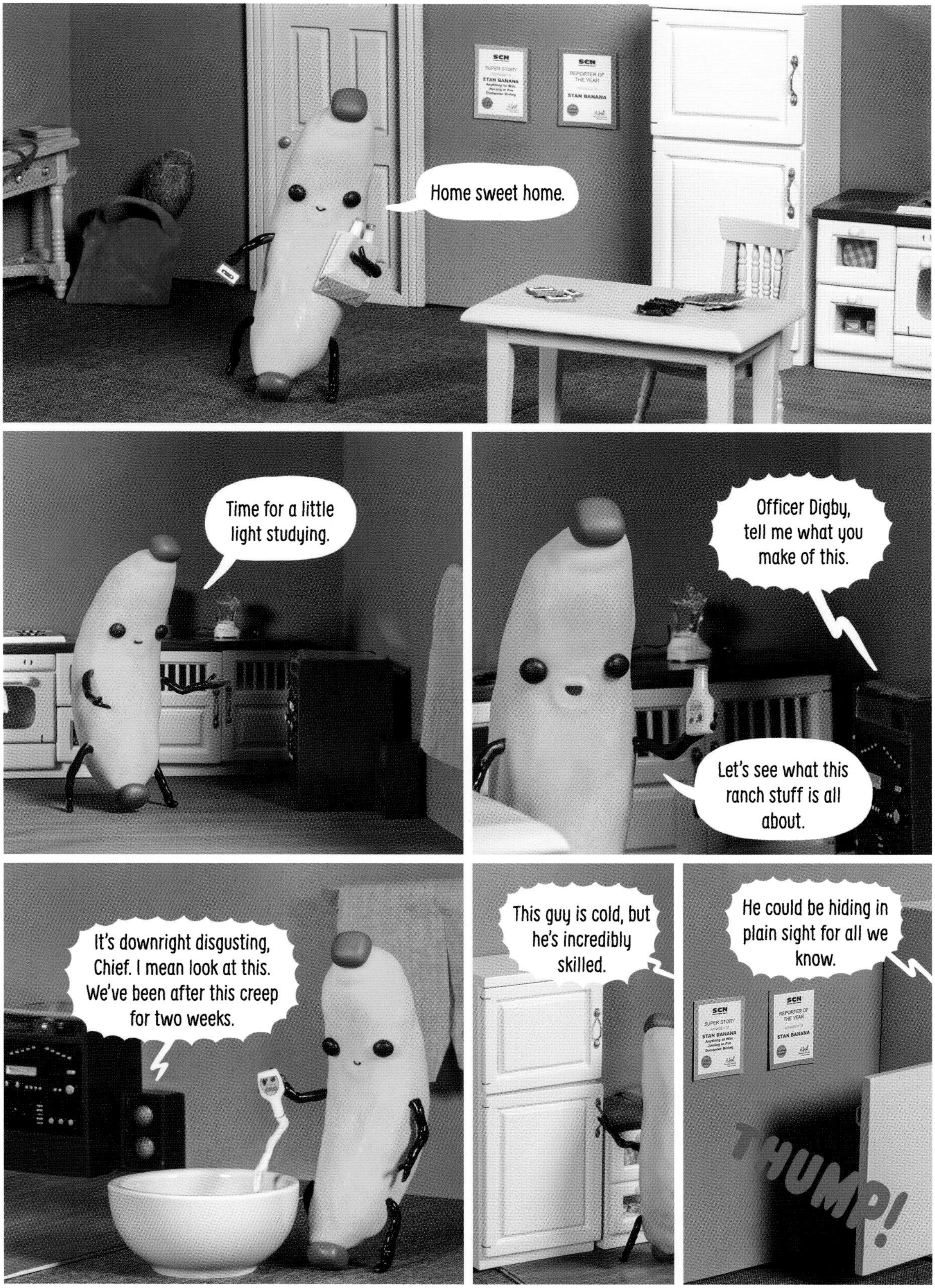
Home sweet home.
Time for a little light studying.
Officer Digby, tell me what you make of this.
Let's see what this ranch stuff is all about.
It's downright disgusting, Chief. I mean look at this. We've been after this creep for two weeks.
This guy is cold, but he's incredibly skilled.
He could be hiding in plain sight for all we know.
THUMP!

What worries me most is that things are starting to escalate. Officer Radish just radioed me.

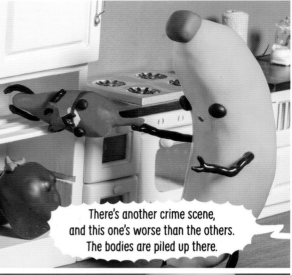

There's another crime scene, and this one's worse than the others. The bodies are piled up there.

At least he's sticking to foods that go great with chocolate. Everyone else should be safe.

This is getting out of control, boss. We need to stop this guy.

You're telling me, Digby. That's why I'm teaming you up with someone.

Aaaaaah!

Who?

That's him over there.

Delicious idea, Digby.

Thanks for helping me expand my palate. See you tomorrow...

THE END.

110

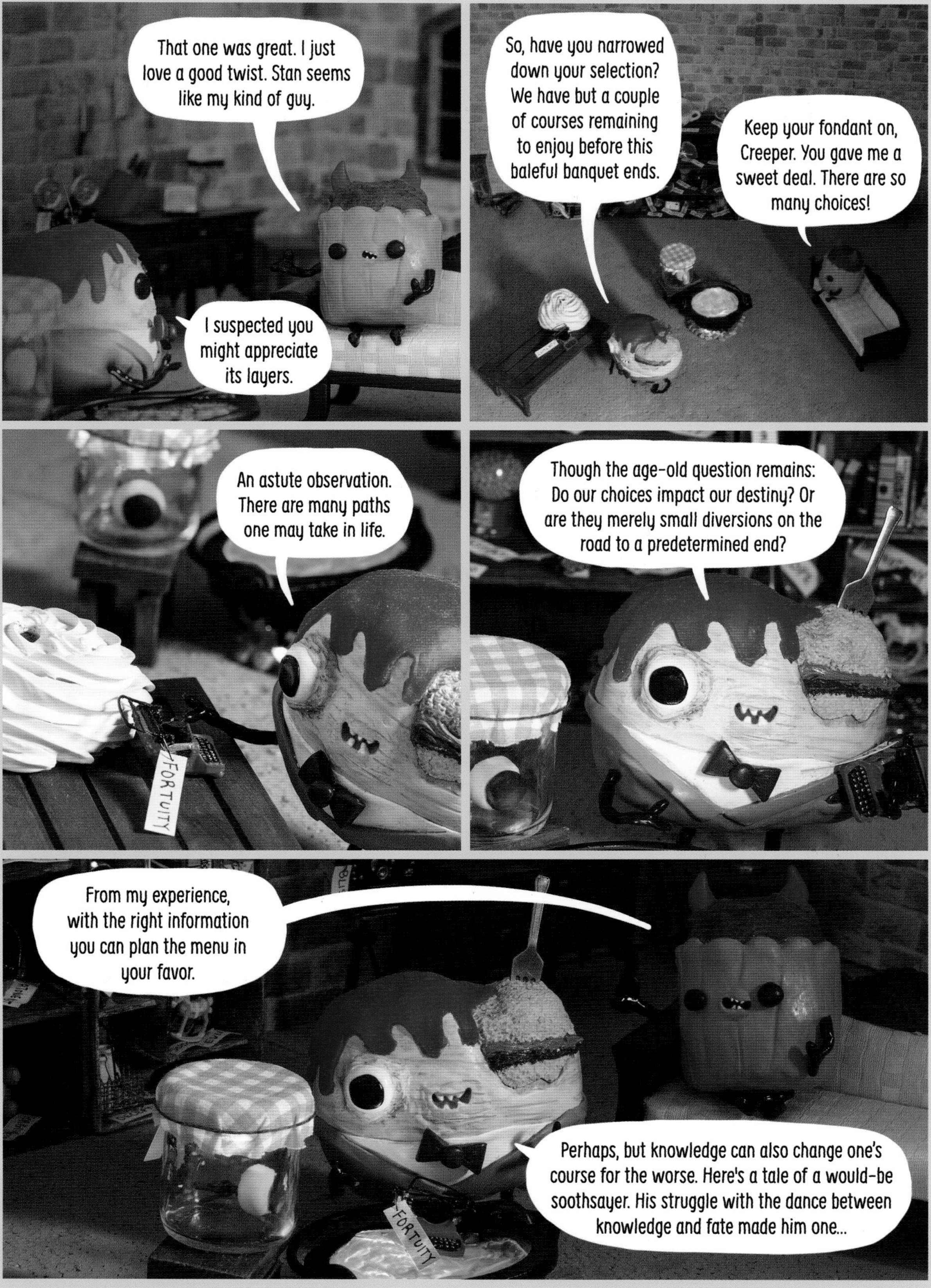

That one was great. I just love a good twist. Stan seems like my kind of guy.
I suspected you might appreciate its layers.
So, have you narrowed down your selection? We have but a couple of courses remaining to enjoy before this baleful banquet ends.
Keep your fondant on, Creeper. You gave me a sweet deal. There are so many choices!
An astute observation. There are many paths one may take in life.
FORTUITY
Though the age-old question remains: Do our choices impact our destiny? Or are they merely small diversions on the road to a predetermined end?
From my experience, with the right information you can plan the menu in your favor.
Perhaps, but knowledge can also change one's course for the worse. Here's a tale of a would-be soothsayer. His struggle with the dance between knowledge and fate made him one...
FORTUITY

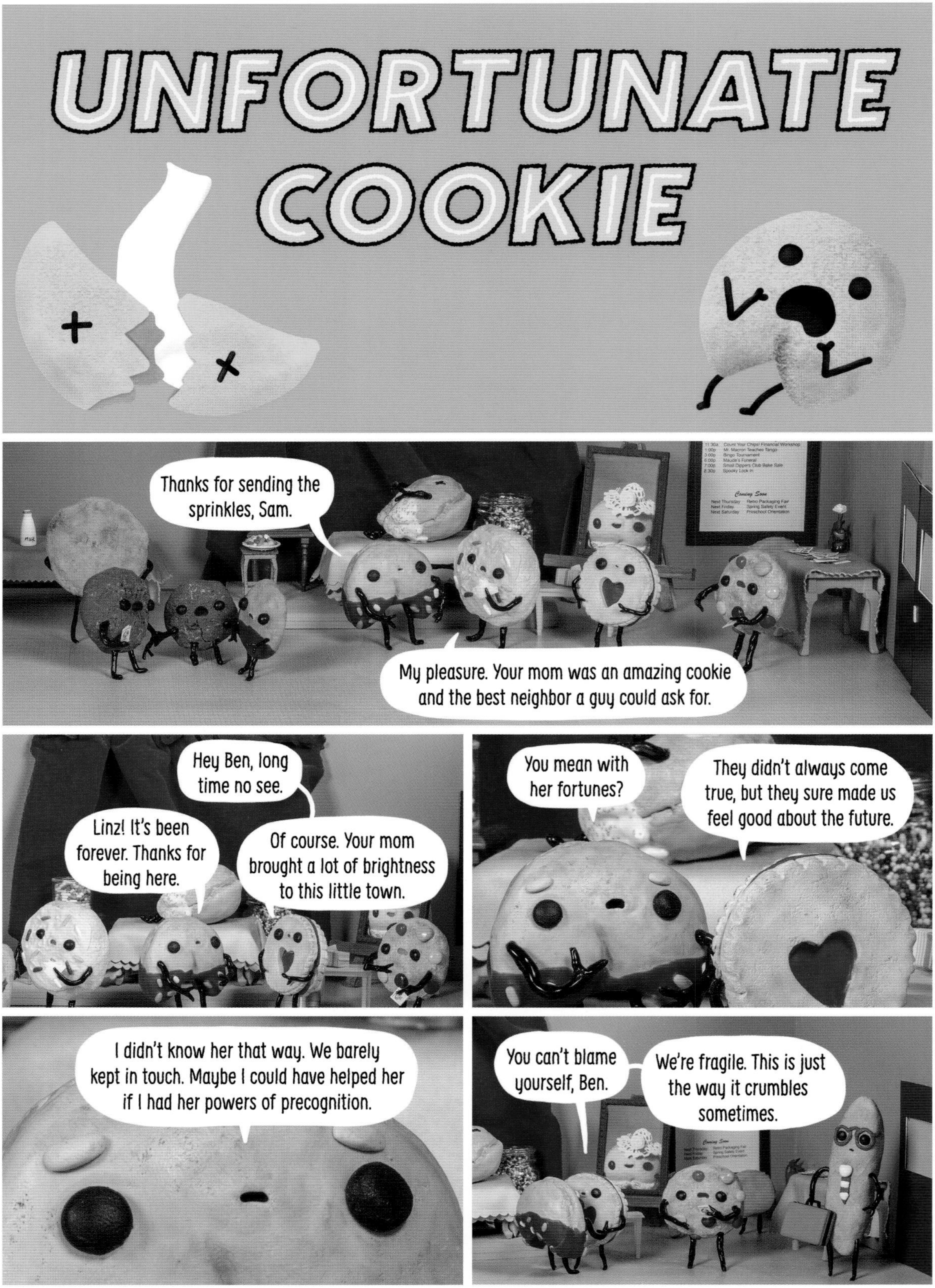
UNFORTUNATE COOKIE
Thanks for sending the sprinkles, Sam.
My pleasure. Your mom was an amazing cookie and the best neighbor a guy could ask for.
Hey Ben, long time no see.
Linz! It's been forever. Thanks for being here.
Of course. Your mom brought a lot of brightness to this little town.
You mean with her fortunes?
They didn't always come true, but they sure made us feel good about the future.
I didn't know her that way. We barely kept in touch. Maybe I could have helped her if I had her powers of precognition.
You can't blame yourself, Ben.
We're fragile. This is just the way it crumbles sometimes.

We can delay the proceedings a little longer if you need a few moments.

That's OK, Vincent. Let's get started.

Good evening, friends. As Maude's attorney, I will now read her inner fortune to reveal her last will and testament.

Doug, would you please assist me?

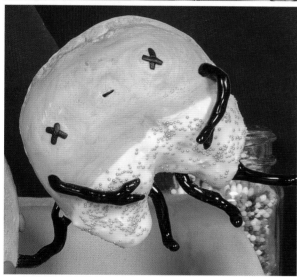

SNP!

"I leave my power of second sight to my son, Ben. Use it to spread joy. Let the rest unfold on its own."

Gasp!

Oh my!

Can that happen?

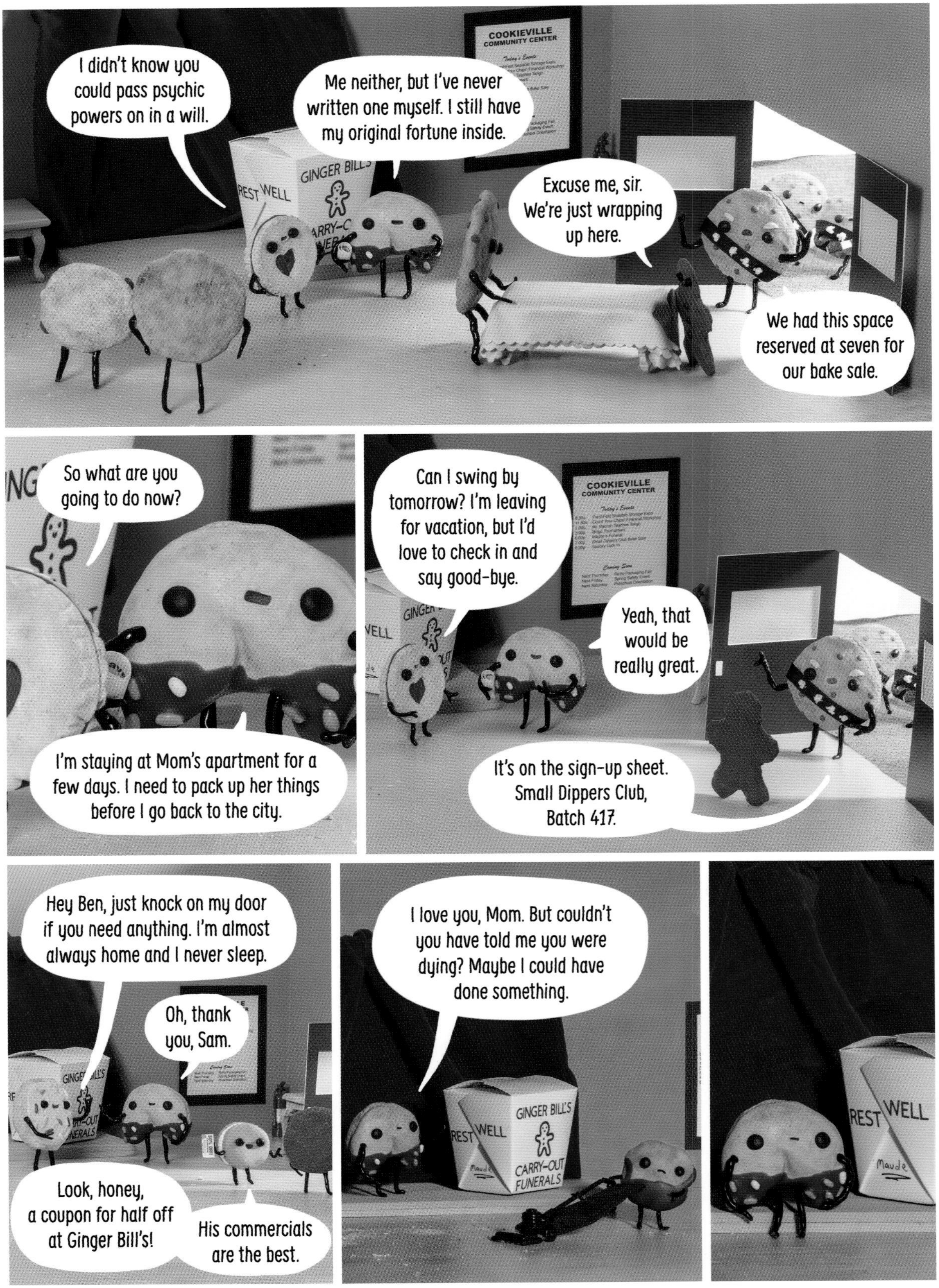
COOKIEVILLE COMMUNITY CENTER
I didn't know you could pass psychic powers on in a will.
Me neither, but I've never written one myself. I still have my original fortune inside.
GINGER BILL'S
REST WELL
Excuse me, sir. We're just wrapping up here.
We had this space reserved at seven for our bake sale.
So what are you going to do now?
I'm staying at Mom's apartment for a few days. I need to pack up her things before I go back to the city.
Can I swing by tomorrow? I'm leaving for vacation, but I'd love to check in and say good-bye.
COOKIEVILLE COMMUNITY CENTER
Yeah, that would be really great.
It's on the sign-up sheet. Small Dippers Club, Batch 417.
Hey Ben, just knock on my door if you need anything. I'm almost always home and I never sleep.
Oh, thank you, Sam.
Look, honey, a coupon for half off at Ginger Bill's!
His commercials are the best.
I love you, Mom. But couldn't you have told me you were dying? Maybe I could have done something.
GINGER BILL'S
REST WELL
CARRY-OUT FUNERALS
Maude
REST WELL
Maude

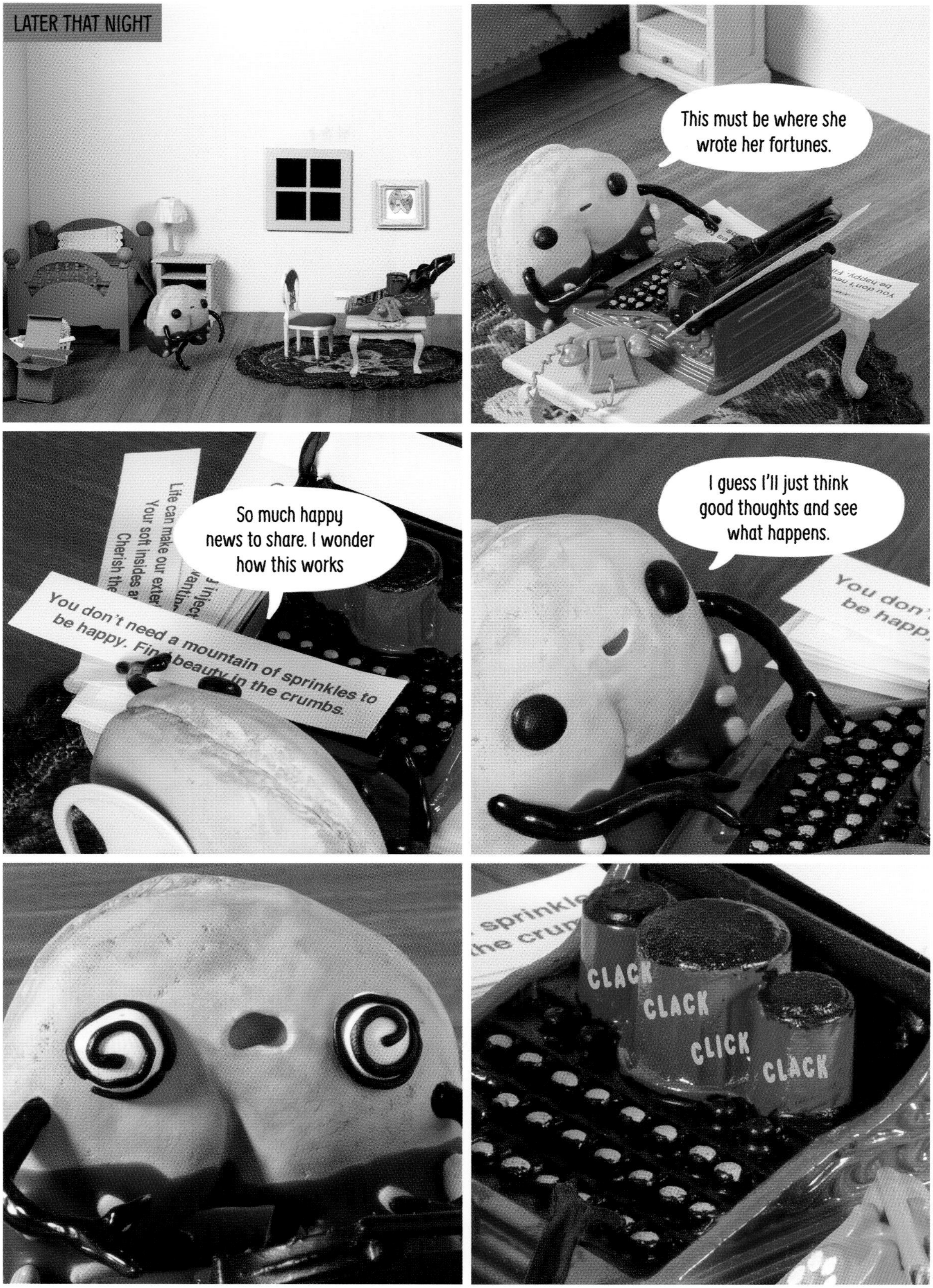
LATER THAT NIGHT
This must be where she wrote her fortunes.
So much happy news to share. I wonder how this works
I guess I'll just think good thoughts and see what happens.
CLACK
CLACK
CLICK
CLACK

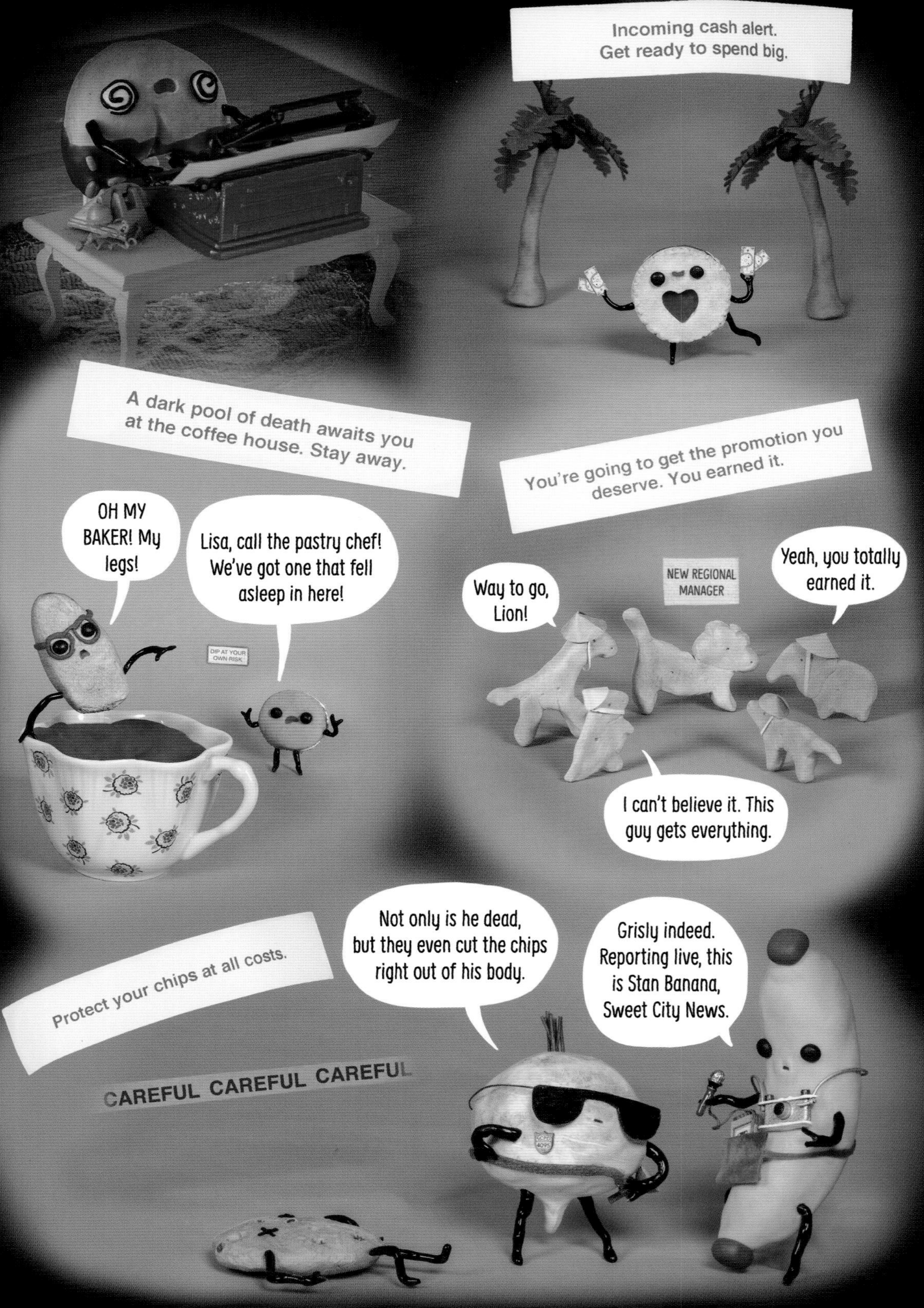

Incoming cash alert. Get ready to spend big.
A dark pool of death awaits you at the coffee house. Stay away.
OH MY BAKER! My legs!
Lisa, call the pastry chef! We've got one that fell asleep in here!
DIP AT YOUR OWN RISK
You're going to get the promotion you deserve. You earned it.
Way to go, Lion!
NEW REGIONAL MANAGER
Yeah, you totally earned it.
I can't believe it. This guy gets everything.
Protect your chips at all costs.
CAREFUL CAREFUL CAREFUL
Not only is he dead, but they even cut the chips right out of his body.
Grisly indeed. Reporting live, this is Stan Banana, Sweet City News.

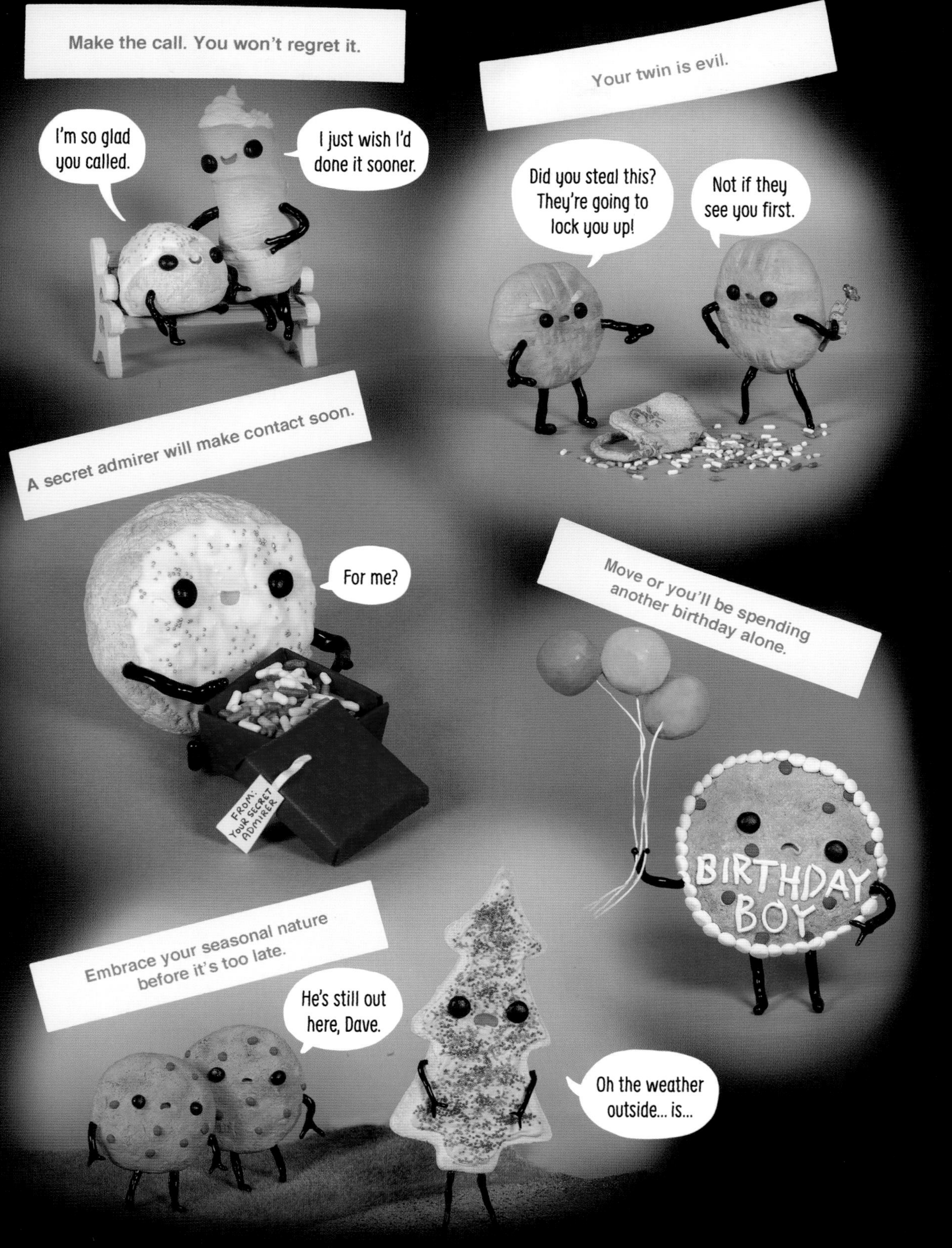
Make the call. You won't regret it.
I'm so glad you called.
I just wish I'd done it sooner.
Your twin is evil.
Did you steal this? They're going to lock you up!
Not if they see you first.
A secret admirer will make contact soon.
For me?
FROM: YOUR SECRET ADMIRER
Move or you'll be spending another birthday alone.
BIRTHDAY BOY
Embrace your seasonal nature before it's too late.
He's still out here, Dave.
Oh the weather outside... is...

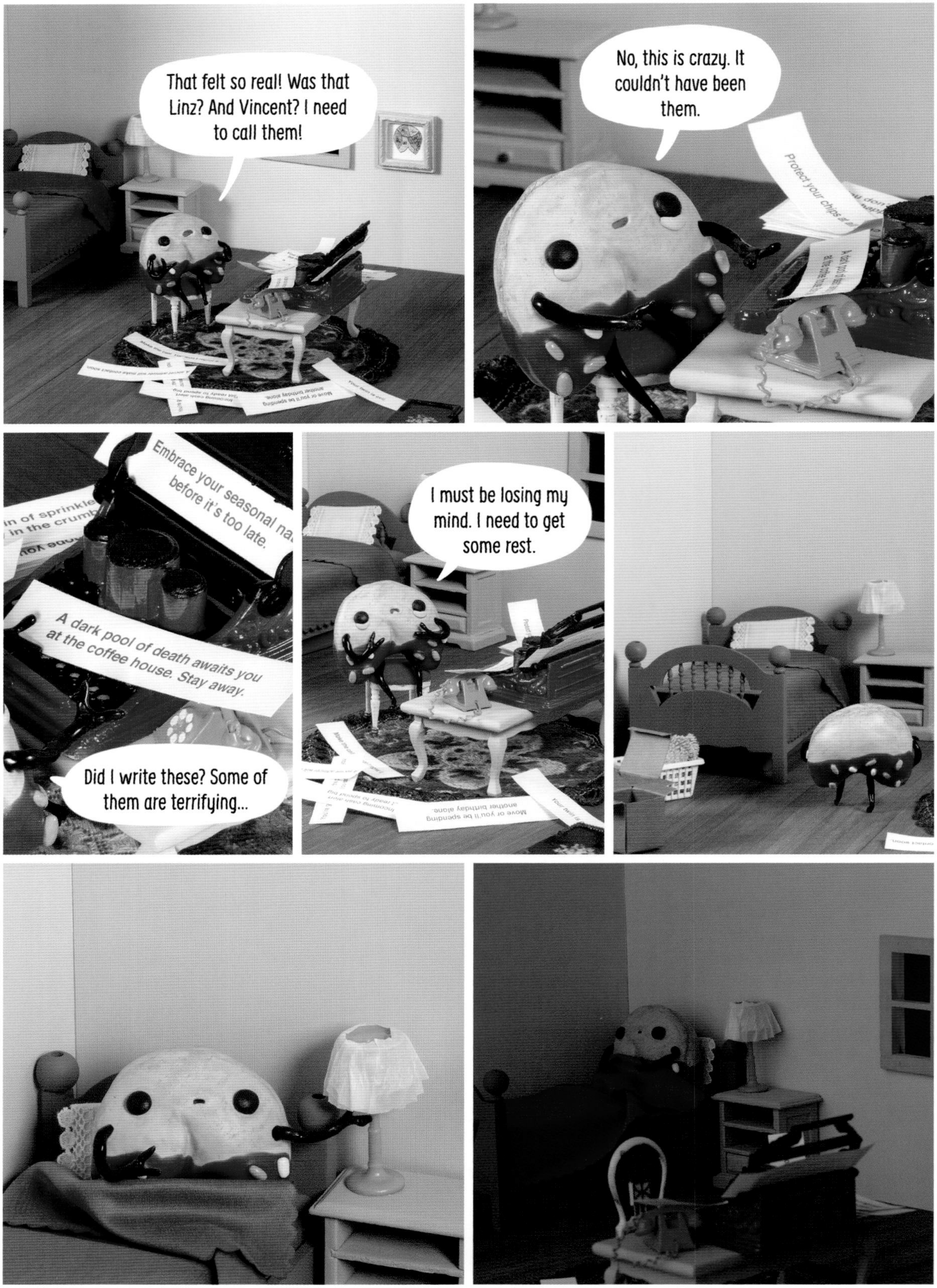
That felt so real! Was that Linz? And Vincent? I need to call them!
No, this is crazy. It couldn't have been them.
A dark pool of death awaits you at the coffee house. Stay away.
Did I write these? Some of them are terrifying...
I must be losing my mind. I need to get some rest.

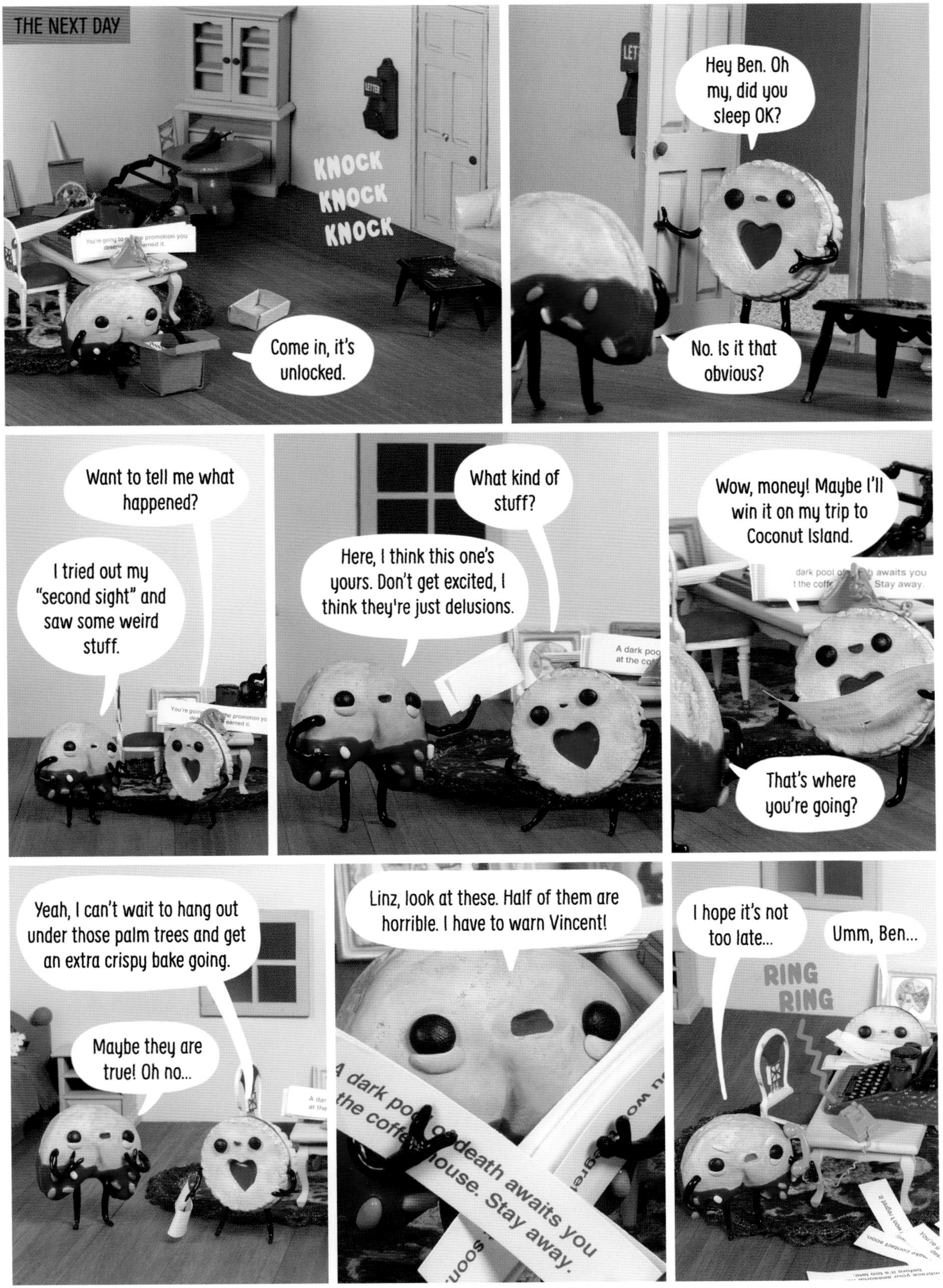
THE NEXT DAY
KNOCK
KNOCK
KNOCK
Come in, it's unlocked.
Hey Ben. Oh my, did you sleep OK?
No. Is it that obvious?
Want to tell me what happened?
I tried out my "second sight" and saw some weird stuff.
What kind of stuff?
Here, I think this one's yours. Don't get excited, I think they're just delusions.
Wow, money! Maybe I'll win it on my trip to Coconut Island.
That's where you're going?
Yeah, I can't wait to hang out under those palm trees and get an extra crispy bake going.
Maybe they are true! Oh no...
Linz, look at these. Half of them are horrible. I have to warn Vincent!
A dark pool of death awaits you the coffee house. Stay away.
I hope it's not too late...
Umm, Ben...
RING
RING

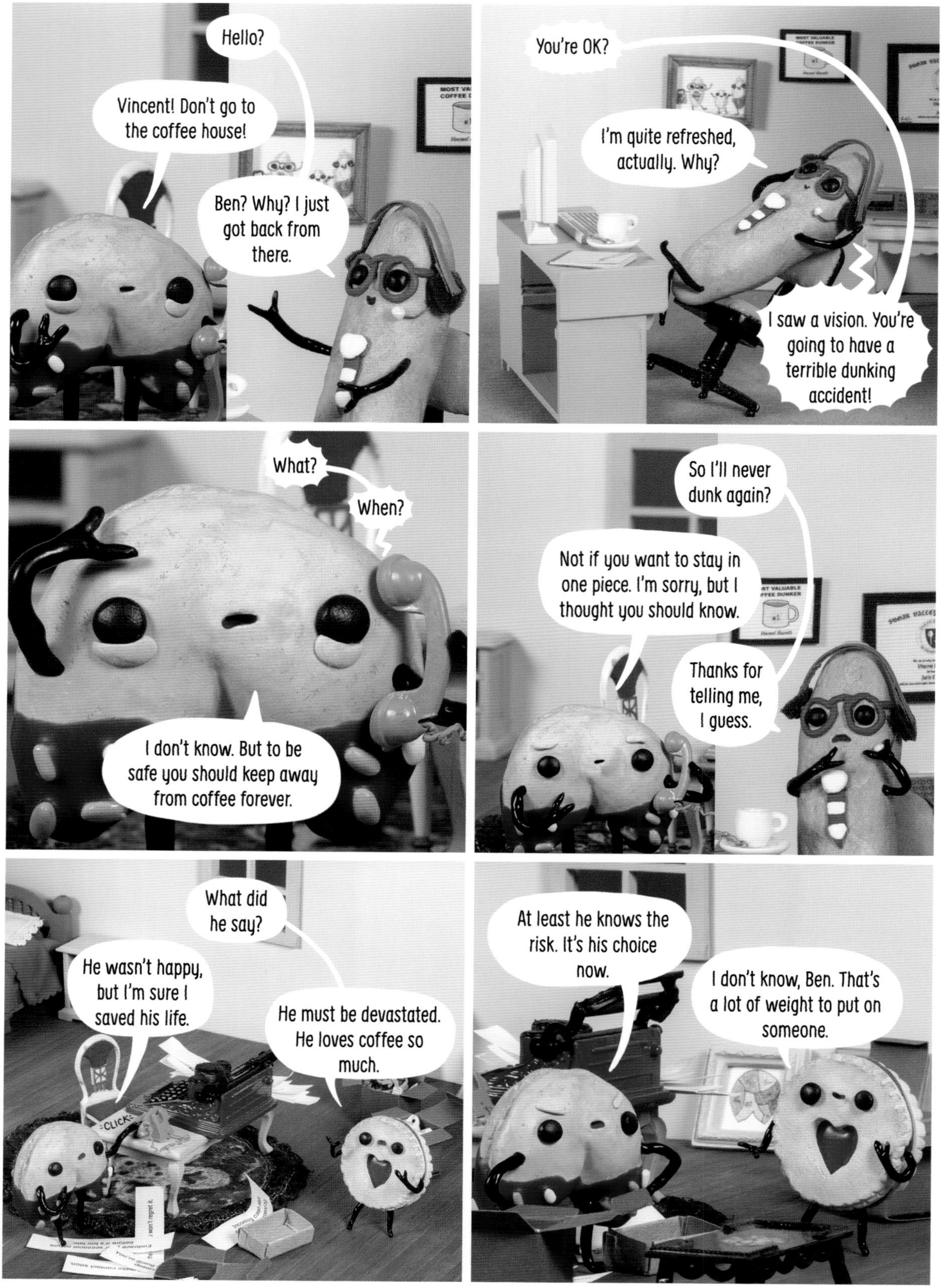
Hello?
Vincent! Don't go to the coffee house!
Ben? Why? I just got back from there.
You're OK?
I'm quite refreshed, actually. Why?
I saw a vision. You're going to have a terrible dunking accident!
What?
When?
I don't know. But to be safe you should keep away from coffee forever.
So I'll never dunk again?
Not if you want to stay in one piece. I'm sorry, but I thought you should know.
Thanks for telling me, I guess.
What did he say?
He wasn't happy, but I'm sure I saved his life.
He must be devastated. He loves coffee so much.
CLICK
At least he knows the risk. It's his choice now.
I don't know, Ben. That's a lot of weight to put on someone.

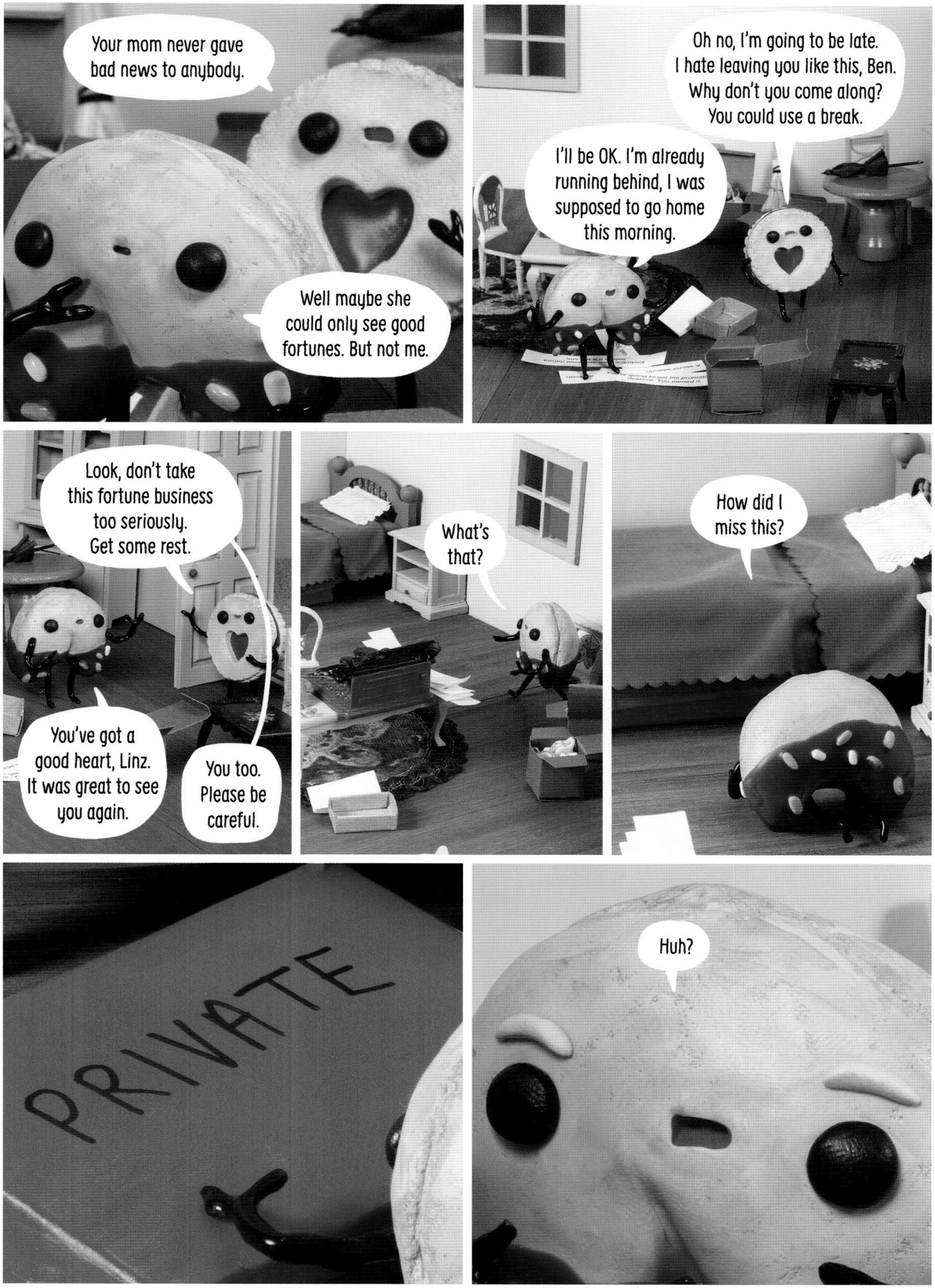
Your mom never gave bad news to anybody.
Well maybe she could only see good fortunes. But not me.
Oh no, I'm going to be late. I hate leaving you like this, Ben. Why don't you come along? You could use a break.
I'll be OK. I'm already running behind, I was supposed to go home this morning.
Look, don't take this fortune business too seriously. Get some rest.
You've got a good heart, Linz. It was great to see you again.
You too. Please be careful.
What's that?
How did I miss this?
PRIVATE
Huh?

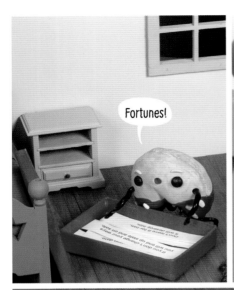

Fortunes!

All of them are bad! Why would she hide these?

Did you try to warn them, Mom?

If you don't change your ways you will end up stale and on sale.

...ling pin isn't finished with you yet.

You will lose all of your cream in the divorce.

Poison raisins have been added to your mix.

Don't leave it for him. It will destroy him.

Beware the Baker's Dozen.

Don't trust his expiration date. He's mislabeled.

That does it. Nobody else is dying on my watch.

Come on, fortune magic. Let's save some lives.

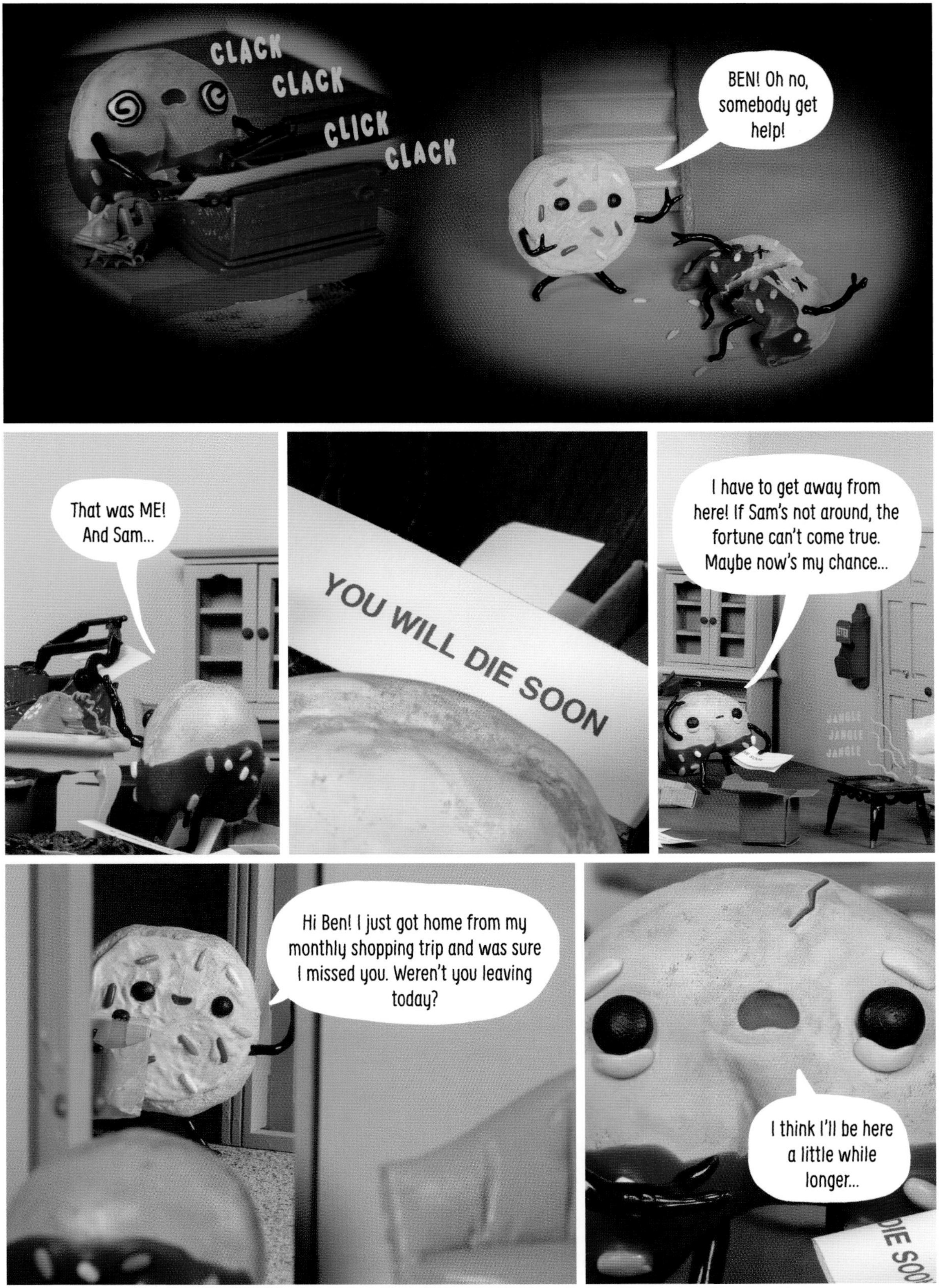
CLACK
CLACK
CLICK
CLACK
BEN! Oh no, somebody get help!
That was ME! And Sam...
YOU WILL DIE SOON
I have to get away from here! If Sam's not around, the fortune can't come true. Maybe now's my chance...
JANGLE JANGLE JANGLE
Hi Ben! I just got home from my monthly shopping trip and was sure I missed you. Weren't you leaving today?
I think I'll be here a little while longer...

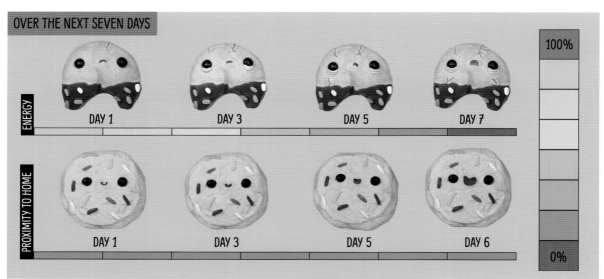

OVER THE NEXT SEVEN DAYS

ENERGY — DAY 1, DAY 3, DAY 5, DAY 7

PROXIMITY TO HOME — DAY 1, DAY 3, DAY 5, DAY 6

100% — 0%

DAY EIGHT

He's never going to leave and I'm starving to death.

It's quiet. I have to do it now.

Just a few more steps and I'm free.

CREAK

Hey Ben!

Aaaaaaaah!

KRAK

BEN!

Oh no, somebody get help!

Always listen to your mother. She knows best.

THE END.

124

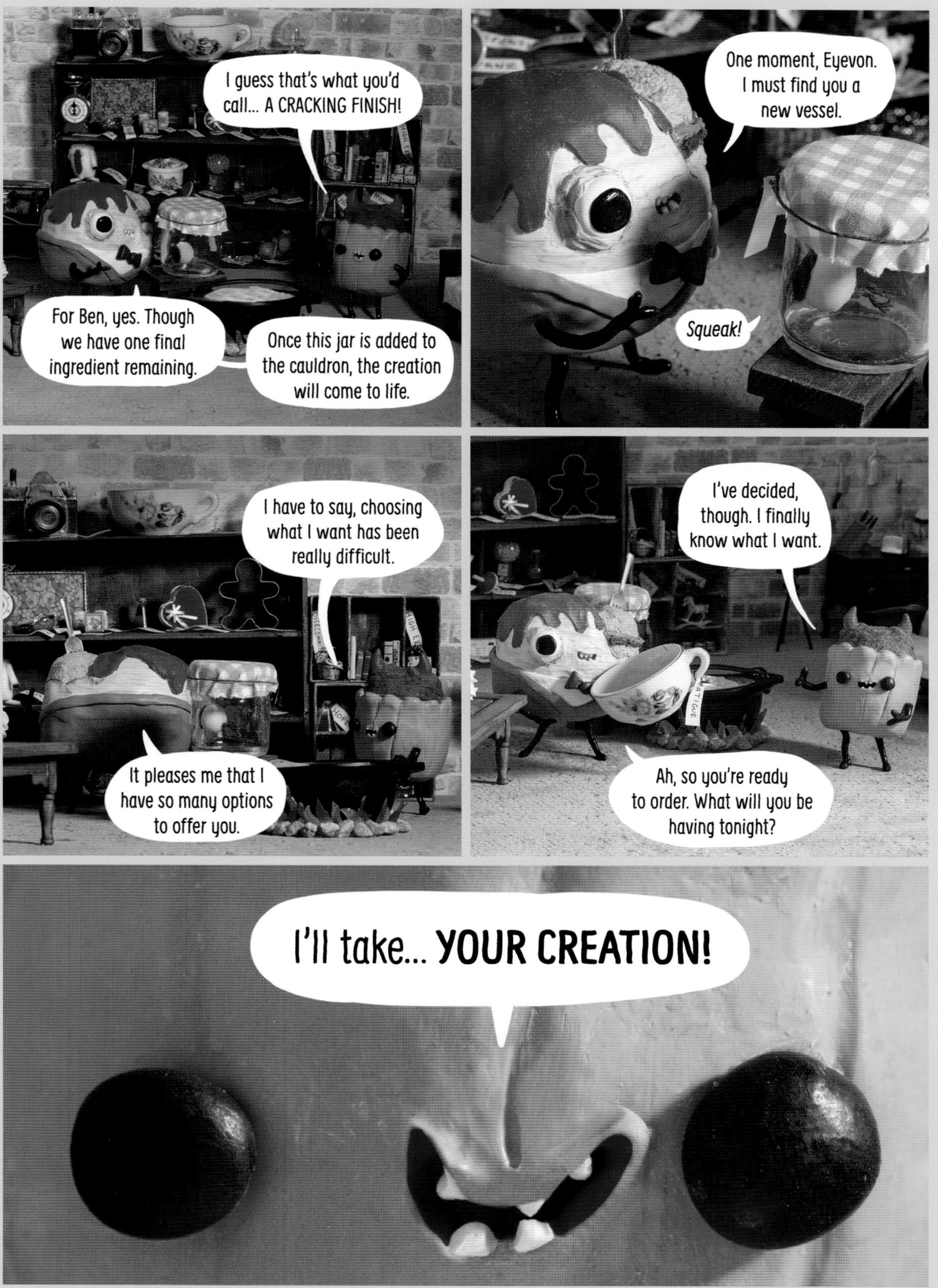

I guess that's what you'd call... A CRACKING FINISH!
For Ben, yes. Though we have one final ingredient remaining.
Once this jar is added to the cauldron, the creation will come to life.
One moment, Eyevon. I must find you a new vessel.
Squeak!
I have to say, choosing what I want has been really difficult.
It pleases me that I have so many options to offer you.
I've decided, though. I finally know what I want.
Ah, so you're ready to order. What will you be having tonight?
I'll take... YOUR CREATION!

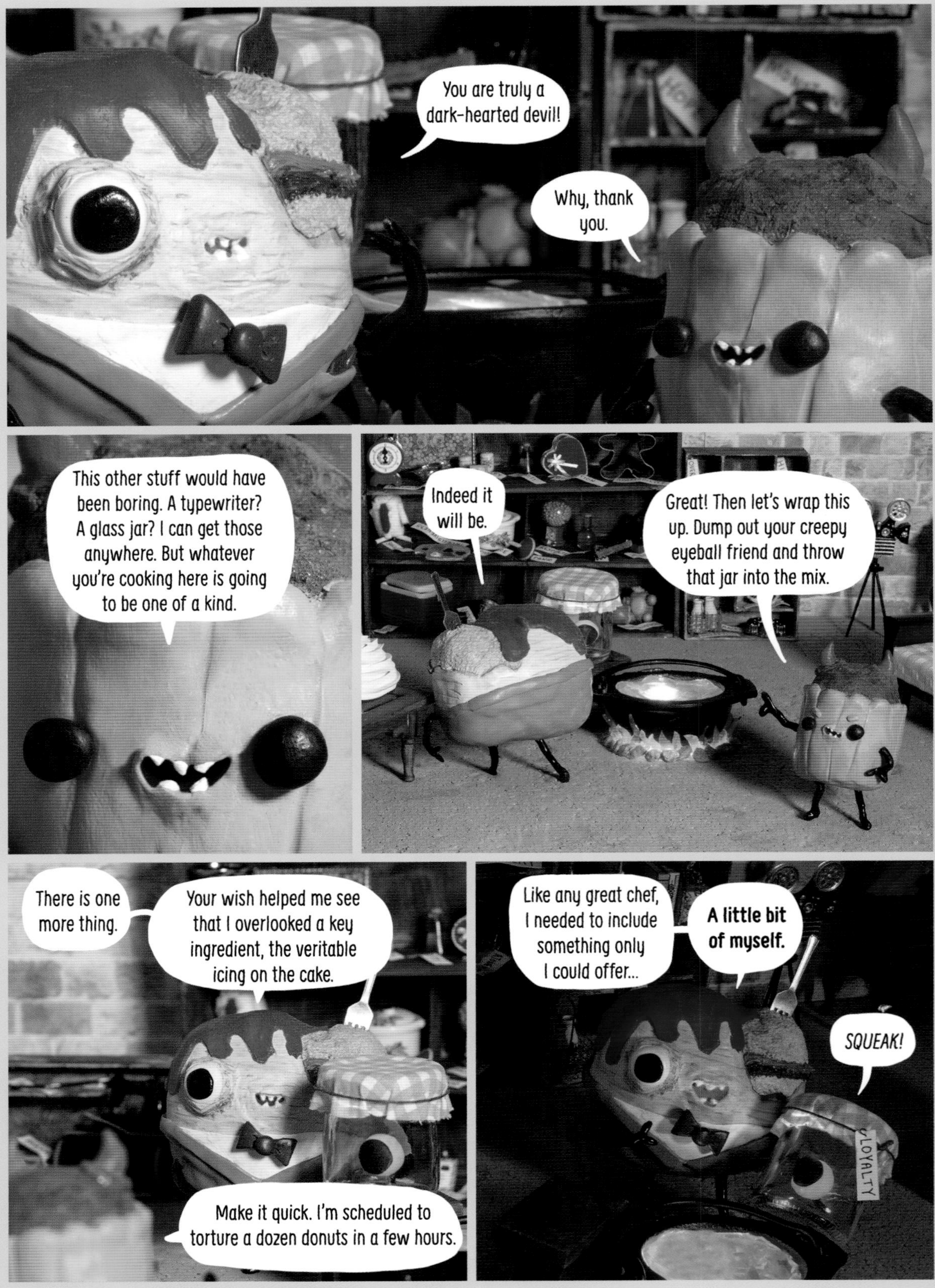
You are truly a dark-hearted devil!
Why, thank you.
This other stuff would have been boring. A typewriter? A glass jar? I can get those anywhere. But whatever you're cooking here is going to be one of a kind.
Indeed it will be.
Great! Then let's wrap this up. Dump out your creepy eyeball friend and throw that jar into the mix.
There is one more thing.
Your wish helped me see that I overlooked a key ingredient, the veritable icing on the cake.
Make it quick. I'm scheduled to torture a dozen donuts in a few hours.
Like any great chef, I needed to include something only I could offer...
A little bit of myself.
SQUEAK!
LOYALTY

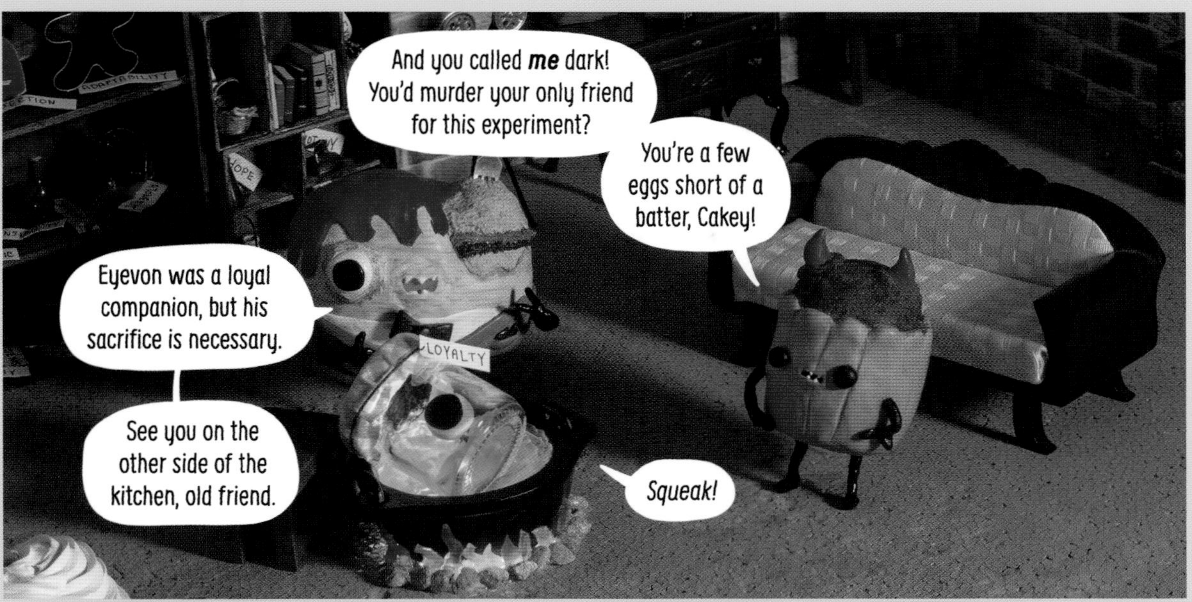
And you called **me** dark! You'd murder your only friend for this experiment?
You're a few eggs short of a batter, Cakey!
Eyevon was a loyal companion, but his sacrifice is necessary.
See you on the other side of the kitchen, old friend.
Squeak!
LOYALTY
HOPE

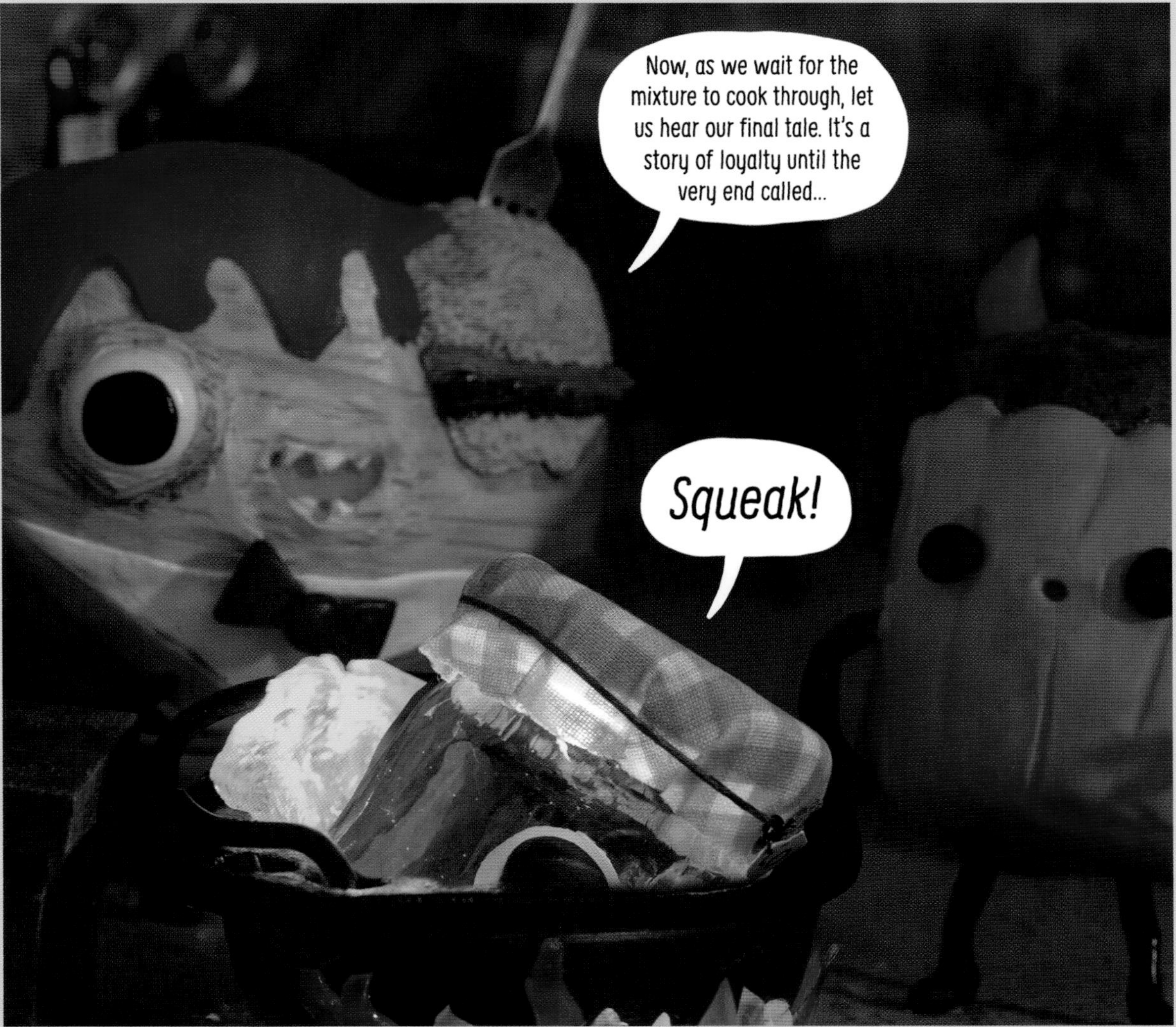
Now, as we wait for the mixture to cook through, let us hear our final tale. It's a story of loyalty until the very end called...
Squeak!

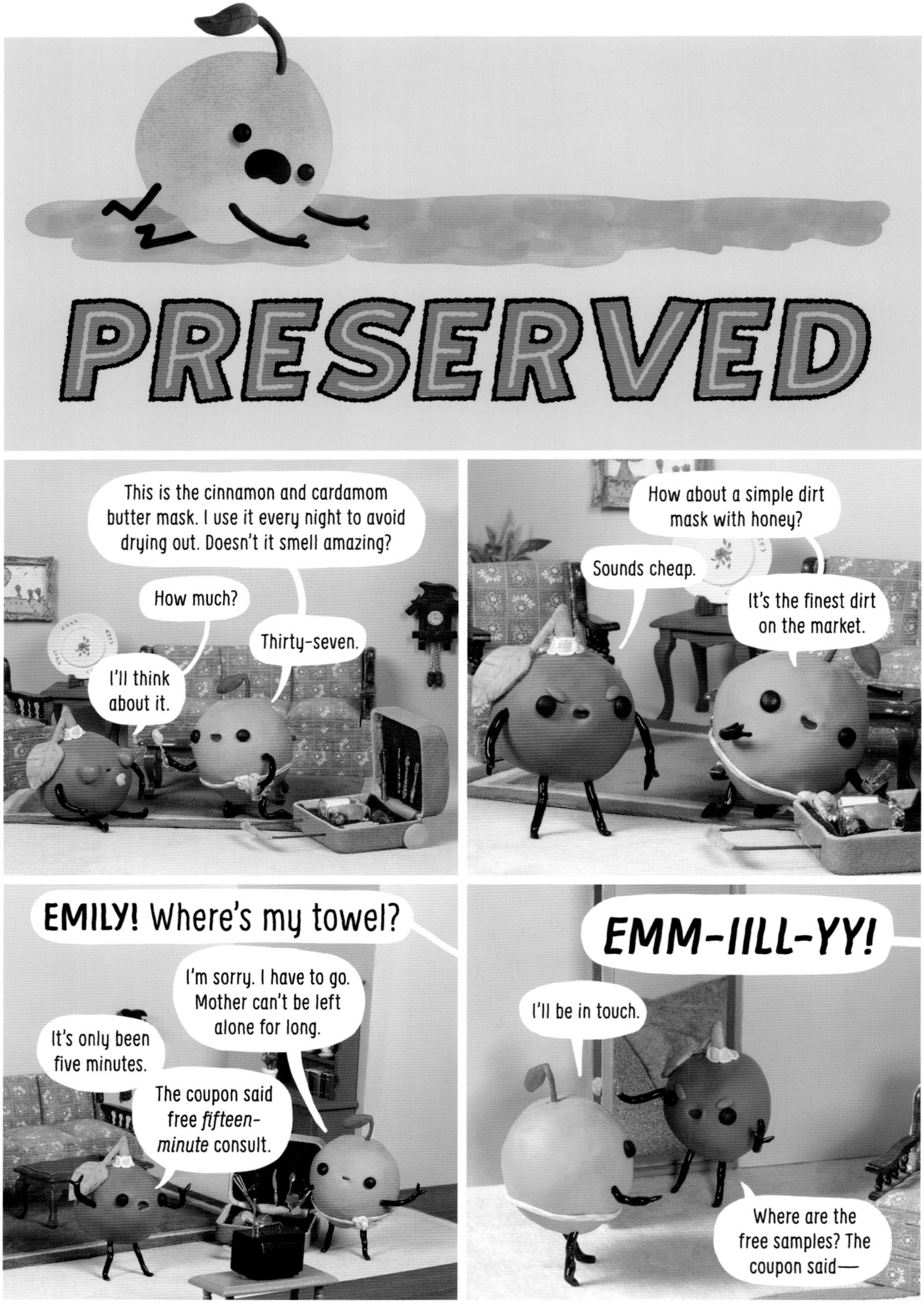
PRESERVED
This is the cinnamon and cardamom butter mask. I use it every night to avoid drying out. Doesn't it smell amazing?
How much?
Thirty-seven.
I'll think about it.
How about a simple dirt mask with honey?
Sounds cheap.
It's the finest dirt on the market.
EMILY! Where's my towel?
I'm sorry. I have to go. Mother can't be left alone for long.
It's only been five minutes.
The coupon said free *fifteen-minute* consult.
EMM-IILL-YY!
I'll be in touch.
Where are the free samples? The coupon said—

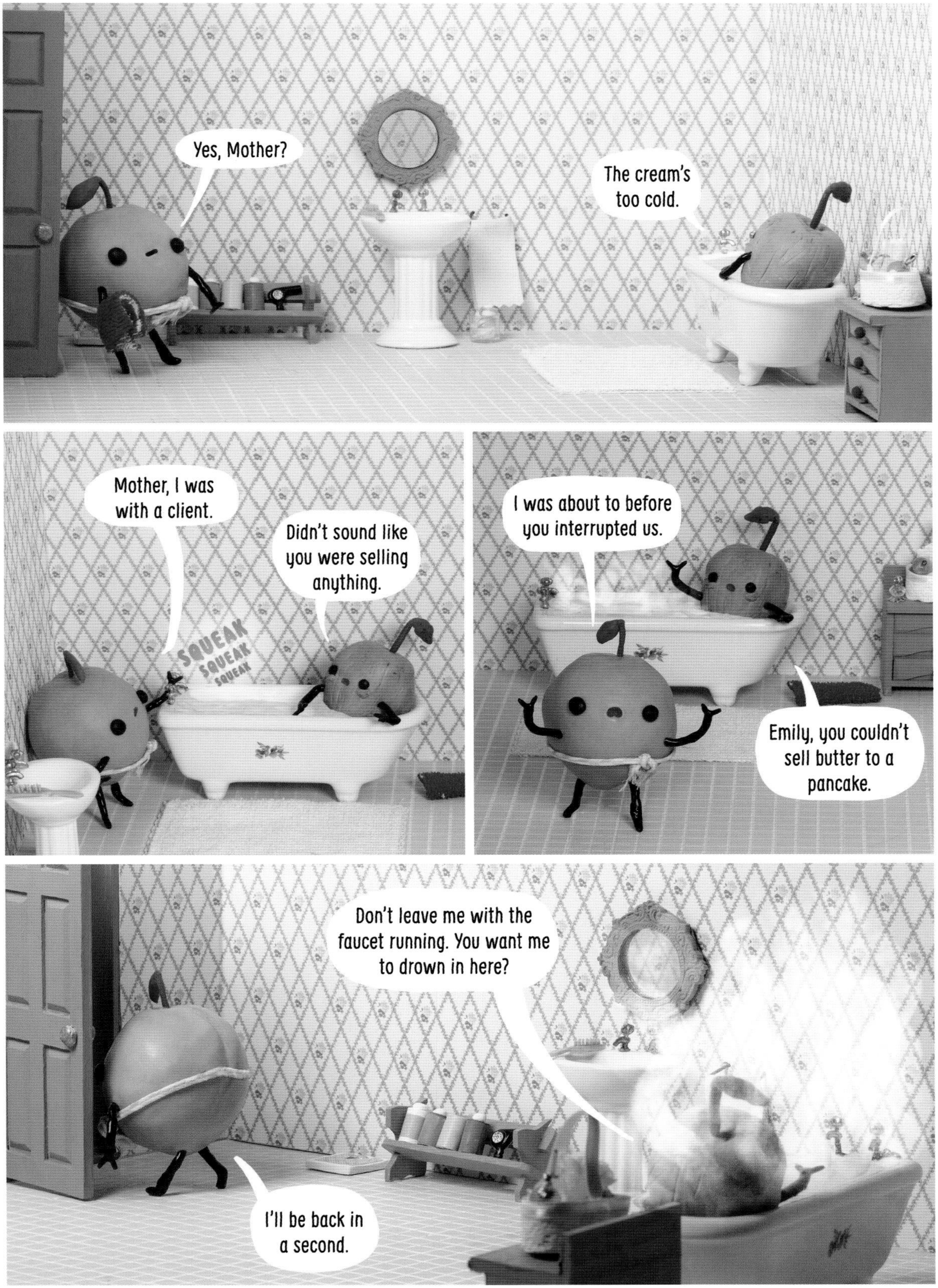
Yes, Mother?
The cream's too cold.
Mother, I was with a client.
SQUEAK SQUEAK SQUEAK
Didn't sound like you were selling anything.
I was about to before you interrupted us.
Emily, you couldn't sell butter to a pancake.
Don't leave me with the faucet running. You want me to drown in here?
I'll be back in a second.

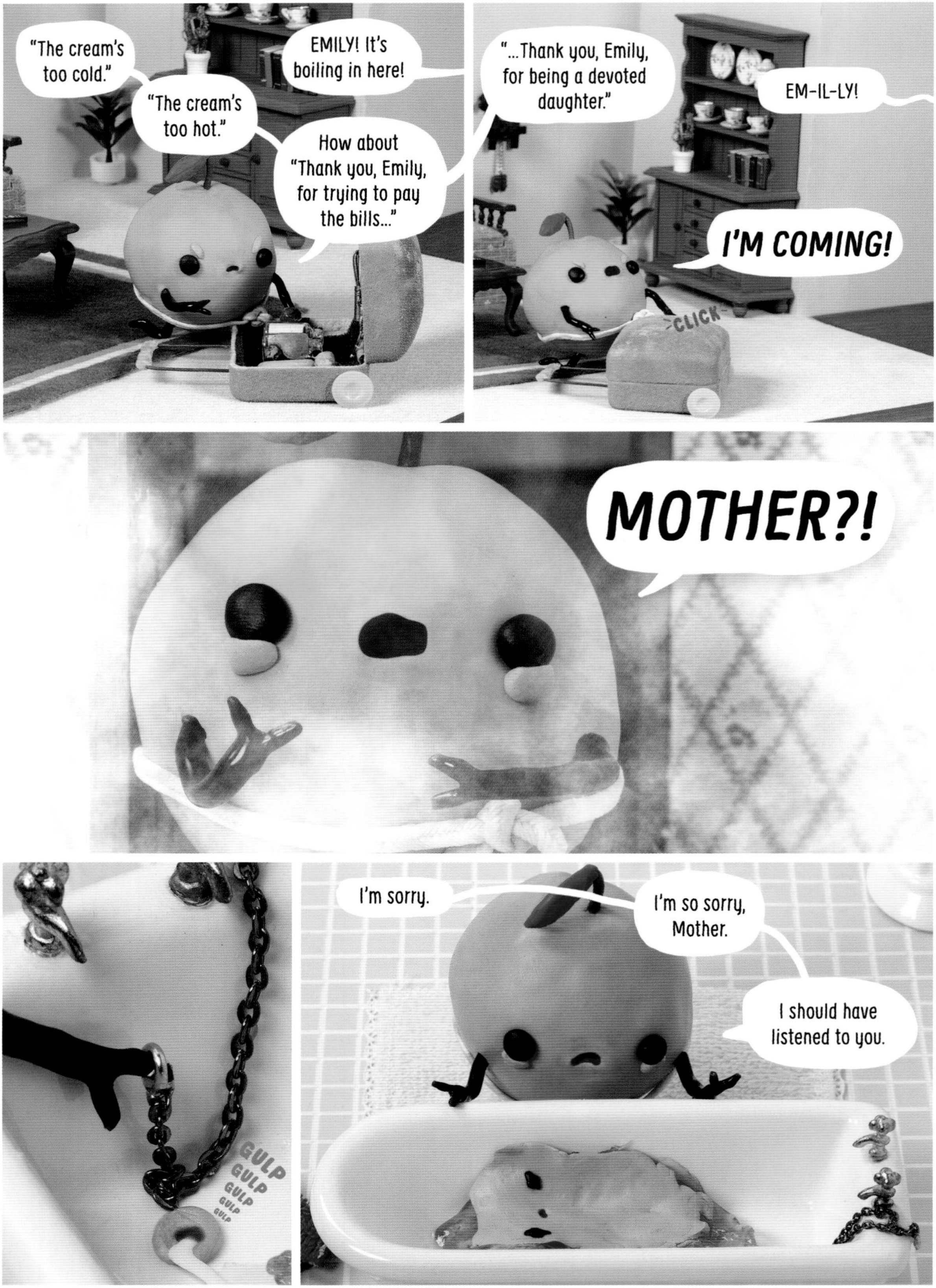
"The cream's too cold."
"The cream's too hot."
EMILY! It's boiling in here!
How about "Thank you, Emily, for trying to pay the bills..."
"...Thank you, Emily, for being a devoted daughter."
EM-IL-LY!
I'M COMING!
CLICK
MOTHER?!
GULP GULP GULP GULP GULP
I'm sorry.
I'm so sorry, Mother.
I should have listened to you.

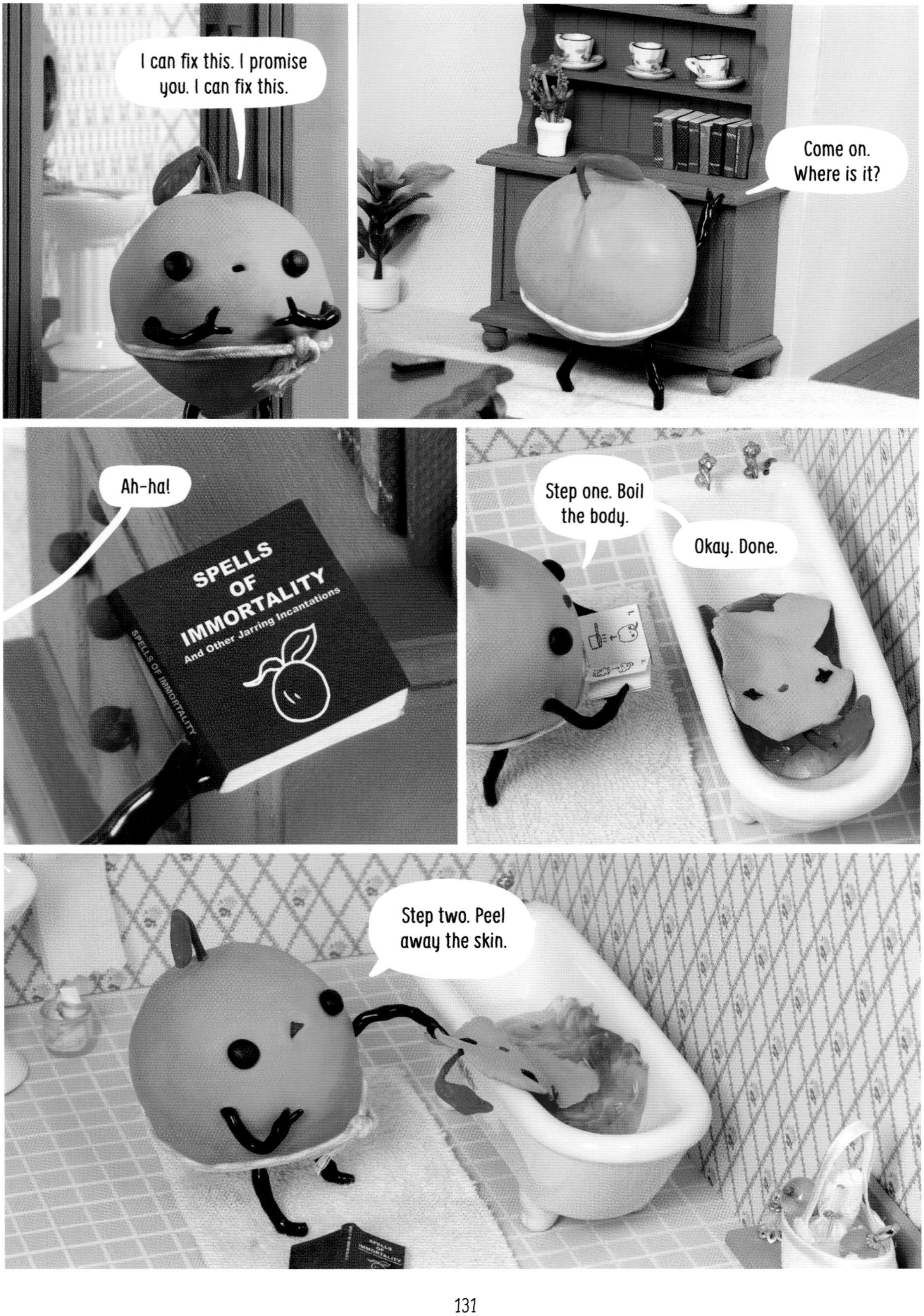
I can fix this. I promise you. I can fix this.
Come on. Where is it?
Ah-ha!
SPELLS OF IMMORTALITY
And Other Jarring Incantations
SPELLS OF IMMORTALITY
Step one. Boil the body.
Okay. Done.
Step two. Peel away the skin.

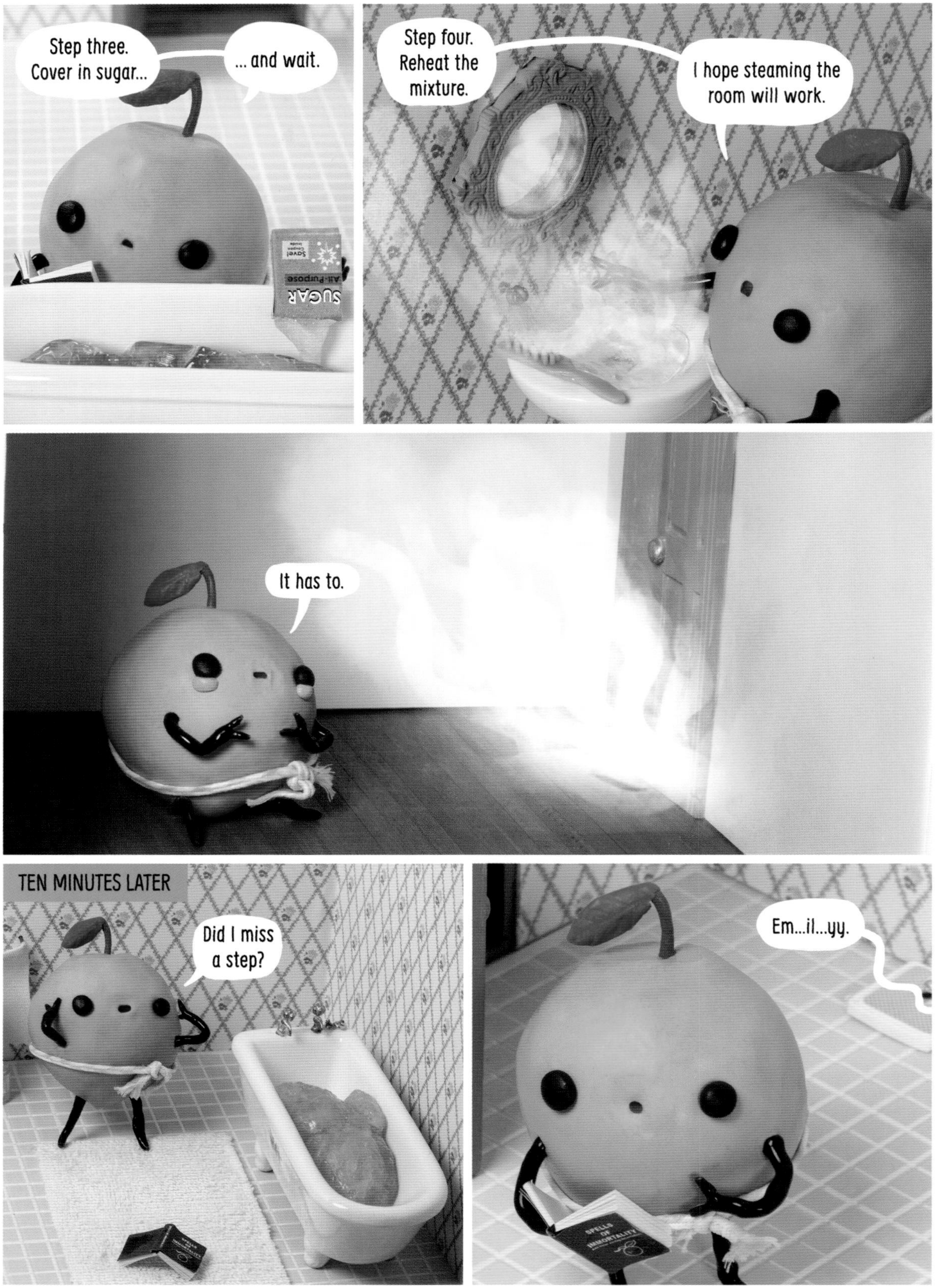
Step three.
Cover in sugar...
... and wait.
SUGAR
All-Purpose
Save!
Step four.
Reheat the
mixture.
I hope steaming the
room will work.
It has to.
TEN MINUTES LATER
Did I miss
a step?
Em...il...yy.
SPELLS
OF
IMMORTALITY

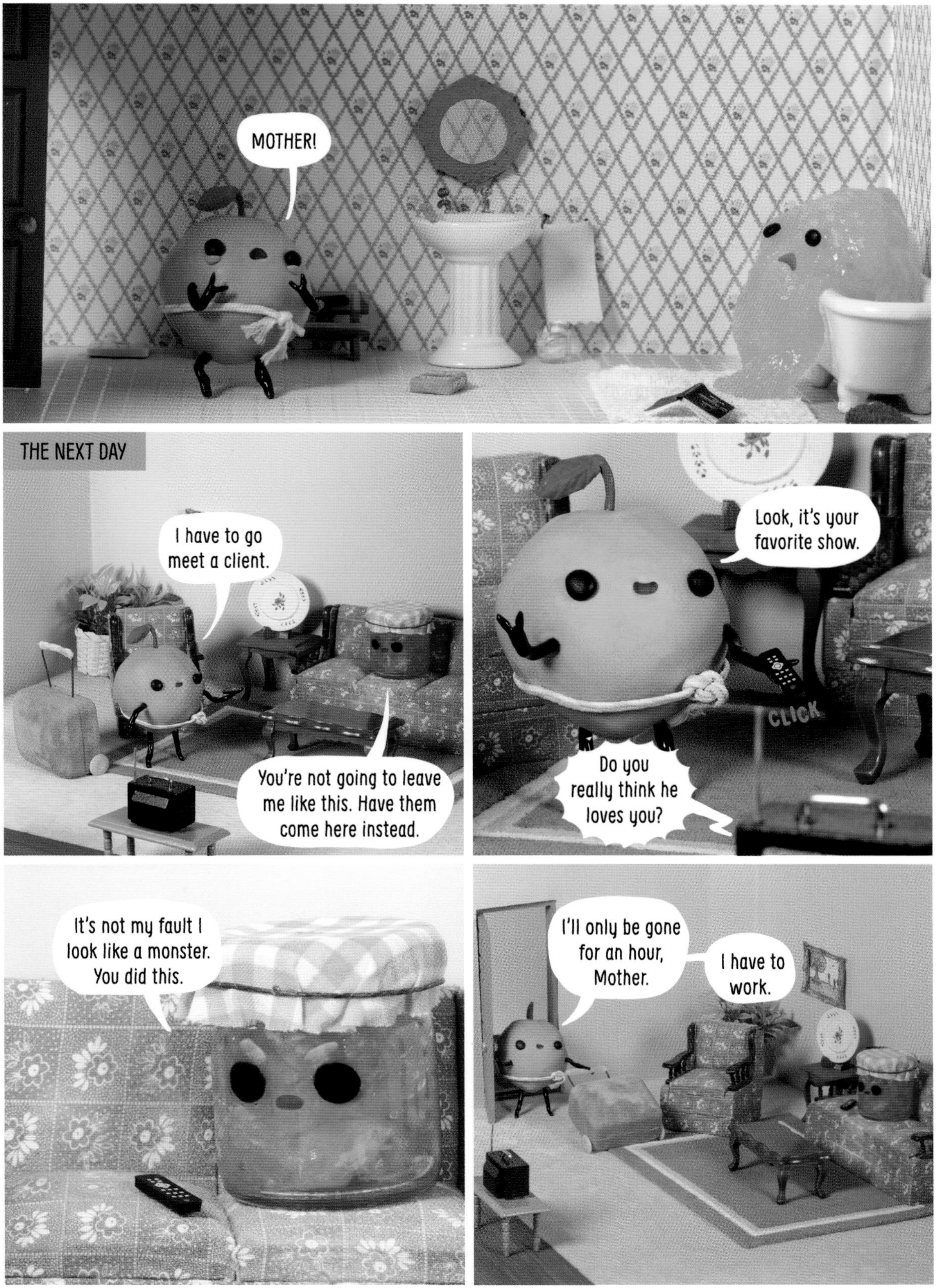
MOTHER!
THE NEXT DAY
I have to go meet a client.
You're not going to leave me like this. Have them come here instead.
Look, it's your favorite show.
CLICK
Do you really think he loves you?
It's not my fault I look like a monster. You did this.
I'll only be gone for an hour, Mother.
I have to work.

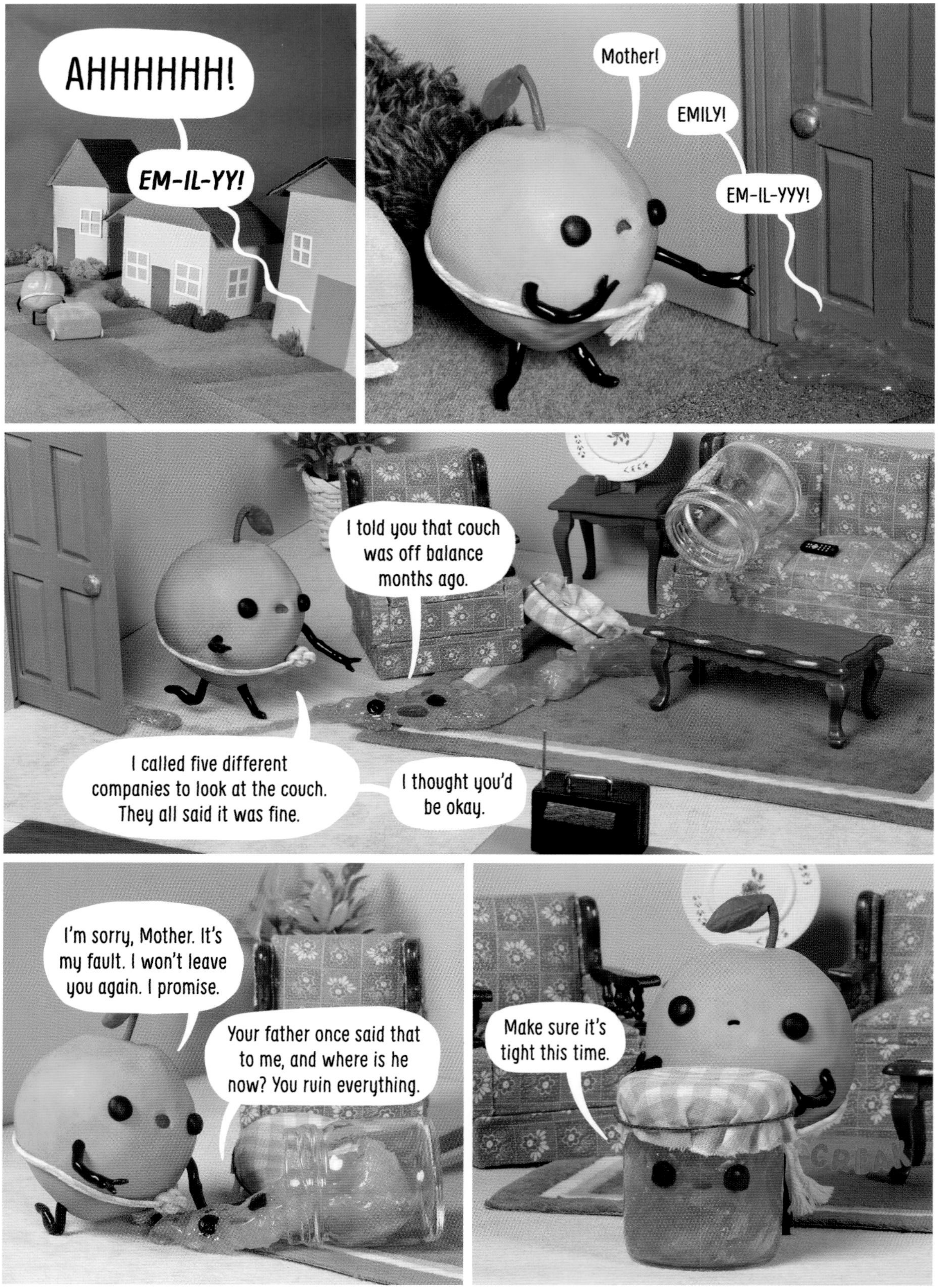
AHHHHHH!
EM-IL-YY!
Mother!
EMILY!
EM-IL-YYY!
I told you that couch was off balance months ago.
I called five different companies to look at the couch. They all said it was fine.
I thought you'd be okay.
I'm sorry, Mother. It's my fault. I won't leave you again. I promise.
Your father once said that to me, and where is he now? You ruin everything.
Make sure it's tight this time.

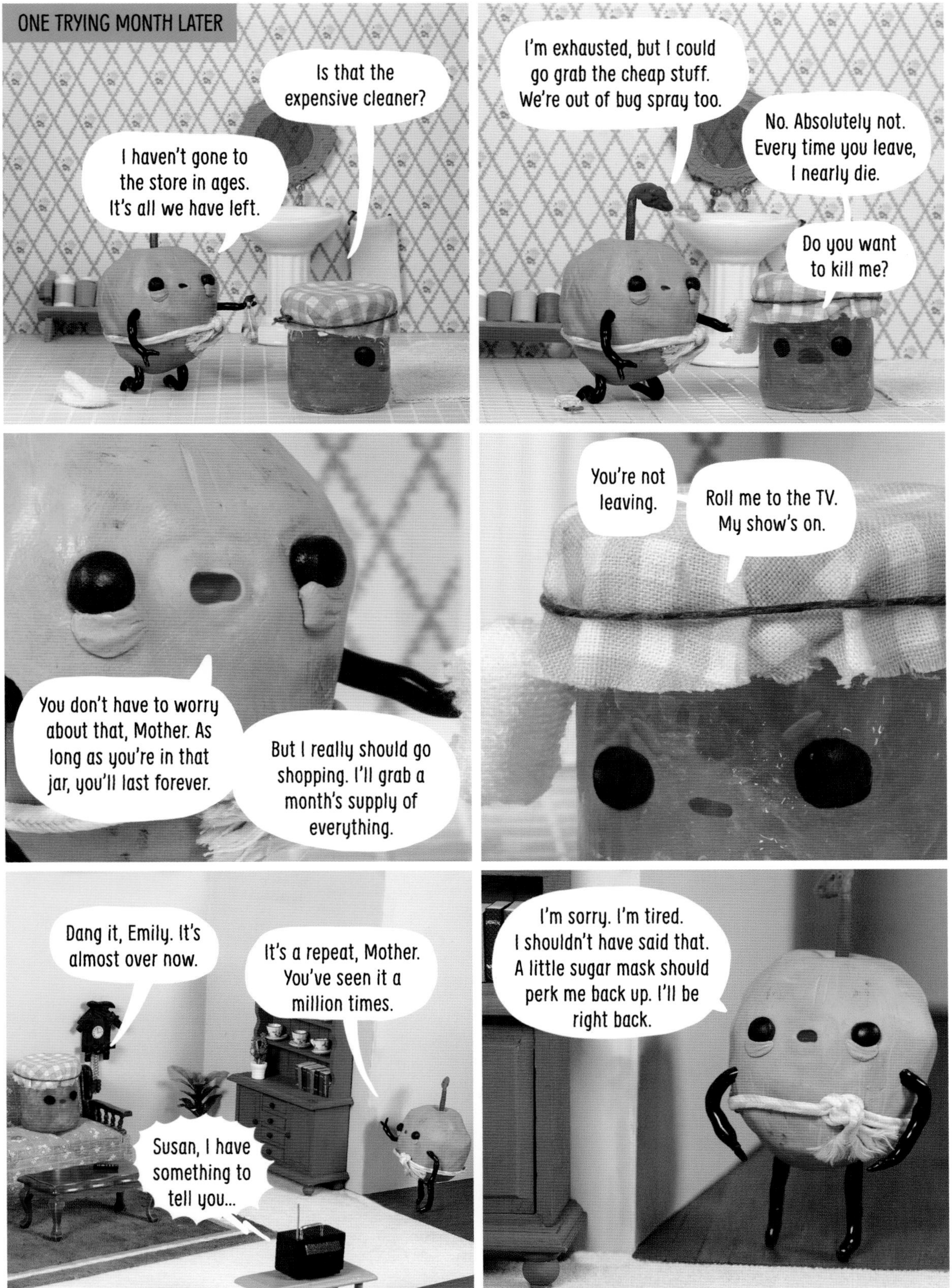
ONE TRYING MONTH LATER
Is that the expensive cleaner?
I haven't gone to the store in ages. It's all we have left.
I'm exhausted, but I could go grab the cheap stuff. We're out of bug spray too.
No. Absolutely not. Every time you leave, I nearly die.
Do you want to kill me?
You don't have to worry about that, Mother. As long as you're in that jar, you'll last forever.
But I really should go shopping. I'll grab a month's supply of everything.
You're not leaving.
Roll me to the TV. My show's on.
Dang it, Emily. It's almost over now.
It's a repeat, Mother. You've seen it a million times.
Susan, I have something to tell you...
I'm sorry. I'm tired. I shouldn't have said that. A little sugar mask should perk me back up. I'll be right back.

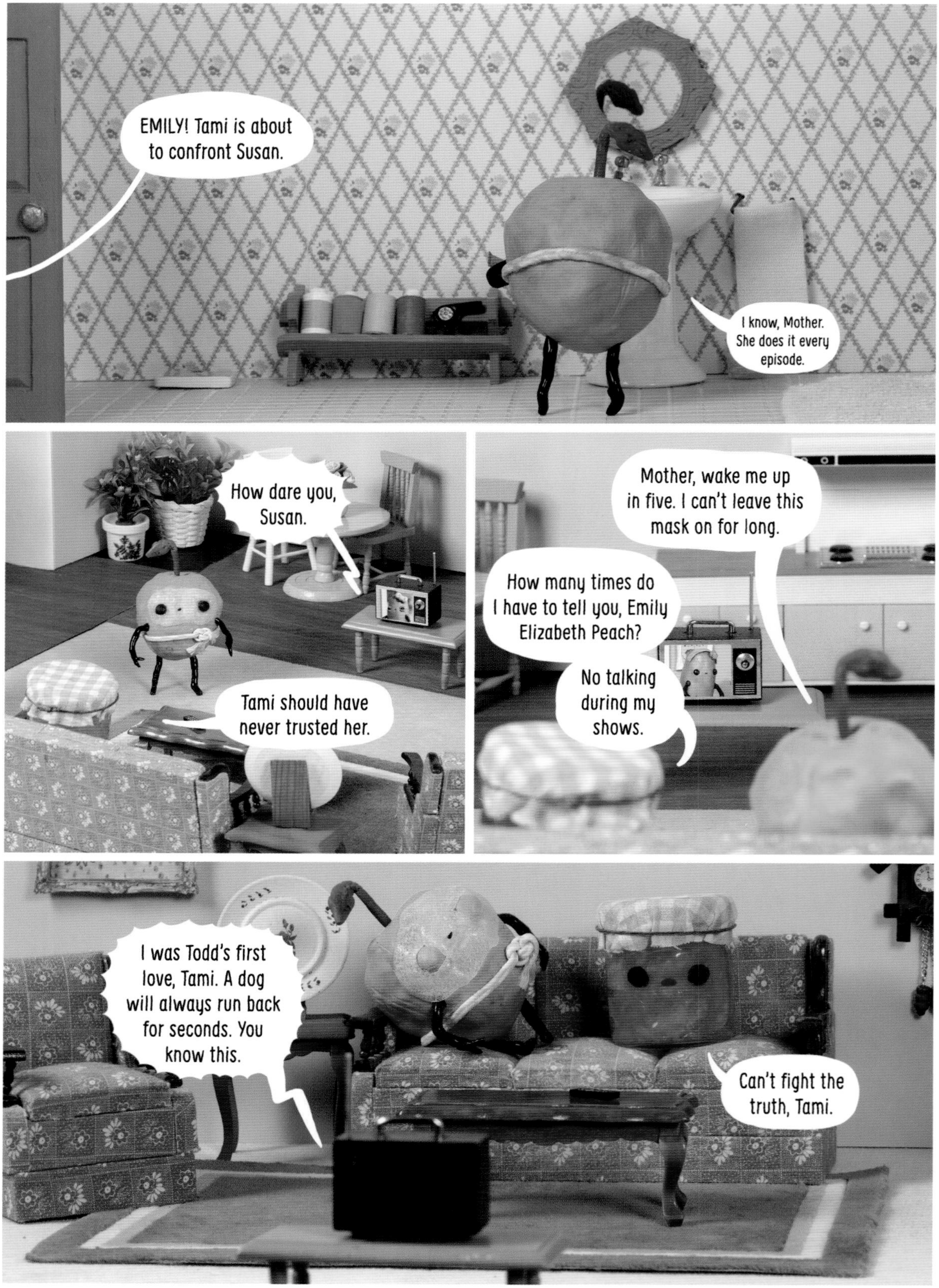
EMILY! Tami is about to confront Susan.
I know, Mother. She does it every episode.
How dare you, Susan.
Tami should have never trusted her.
Mother, wake me up in five. I can't leave this mask on for long.
How many times do I have to tell you, Emily Elizabeth Peach?
No talking during my shows.
I was Todd's first love, Tami. A dog will always run back for seconds. You know this.
Can't fight the truth, Tami.

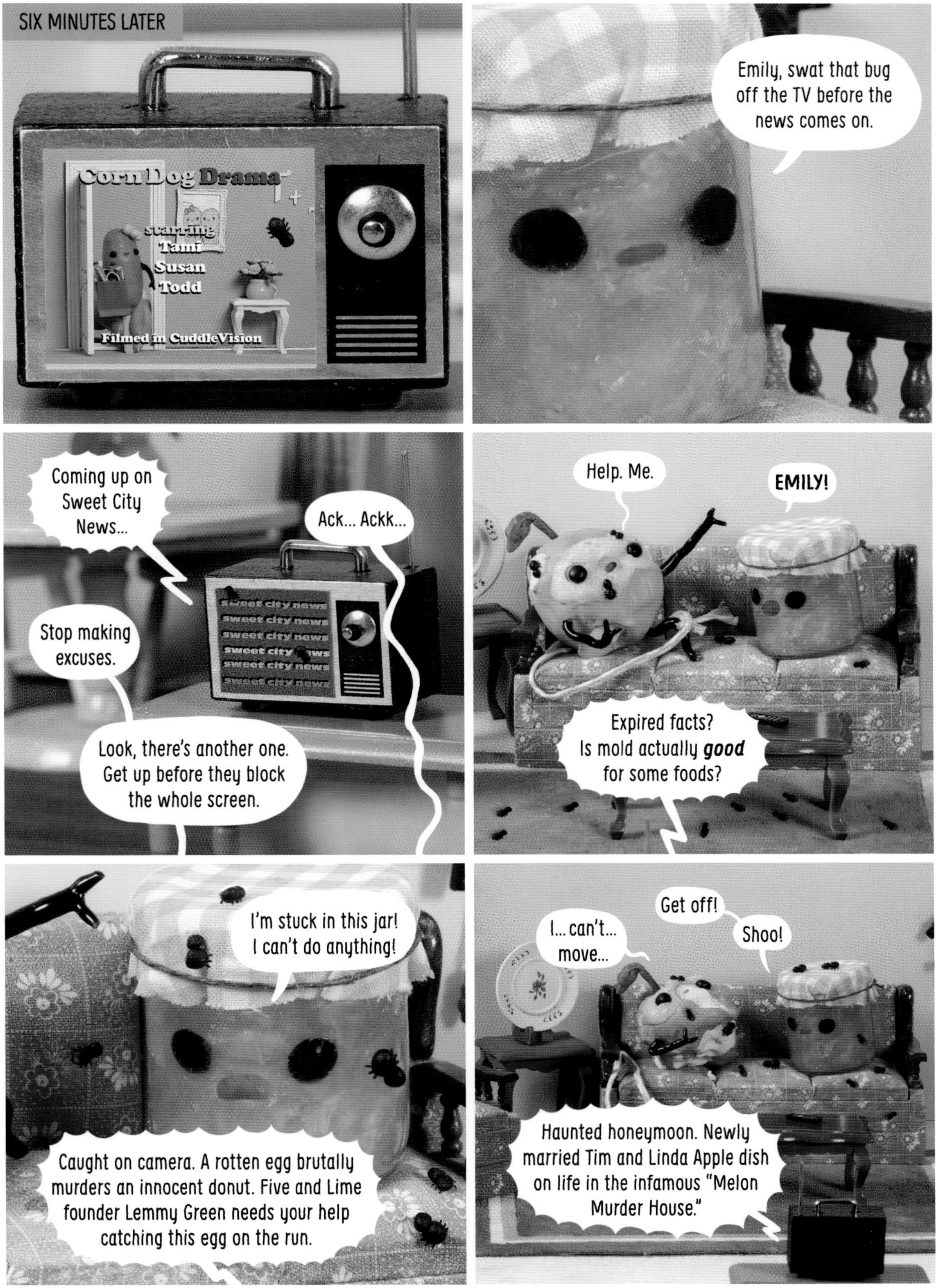
SIX MINUTES LATER
Corn Dog Drama
starring
Tami
Susan
Todd
Filmed in CuddleVision
Emily, swat that bug off the TV before the news comes on.
Coming up on Sweet City News...
Ack... Ackk...
Stop making excuses.
Look, there's another one. Get up before they block the whole screen.
Help. Me.
EMILY!
Expired facts? Is mold actually **good** for some foods?
I'm stuck in this jar! I can't do anything!
Caught on camera. A rotten egg brutally murders an innocent donut. Five and Lime founder Lemmy Green needs your help catching this egg on the run.
Get off!
I... can't... move...
Shoo!
Haunted honeymoon. Newly married Tim and Linda Apple dish on life in the infamous "Melon Murder House."

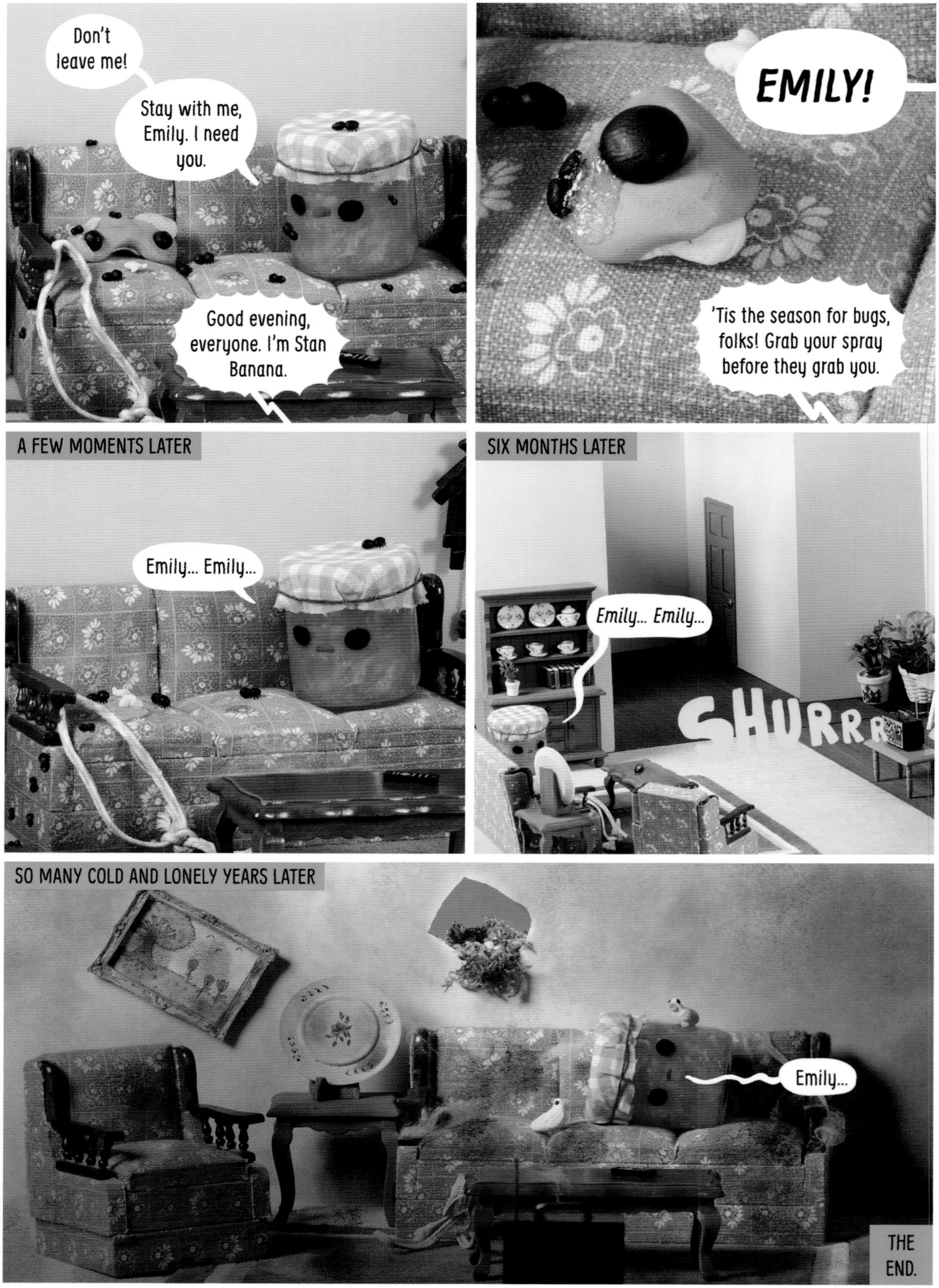
Don't leave me!
Stay with me, Emily. I need you.
Good evening, everyone. I'm Stan Banana.
EMILY!
'Tis the season for bugs, folks! Grab your spray before they grab you.
A FEW MOMENTS LATER
Emily... Emily...
SIX MONTHS LATER
Emily... Emily...
SHURRR
SO MANY COLD AND LONELY YEARS LATER
Emily...
THE END.

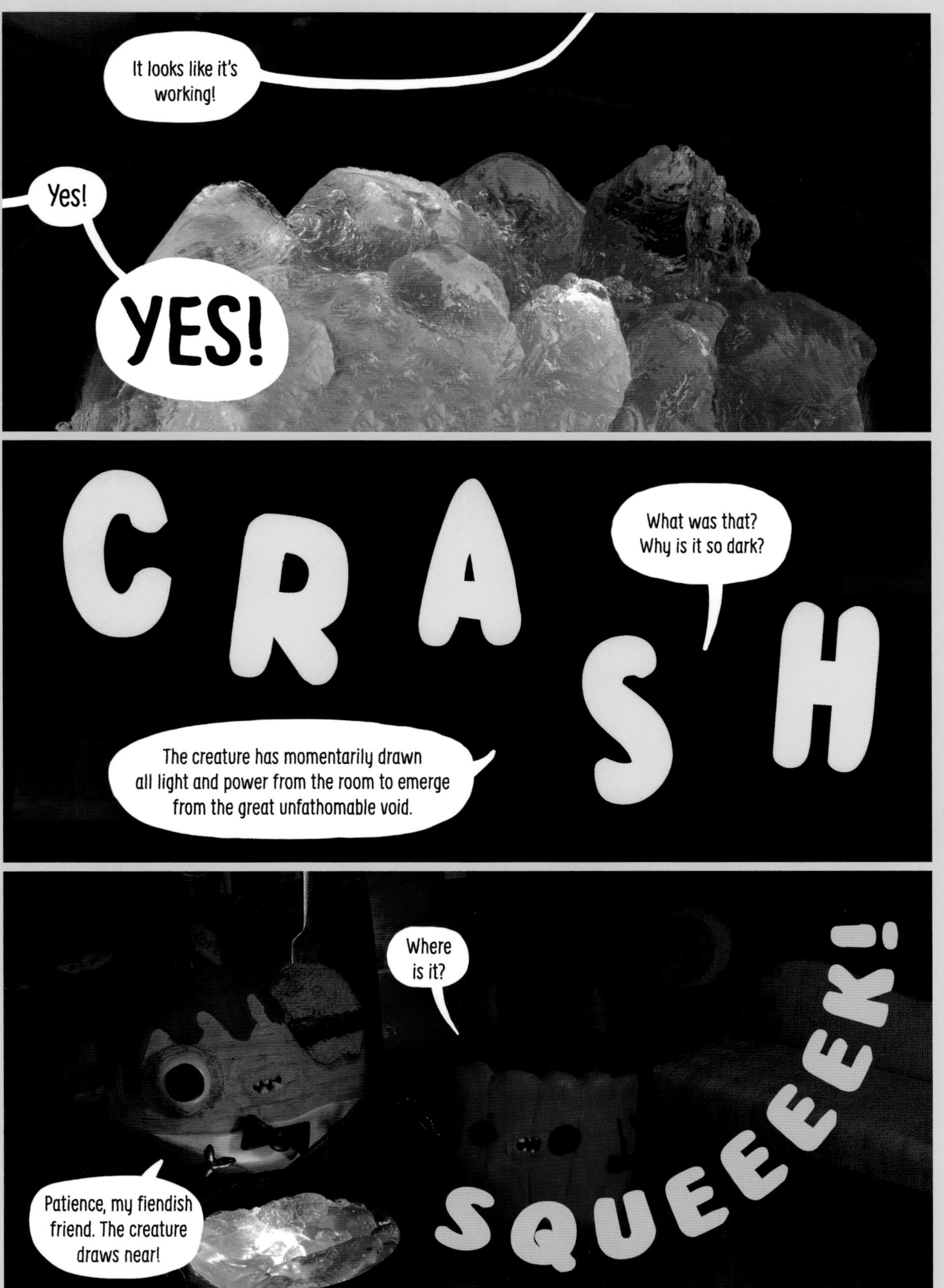
It looks like it's working!
Yes!
YES!
CRASH
What was that? Why is it so dark?
The creature has momentarily drawn all light and power from the room to emerge from the great unfathomable void.
Where is it?
SQUEEEEK!
Patience, my fiendish friend. The creature draws near!

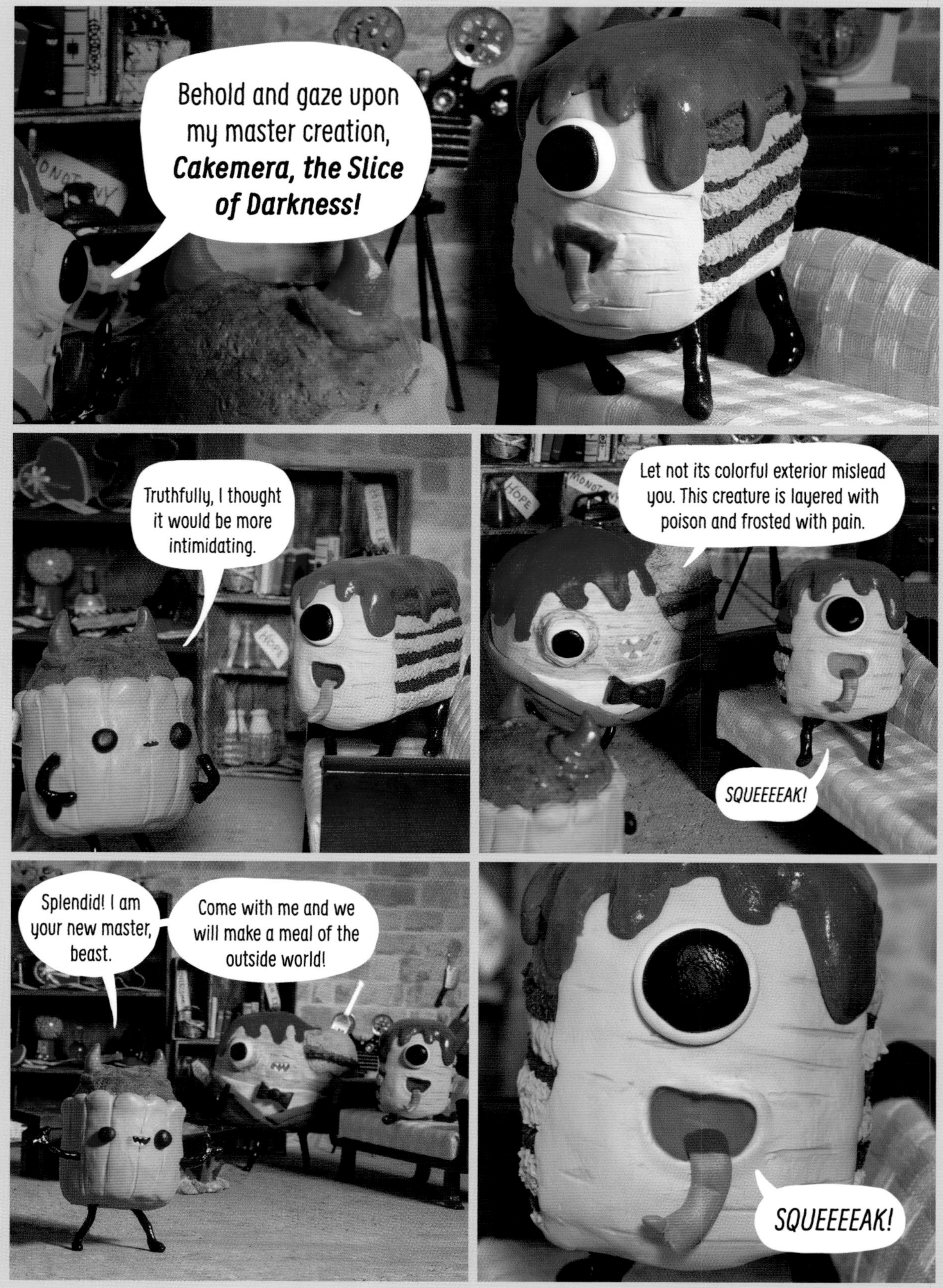
Behold and gaze upon my master creation, ***Cakemera, the Slice of Darkness!***
Truthfully, I thought it would be more intimidating.
Let not its colorful exterior mislead you. This creature is layered with poison and frosted with pain.
SQUEEEEAK!
Splendid! I am your new master, beast.
Come with me and we will make a meal of the outside world!
SQUEEEEAK!

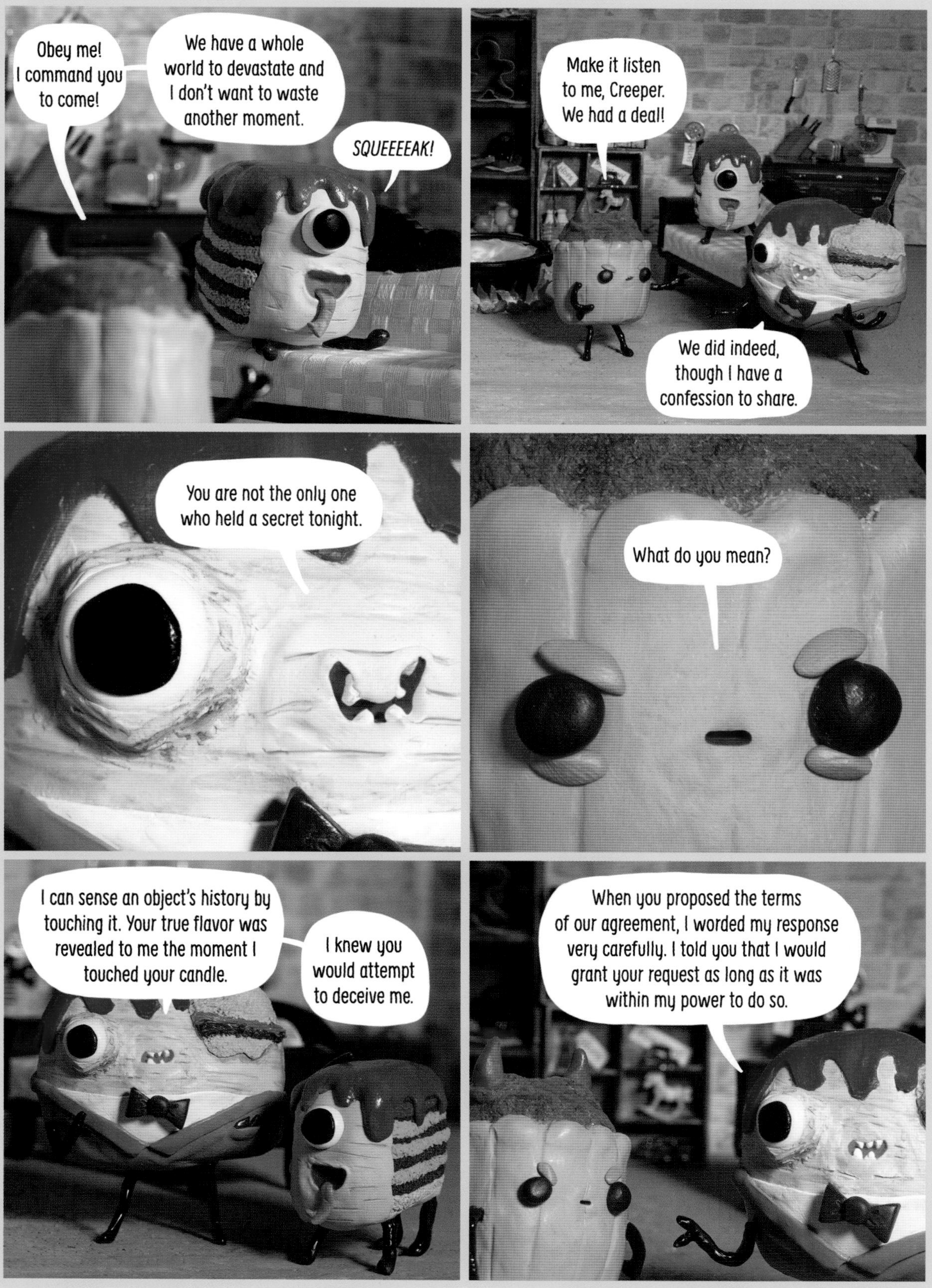
Obey me! I command you to come!
We have a whole world to devastate and I don't want to waste another moment.
SQUEEEEAK!
Make it listen to me, Creeper. We had a deal!
We did indeed, though I have a confession to share.
You are not the only one who held a secret tonight.
What do you mean?
I can sense an object's history by touching it. Your true flavor was revealed to me the moment I touched your candle.
I knew you would attempt to deceive me.
When you proposed the terms of our agreement, I worded my response very carefully. I told you that I would grant your request as long as it was within my power to do so.

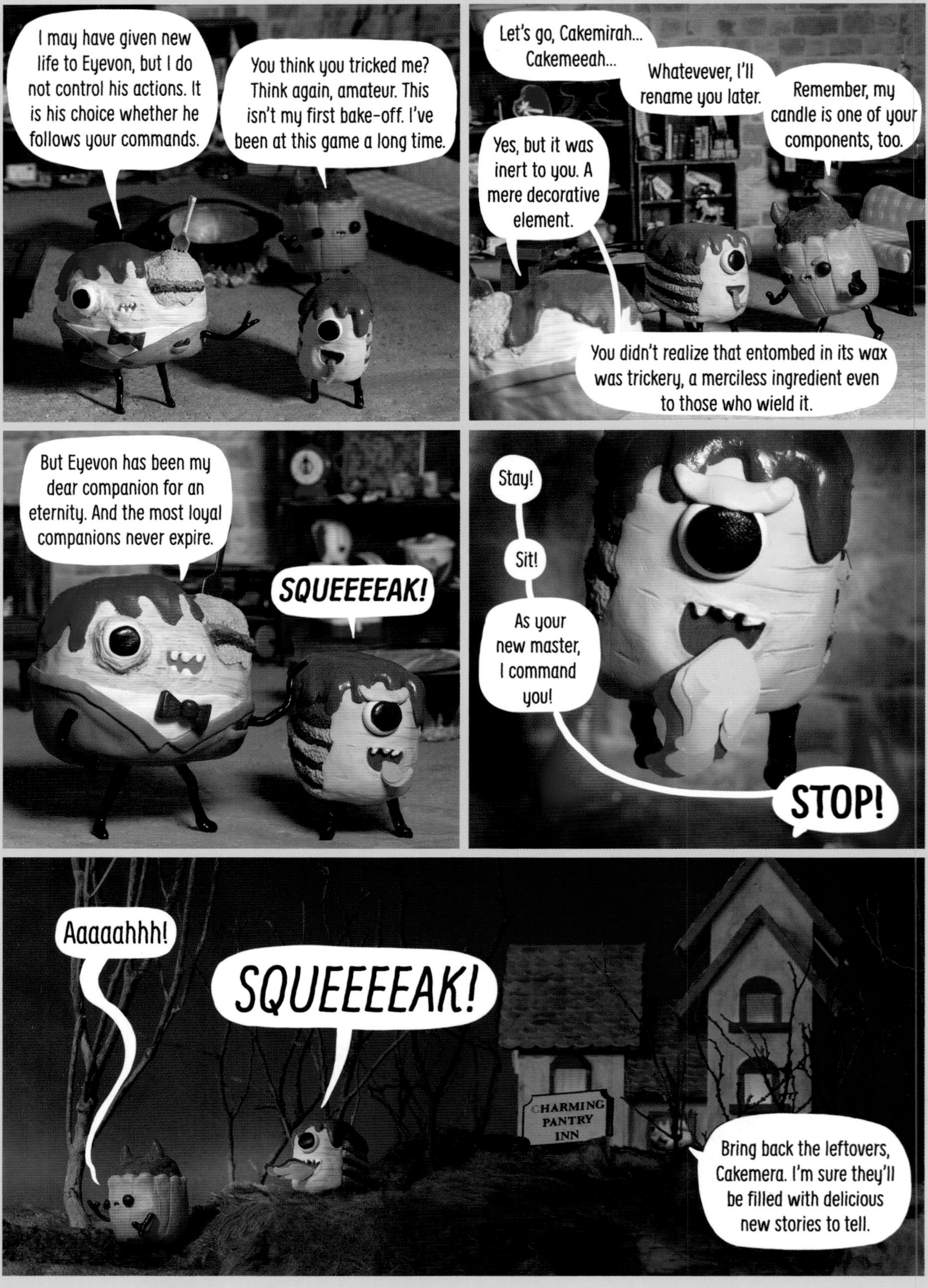

I may have given new life to Eyevon, but I do not control his actions. It is his choice whether he follows your commands.
You think you tricked me? Think again, amateur. This isn't my first bake-off. I've been at this game a long time.
Let's go, Cakemirah... Cakemeeah...
Whatevever, I'll rename you later.
Remember, my candle is one of your components, too.
Yes, but it was inert to you. A mere decorative element.
You didn't realize that entombed in its wax was trickery, a merciless ingredient even to those who wield it.
But Eyevon has been my dear companion for an eternity. And the most loyal companions never expire.
SQUEEEEAK!
Stay!
Sit!
As your new master, I command you!
STOP!
Aaaaahhh!
SQUEEEEAK!
CHARMING PANTRY INN
Bring back the leftovers, Cakemera. I'm sure they'll be filled with delicious new stories to tell.

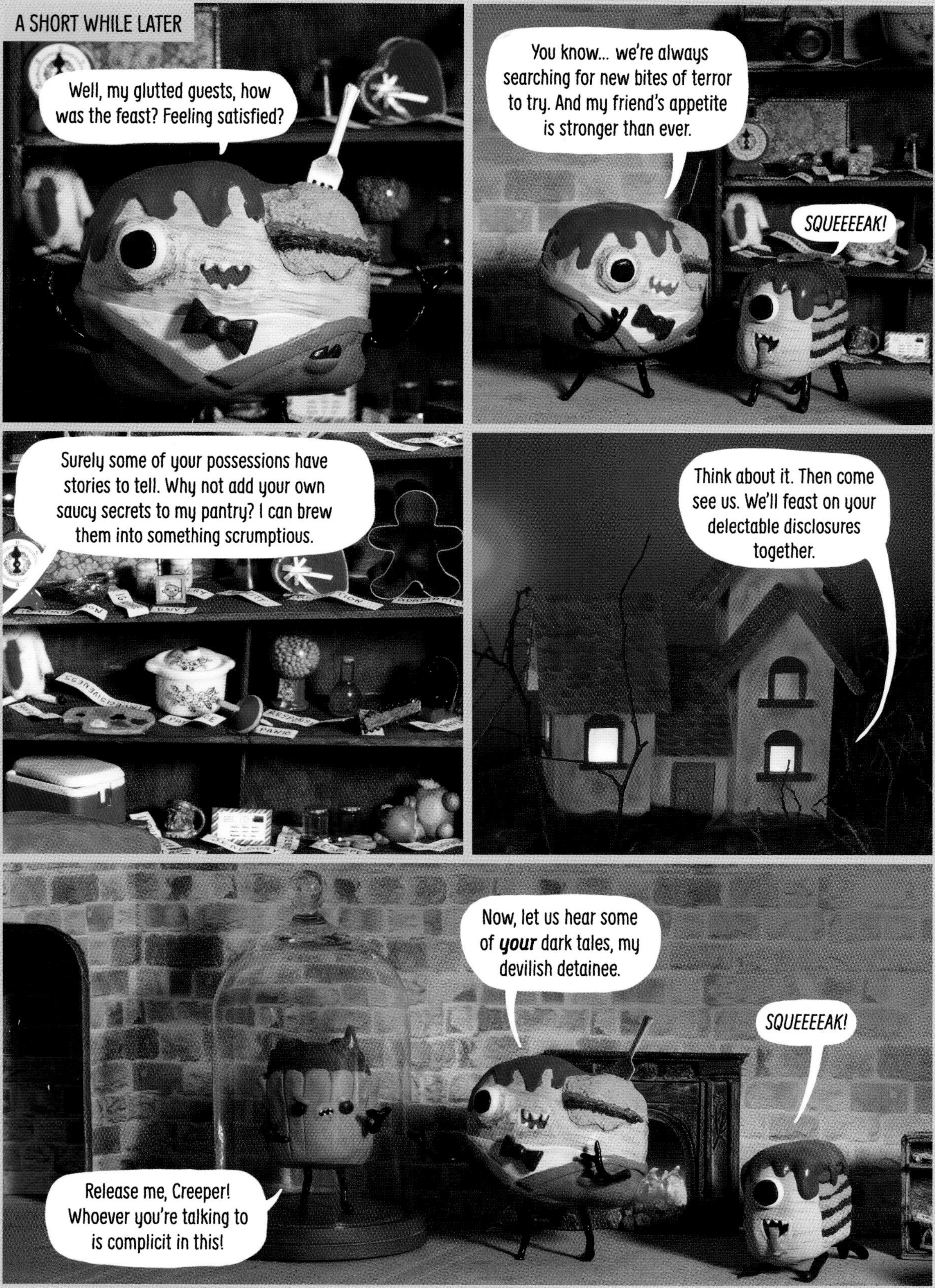
A SHORT WHILE LATER
Well, my glutted guests, how was the feast? Feeling satisfied?
You know... we're always searching for new bites of terror to try. And my friend's appetite is stronger than ever.
SQUEEEEAK!
Surely some of your possessions have stories to tell. Why not add your own saucy secrets to my pantry? I can brew them into something scrumptious.
Think about it. Then come see us. We'll feast on your delectable disclosures together.
Now, let us hear some of ***your*** dark tales, my devilish detainee.
SQUEEEEAK!
Release me, Creeper! Whoever you're talking to is complicit in this!

ACKNOWLEDGMENTS

A huge cake-filled THANK YOU to Rick Chillot, Andie Reid, Jhanteigh Kupihea, Jane Morley, and the whole team at Quirk Books. Your encouragement and feedback on this dream project warmed our strange little hearts. We owe you many delicious desserts.

To Charlie Olson and Inkwell for being so supportive of our ideas and for introducing us to the best pizza in Brooklyn.

To Phil Nobile Jr. for his contribution to this book, and to the whole team at Fangoria for helping to keep horror and physical media out of the grave.

To the many wonderful people who have supported our work and allowed us to share our stories: Warren Bernard, Linda Bernard, MDT, and Sam Marx and the wonderful Small Press Expo; Kate Feirtag, the Society of Illustrators, and the MoCCA Arts Festival; Seth Unger, George Motz, and everyone at the Food Film Fest; and Ben Penrod and the Awesome Con crew.

To our parents, who fed us a steady diet of delicious treats and horror, thank you for spawning our food and film obsessions.

To our friends Ryan and Emily Sears, Matthew Winner, Laurie Keith, the ITMODcast crew, and our Alamo Drafthouse Film Club pals wrangled by Andy Gyurisin in Winchester, VA, and Bryan Loy in Ashburn, VA. Your love of film stuffs our souls with cinematic joy.

To our pets, Kio and Biscotti. Thank you for making every day an adventure.

And to our beloved London. Much of this book came from our love for you and the deep loss we felt when we had to say goodbye. You will forever be our best friend. We miss you every day and will always save the last bite of pizza for you.

For bonus material and a behind-the-scenes look
at the making of this book, visit bitesofterror.com